School Choice

The End of Public Education?

Mercedes K. Schneider

Foreword by Karen GJ Lewis

TEACHERS COLLEGE PRESS

TEACHERS COLLEGE | COLUMBIA UNIVERSITY

NEW YORK AND LONDON

Published by Teachers College Press, 1234 Amsterdam Avenue, New York, NY 10027

Cover photos: Bulldozer by Maria Jeffs / Shutterstock. Bricks by garycycles8 under a creative commons attribution license / Flickr.

Grateful acknowledgment is made to reprint the following:

Excerpts in Chapter 4 from Solo, Robert A., ed. *Economics and the Public Interest: Practical Applications of Economics to Problems of Public Welfare.* Copyright © 1955, 1983 by Robert A. Solo. Reprinted by permission of Rutgers University Press.

Excerpt in Chapter 5 from Budde, Ray. The evolution of the charter concept, *Phi Delta Kappan, 78*(1), 72–73. Reprinted with permission of Phi Delta Kappa International, www.pdkintl.org. All rights reserved.

Excerpt in Chapter 6 from Public Interest report, "Cashing in on Kids" (cashinginonkids.com). Used with permission.

Excerpts in Chapter 9 from Goodman, Joan F. Charter management organizations and the regulated environment: Is it worth the price? *Educational Researcher, 42*(2), 89–96. Reprinted by permission of SAGE Publications, Inc. Retrieved from edr.sagepub.com/content/42/2/89.full.pdf

Excerpts in Chapter 9 from EduShyster (edushyster.com) blog entry by Jennifer Berkshire. Used with permission of the author.

Library of Congress Cataloging-in-Publication Data is available at loc.gov

ISBN 978-0-8077-5725-3 (paper)
ISBN 978-0-8077-7424-3 (ebook)

Printed on acid-free paper
Manufactured in the United States of America

23 22 21 20 19 18 17 16   8 7 6 5 4 3 2 1

For Billy, Rita, Anna, and Johnny

Folly is set in great dignity and in high places.

—Ecclesiastes 10:6a

Contents

Foreword

If you have the opportunity to meet Mercedes [Mer-suh-DEEZ] Schneider, she will charm you with her Southern Louisiana drawl and her lady-like, "good home training" manners, but what you will find is her laser focus on the defense of public education. Having taken on the origins of the Common Core State Standards and the politicians and oligarchs whose mission is the abject destruction of the democratic ideal of American public education, she turns that focus on the concept of school choice in the form of vouchers and charters.

While deftly annotated, this is no overwhelming scholarly tome for which you'll need your dictionary. This book is designed to be a comprehensive, accessible explanation of what school choice really is, beginning with its origins in sex segregation in the Massachusetts Bay Colony as a way to keep boys out of trouble—even as compulsory education for girls was nonexistent. Schneider clearly notes early and often that public education was seen as "a means of turning Americans, whether 'native' or 'foreign born,' rural or urban—into patriotic and law-abiding citizens, thereby achieving the Jeffersonian goal of securing the republic."

Schneider further draws on the wisdom of Horace Mann, who believed that universal public education could "counter act the domination of capital and the servility of labor." Mann used the term "the great equalizer," a phrase that sounds all too familiar to those of us engaged in the skirmishes of the current education wars. Mann was also concerned about the physical conditions of schools, what we consider working conditions that are part and parcel of modern union contracts.

Schneider lets us know that as early as 1855, Massachusetts outlawed racial segregation in public schools, but she also reminds us that it wasn't until 1954 with *Brown v. Board of Education* that racial segregation was outlawed federally. Interestingly, this led to the development of schools of choice throughout the South and the first use of public dollars for private segregated "academies."

Schneider adds, "When I read that school choice is being termed 'a civil rights issue' in the 21st century, I find the irony profound given that school

choice was a tool used in certain states to intentionally defy federal desegregation mandates in the latter 20th century." Schneider lists plan after
plan, each attempting to skirt desegregation and preserve White supremacy
and its proponents. Each plan found ways to institute "school choice" by
providing scholarships for White students to attend nonsectarian private
schools. These measures subverted the intention of desegregating schools
until the 1960s. Schneider also puts the market fundamentalism of Milton
Friedman, considered the father of modern school choice, under her micro-
scope and finds it not only wanting but detrimental to the ultimate goal of
desegregation.

Schneider moves on to take on the concept of charter, which, as many
know, began as a concept put forth by educators Ray Budde and Albert
Shanker (the former a professor at the University of Massachusetts Amherst
and the latter a former president of the American Federation of Teachers),
who both saw the value of teacher-led schools freed from the restraints of
district and government mandates that stifled innovation. Unfortunately,
the charter movement was quickly coopted by the voucher movement
and Friedman neoliberal market fundamentalists. Frankly, it all sounds so
very good on paper: "Why should poor children be "trapped" in failing
schools?" It's such a common refrain that appeals to a wide range of folks.
The answer is they shouldn't. But charter schools are no more successful at
helping all children than traditional public schools. What they're good at,
Schneider demonstrates, is selecting their students carefully and spending
public money outside of public purview. Charter schools, with their un-
elected boards and conflicts of interest—some folks on these boards have
businesses that benefit from having access to all those public dollars—tend
toward corruption. She cites case after case and includes dollar amounts of
monies stolen from the public coffers and transferred to smooth operators
with no moral compasses. Unfortunately, Budde and Shanker's vision has
gone completely awry.

I've always wondered why choice-promoting, billionaire philanthro-
pists who so often shed crocodile tears over the plight of poor children just
don't pool their resources and fund public schools in an effort to simulate
the schools where they send their own children. Schneider doesn't provide
the answer–she's way too good a teacher for that—but she arms readers
with facts. It's up to us to take this wealth of information, use it, and create
a movement that fights for democracy, real accountability, and ultimately,
excellent public schools for all.

—Karen GJ Lewis

Acknowledgments

This book is the third that I have written over the course of three summers—one book per summer. An amazing accomplishment, one for which I thank the Lord Jesus Christ first and foremost, for it is He who gave me the intelligence, stamina, and people to help me publish all three.

Next, I would like to thank an individual who has been a wonderful support for the writing of this book and who has asked to remain anonymous. Even though I would prefer to acknowledge this most valued contributor by name, I will respectfully honor this person's request.

In addition, my heartfelt gratitude goes out to my colleague, Janna Robertson, for her kind efforts in raising the funds to pay for the indexing of this book, and for the generous donors to that effort: Elaine Cooper, Mark Joyce, Christine Langhoff, Ray Nichols, Karen Oil, Ann Porter, Denise S., Virginia Tibbetts, Alison Thompson, and several anonymous contributors.

I am also indebted to editor extraordinaire, Jean Ward, for her support, expertise, and care in transforming manuscript into published work, and I thank all at Teachers College Press who contributed to this work.

Finally, a special acknowledgement of my friends, Jennifer Berkshire and Belinda Breaux, who made me smile on numerous occasions with their almost-convincing protestations that this book should indeed be dedicated to them.

Prologue

What is familiar to us we tend to take for granted. I attended public school from the time I was 5 years old until I was 17 (1973–1985). My parents also attended public schools, though in different eras: My father was a public school student in New Orleans circa 1924–1933. At that time and place, it was common for students to end with eighth grade and continue with some sort of trade school or enter the workforce. My mother attended public school in the New Orleans suburb of Chalmette from 1951 to 1964. As was common for her time, she graduated from high school and almost immediately became a wife and mother. My aunts, uncles, cousins, brothers, and sisters attended public schools, as did most of my neighbors. Some of the children in my neighborhood attended private, Catholic schools, but this was unusual.

When I was growing up, children typically went to the public schools nearest their homes. In our school zone, we had quite the income spread. My family was at the lower end. My father was a disabled veteran, so we lived on Social Security benefits and food stamps. Many of my classmates came from more promising financial situations; their families could afford to eat in restaurants, take vacations, and install in-ground swimming pools.

We were a mix of socioeconomic backgrounds, and it was good for us to interact with and learn from one another. My family moved to a more rural location in southern Louisiana for my high school years; there I was exposed to a greater sense of community in my school and was able to form more friendships with African American classmates. I realize that historically some African American families and students preferred schools for only African Americans, and that this preference might well be rooted in the need to feel safe from racial discrimination. So while it was beneficial for me, I can't know if our integrated school best served all of my classmates.

The change was good for me. Equally important was that the school and school systems were stable. Boundaries were set geographically. While there were school rivalries, there was concerns that some students might be less valued because their capabilities in delivering desirable standardized test scores by which schools would be graded in the name of some so-called healthy, market-driven competition for the best schools to outdo other schools.

American public education can only work if it is able to keep its doors open wide to serve all students no matter who those students are—and without risk of destabilization based on its promise to serve all students and to enroll them whenever they arrive.

Whoever and whenever.

I now teach sophomore English at a traditional public high school in southern Louisiana. A number of times during the school year, new students have joined my class at awkward and inconvenient times. One week prior to the end of a grading period. Halfway through the time that my class was working on a major research project. These students varied in their circumstances, motivation, behavior, and aptitude. Some enrolled with us as a result of a move. Others had been dismissed or otherwise removed from a private school setting. Still others decided against home schooling. No matter the circumstances that brought these students into our front office, American public education has her arms wide open. As difficult as these late enrollments can be for both teacher and student, no child is turned away because of inconvenience to the school schedule. The fact that American students have the right to that free and public education through high school—and the right to enroll in the local public school regardless of the convenience to the school—is a marvelous guarantee of educational opportunity. Indeed, it is an opportunity hard-earned, given the historical difficulties faced by those who were not European-descended, White, male, wealthy, English-speaking, and of average or better intelligence.

Free universal public education is an American ideal and institution that needs our protection to prevent its dismantling. Vested interests have coopted the creative ideas of the pioneering educators who first proposed charter schools and in too many cases, these interests have turned those promising ideas into pathways for their own profiteering at the expense of children.

Preface

School choice. It sounds so simple. Parents choose the taxpayer-funded school that they want their child to attend, and the child attends that school. Or, parents take their part of that tax money in order to choose to send their child to a private school. Parents are empowered and satisfied, and society is all the better for it.

Except, it isn't that simple. Allotting taxpayer money to send children to private schools via school vouchers might be nothing more than a convenient vehicle for enabling segregation, for separating society into "us" and "them." Additionally, school choice through both vouchers and, much more prevalently, through charter schools morphs into an underregulated operation. Money is squandered. Schools churn as charters close and reopen and close again. Charter schools actually become more empowered to choose students than are the parents to choose schools. The market model of education drives what becomes a system that worships test scores, and a lower bottom line to ever-higher test scores becomes more desirable than issues of equity or educational quality. In the end, America's public school system suffers as it bleeds funding, and America's children, families, and communities suffer as well.

In 21st-century America, traditional public education is under attack. In its efforts to serve all, the traditional public school is being branded a monopoly by those who support a dual, resource-draining system of choice that is not designed to serve all students. Indeed, the term *school choice* could well mean that the school is doing the choosing, whether overtly by catering to a specific subgroup of students or covertlyby a creative means of attracting enrollment by some students while avoiding enrollment by others, or by enrolling all and pressuring less-desirable students and their parents into making the choice to leave. The result is often a choice school system and a traditional school system competing for the same financial resources, with the choice system being afforded the advantage of selection and deselection/attrition that all too often is able to pass the neediest, most difficult to educate students onto a traditional system that is continuously branded a failure—even as it accepts all students whenever they happen to arrive.

America has room for only one school system, and it should be the system that complements the democratic foundation of public education for all: the traditional community school. Otherwise, what America will face in the name of school choice is an underfunded, traditional public system catch-all for an unstable, market-driven nonsystem that values students based on their ability to produce high test scores.

School choice centered on test scores cannot possibly accommodate all students. Within such a system there will be few winners and even more losers. The biggest loser will be our nation as a whole. This is the course America follows in the name of school choice, primarily through charter school expansion. The purpose of this book is to closely examine that course across decades and centuries, to offer a brief yet timely view of the history of education in America and the detrimental turning of the corner American public education has taken in the name of school choice, in the form of vouchers and charter schools. The prologue describes my own early experience as a public school student and then teacher in southern Louisiana. Chapter 1 examines the popular message that American education is the key to global competition and examines other countries to which American education is often compared. Chapter 2, The Messy Beauty of American Public Education, offers a brief history of education in America, including the roles of individuals such as Thomas Jefferson, Benjamin Rush, and Horace Mann.

In Chapter 3, School Choice as a Means to Preserve Racial Segregation, the focus is on the history of school vouchers as a means for Southern politicians to avoid federal desegregation orders. Chapter 4, Milton Friedman and His Unrealistic School Choice, turns readers' attention to school choice as it was conceived and promoted by economist Milton Friedman, who is considered the father of school choice. This chapter also examines notable school voucher efforts in other countries (specifically Sweden and Chile), as well as within the United States (Milwaukee, Cleveland, and the District of Columbia).

The primary focus of the next six chapters is charter schools. Chapter 5 explores the evolution of charter schools, from a team of innovative teachers, to a school or group of faculty within a public school, to a stand-alone school under a charter operator. Originators of the seminal ideas that produced charter schools were educators Ray Budde and Al Shanker, with state legislatures promoting charter schools by the mid-1990s. Chapter 6 examines major promoters of charter schools, including both political parties at state and federal levels, the Walton family, the conservative American Legislative Exchange Council (ALEC), and the undeniable financial market interest in charters via hedge funders.

And wherehen the market steps in to promote charter schools, the traditional neighborhood public school suffers, as noted in Chapter 7, The Charter Take-Away from the Neighborhood Public School. In short, Al Shanker's vision of the charter school as a way for teams of teacher leaders to try innovative ideas with groups of students in their schools turned into today's underregulated open door for privately run charter profiteering, which leads into the principal discourse of Chapter 8, For-Profit Charters (and Associated For-Profit Education Business Opportunities).

Chapters 9 and 10 conclude the discussion of charter schools via consideration of two questionable charter entities: those that micromanage student behavior in the name of no excuses (as detailed in Chapter 9) and those run by an elusive Turkish imam who lives in posh seclusion in Pennsylvania, Fethullah Gulen (Chapter 10).

That brings us to Chapter 11, Some Final Thoughts on School Choice. This concluding chapter addresses the current state of vouchers in the United States, as well as the federal push to expand underregulated charter schools via both the proposed and approved reauthorizations of the Elementary and Secondary Education Act of 1965 (ESEA). This book closes with a brief discussion of how one might confront the negative influence of underregulated charters upon public education, while encouraging readers to combat charter-propelled privatization in their own communities and protect the future of public education in these United States.

CHAPTER 1

The Pressure to Compete Globally

At the 2015 Network for Public Education (NPE) conference in Chicago, I heard University of Oregon professor Yong Zhao speak on the perils of education reform driven by test scores. One of his comments regarding the marvel of American public education as compared to education systems around the world was this:

> Public education. Public provision. That is, we allow everybody. . . . That's amazing, right? In other countries, you can't. Other countries' selection system: "If you don't pass my kindergarten readiness test, you don't get to come to kindergarten."[1]

The push for school choice has gained momentum from corporate education reformers focused on the standardized test score as the end-all and best measure of a supposedly successful education—and as some unsubstantiated guarantee of global competitiveness. As a result, American public education is often unfairly compared to the educational systems in other countries and found wanting.

Let us briefly consider three other education systems around the world, as well as what these systems are teaching: China, South Korea, and Finland. I selected these three countries because those who are focused on educational reform driven by test scores are fond of comparing American public education to the educational systems in these countries—and of condemning the American classroom on the way to declaring school choice as a necessary component of fixing what they decided was broken.

CHINA

Education in China was not compulsory until 1986, when the Chinese government passed a law requiring all Chinese children to have 9 years of education.[2] However, it is important to remember that China's communist government directs the education of the Chinese people. Such education includes having young children chant about both "pathetic Europe" and

China, with the directive, "do not make big changes."[3] Conformity is the way to go. Talk of universal rights of human beings is publicly rejected at the university level. Note these words by Chinese Academy of the Social Sciences (CASS) Dean Wang Weiguang, especially his attempt to instill fear in Chinese citizens by equating universal human rights with colonization by capitalists:

> Certain countries in the West advertise their own values as "universal values," and claim that their interpretations of freedom, democracy, and human rights are the standard by which all others must be measured. They spare no expense when it comes to hawking their goods and peddling their wares to every corner of the planet, and stir up "color revolutions" both before and behind the curtain. Their goal is to infiltrate, break down, and overthrow other regimes. At home and abroad certain enemy forces make use of the term "universal values" to smear the Chinese Communist Party, socialism with Chinese characteristics, and China's mainstream ideology. They scheme to use Western value systems to change China, with the goal of letting Chinese people renounce the Chinese Communist Party's leadership and socialism with Chinese characteristics, and allow China to once again become a colony of some developed capitalist country.[4]

Weiguang's message is that to be really Chinese, one must reject notions of universal human rights and trust China's Communist Party. No other thinking is allowed. In fact, Chinese Nobel Peace Prize Laureate Liu Xiaobo sits in a Chinese prison for circulating a document that confronts the Chinese government about a need to recognize and respect the universal rights of human beings.

China scores well on international tests. This is true. Nevertheless, the narrow view that since China scores high on international tests and America does not, America's public school system is failing is a farce used to promote the destabilization of traditional public education. Such declared failure comes from our own government, which sells school choice as the means to compete economically with nations where the concept of universal human rights is publicly dashed and conformity is not only praised but also demanded.

Chinese education traditionally produces conformity, not ingenuity and creativity. Chinese American university professor Yong Zhao views the absence of standardization in American education as a strength.[5] In contrast, the Chinese are so focused on high test scores that one Chinese high school pays for amino acid IVs so that students can study longer, and another has put bars on its upper-story windows to keep students from leaping to their deaths. However, as Zhao notes, the Chinese are seeking to move away from the conformity that produces high test scores at the expense of innovation, autonomy, and ingenuity.[6]

Such details are not included when those advocating school choice declare traditional American public education a failure.

SOUTH KOREA

Another country that consistently scores well on international tests is South Korea. Education in South Korea is compulsory for elementary school (grades 1–6) and middle school (grades 7–9), and Korean children attend local schools. The ages for compulsory education are approximately 7 to 16 years old by Western age equivalents. However, most Koreans continue attending school through high school (around 18 years of age).[7]

In South Korea, students are passed in elementary and middle school regardless of achievement. But the pressure to achieve is still present in the *hagwon*, or independently owned schools, that students attend after the regular school day is over. South Korean middle school students are under pressure to test into desirable high schools, and high school students are pressed to test into top-rated South Korean universities.[8] Thus, like Chinese education, South Korean education is intensely test-centered. South Korean high school students studying for the university entrance exam sleep an average of only 5.5 hours per night.[9] College education is coveted (and expected) in South Korea, with one result that the nation's overabundance of college graduates is out of sync with its job market demands. Thus, South Korean youth are pressured into testing into top universities only to face the very real possibility of being unemployed upon graduation: A February 2014 statistic has the number of "economically inactive" university graduates greater than 3 million—and likely continuing to rise.[10] Unfortunately, South Korea's suicide rate is one of the highest among developing countries, with suicide being the fourth leading cause of death in the nation and the leading cause of death among teens.[11] Moreover, these suicide rates spike in November, when college entrance exams are held.[12]

None of these facts support wholesale condemnation of traditional American public education; rather, they point to the extreme human cost of South Korea's high international test scores.

FINLAND

Let us now consider the education system in Finland. Many educators admire the Finnish education system. I am among them. Finland is a parliamentary democracy;[13] from preschool to the university level, Finnish schools are nationally funded based on the number of students,[14] with the only education possibly requiring payment from individuals being adult education.[15] Even though Finnish students score well on international tests, their nation's education system is not test-centric, which means that Finnish students are not pressured to chase after high test scores. As education historian Diane Ravitch notes in *Reign of Error*:

> Finns place a high premium on creativity, the arts, and problem solving and still manage to do well on international tests, without subjecting their students to a steady diet of standardized testing.[16]

Ironically, it seems that American-based educational research prompted the currently celebrated positive change in the Finnish education system[17]—research that Finland applied and that the United States has largely ignored in favor of standardized test scores as the ultimate mark of educational success.

The supposed threat of the United States as being less globally competitive because of the success of the Finnish education system is absurd. However, the United States can learn some lessons from the Finnish education system. For example, as Finnish educator Pasi Sahlberg notes in Darling-Hammond and Rothman's *Teaching in the Flat World*, "Finns regard teaching as a noble, prestigious profession—akin to medicine, law, or economics—and one, like medicine, driven by moral purpose rather than material interests."[18]

Such an altruistic perspective provides a stark contrast to the goal of some Americans winning a largely imagined international competition for the highest test scores. But in order for U.S. schools to compete with the Finnish educational system in ways that really matter for students, American teachers would need to be released from ever-rising test-score pressures to perform for the sake of their own jobs and the welfare of their schools.

Sahlberg also notes that teaching in Finland involves "recruiting the best"[19] to become teachers. Of course, one could easily take Sahlberg's words and twist them to form an indictment of the traditional career teacher in the United States. In other words, if only America would also "recruit the best" teachers, then the United States would indeed attain those globally competitive test scores. However, such a test-centric goal is not part of the Finnish view of teaching as a respected profession deserving of the best individuals—which extends beyond required content and pedagogic knowledge to include emphasis on "excellent interpersonal skills and a deep personal commitment to teach and work in schools."[20] In short, the respect accorded to Finnish teachers is not shakily constructed on top-down, punitive, test-score-driven demands. Instead, it is an integral component of the Finnish culture and worldview.

In Finland, there is no effort to single out so-called "low-performing" schools for punitive action based on test scores. The test-centrism is simply not there. Neither is the mindset that those perceived as weak—whether students, teachers, or schools—should be actively hunted and speedily replaced.

Even Finnish principal and teacher evaluation is much more likely to be a qualitative process, and test-based measurements are, as Sahlberg describes, "alien to the Finnish education system."[21]

In contrast to Finland, 21st-century America has latched onto the standardized test score as the end-all, be-all of educational value, and that focus has notably contributed to the declaration that traditional public education is failing and needs to be replaced by a market-driven decentralization of schools that often lack adequate oversight. This we call "school choice." However, the roots of school choice were planted long before America became obsessed with standardized tests. As we journey toward examining the history of school choice in the United States, let us first consider the emergence of public education in America.

The Messy Beauty of American Public Education

Traditional American public education is a democratic cornerstone–and one not easily established historically. In order to better understand as much, one must become familiar with the history of education in these United States. Thus, in this second chapter, let us briefly consider the origin of the American public school.

In the title of the prologue, I noted that American public education is "messy." The messiness of American public education is certainly true in the case of accepting all children into the classroom, whoever they are and whenever they arrive during the school year. Such is also true when one considers American public education's history. Some might think that not long after the United States became a country, the promise of a free and public education for all members of society and the goal of such education to afford American citizens the opportunity to become creative and critical thinkers have evolved over time. In fact, the Constitution does not guarantee citizens the right to a public education.[1] However, by 1973, in the U.S. Supreme Court case concerning school funding, *San Antonio Independent School District v. Rodriguez*, Justice Lewis Powell stated, "Education is one of the most important services performed by the State." Powell cites the importance of the Supreme Court case, *Brown v. Board of Education*:

> In *Brown v. Board of Education*, 347 U.S. 483 (1954), a unanimous Court recognized that "education is perhaps the most important function of state and local governments." What was said there in the context of racial discrimination has lost none of its vitality with the passage of time:
>
> Compulsory school attendance laws and the great expenditures for education both demonstrate our recognition of the importance of education to our democratic society. It is required in the performance of our most basic public responsibilities, even service in the armed forces. It is the very foundation of good citizenship. Today it is a principal instrument in awakening the child to cultural values, in preparing him for later professional training, and in helping him to adjust normally to his environment. In these days, it is doubtful that any child may reasonably be expected to succeed in life if he is denied the opportunity of

an education. Such an opportunity, where the state has undertaken to provide it, is a right which must be made available to all on equal terms.[2]

It is interesting that the U.S. Constitution does not guarantee taxpayer-funded education for all of its citizens. However, based upon Supreme Court Judge Powell's words above, the federal government clearly expects state governments to provide public education for their citizens.

Nevertheless, historically speaking, such is easier spoken than accomplished.

EDUCATION AS A PUBLIC RESPONSIBILITY

On April 14, 1642, the Massachusetts Bay Colony passed its first law: all children should be taught to read and write, thus founding the idea on what would become U.S. soil that educating youth is a public responsibility.[3] However, before passage of this law, in 1635, the first public school opened in Boston, known as the Boston Latin School. Unusual for its time, Boston Latin School was not founded by a church. It was the result of a decision of the Boston Town Meeting. Other Massachusetts towns also established citizen-funded schools. These first schools, commonly called "grammar schools," chiefly served boys. The idea that all children should learn to read and write was expected to take place in the home.

Concerned that the expected home education was not happening, in 1647, the Massachusetts Bay Colony mandated that any town of 50 families was to have an elementary school, complete with its own schoolmaster. Towns of 100 or more were required to hire a schoolmaster who could also teach Latin.

Even in colonial America, responsibility for education shifted notably from the home to the municipality. Still, it is important to note that these schools mainly served White males. Furthermore, though the schools were public, not all were free. Families often were required to contribute financially (or with goods or services) toward their grammar school attendance. Too, this early public education was not compulsory in the sense that parents were not required by law to send their children to school.

Not all towns of 50 or more families complied with the Massachusetts Bay Colony mandate to provide a grammar school. The result was that these towns were fined, and some towns did not seem to mind. They did not want to establish schools.[4]

In 1780, John Adams provided for public education as part of the Massachusetts Constitution.[5] In 1785, Adams wrote the following in his letter to London physician John Jebb, concerning the responsibility of public education:

> The whole people must take upon themselves the education of the whole people and must be willing to bear the expense of it. There should not be a district one

mile square, without a school in it, not founded by a charitable individual, but maintained at the expense of the people themselves.[6]

In 1789, Massachusetts became the first state to pass a law providing for comprehensive education directed by a town committee, a precursor to district-directed education. The Massachusetts Education Act of 1789 also led to the practice of tax support for a town's schools.[7]

The question of comprehensive public education had become a national issue. As McGill University professor Jason Opal notes in his book *Beyond the Farm: National Ambitions in Rural New England*:

> Many post-Revolutionary leaders valued schools as pillars of republican society. At least in theory, they wanted every citizen to have a common educational experience and to learn "that he does not belong to himself, but that he is a public property." They meant, more specifically, *national* property. To accomplish this, reformers like Benjamin Rush and Thomas Jefferson called for three-tiered state systems, with free elementary schools at the base, regional academies for more advanced pupils in the middle, and, at the pinnacle, state colleges for the best and brightest. . . .
>
> Most of their designs quickly ran aground, however. In New York, a 1795 plan to improve common schools withered five years later when the legislature refused to fund it. In Massachusetts and New Hampshire, as well, *de jure* educational reform was modest in both intent and effect. Only in urban centers did education reform gain traction, primarily as a device for keeping poor children in line.[8]

Even in the early days of our nation, public education was a "messy" endeavor.

Opal continues by noting that "day-to-day questions of schooling" fell to the townspeople, including at what age students should start school, whether girls should be taught to write, and who would teach during the summer. The credentials of teachers varied from town to town, with taxpayer money having the last word. What was considered acceptable discipline and instruction also varied, as did the length of the school year and the degree of crowding in classrooms.

Concerning the provision of public schools with tax support—and the resistance to this idea—one of the founding fathers to which Opal alludes, physician and Pennsylvania statesman Benjamin Rush,[9] asserted in his essay *Education Agreeable to a Republican Form of Government* (1786) that taxes should be viewed as an investment:

> But, shall the estates of orphans, bachelors, and persons who have no children, be taxed for the support of schools from which they can derive no benefit? I answer in the affirmative. . . . It will be true economy in individuals to support

public schools. The bachelor will in time save his tax for this purpose, by being able to sleep with fewer bolts and locks to his doors—the estates of orphans will in time be benefited, by being protected from the ravages of unprincipled and idle boys, and the children of wealthy parents will be less tempted, by bad company, to extravagance. . . . I believe it could be proved, that the expenses of confining, trying, and executing criminals, amount every year, in most counties, to more money than would be sufficient to maintain all the schools that would be necessary in each county.[10]

Rush envisioned public education (of males) as a means for ensuring a safe and productive society. He also viewed such as a civic responsibility of citizens who had the financial means to promote such societal security. All people need money in order to live, and Rush viewed public education as an indispensable avenue for tempering criminal activity that would otherwise have negatively affected all living in community, the wealthy included.

The positions of another of the founding fathers of American public education to whom Opal alludes, Thomas Jefferson, can best be understood if one keeps in mind the context in which he lived. Jefferson was a statesman in a newly formed republic at a time in which the general education of women and Blacks was not the norm. Also previously unheard of was the idea of educating children of laboring families with the aim of determining what these children might become. Jefferson is often negatively cited for his comment about "raking genius from the rubbish." However, keeping in mind the context of Jefferson's life and of his role in trying to establish a free, basic education for all—and a means for recognizing that academic giftedness is not a quality to be confused with one's economic station—it is possible to weigh Jefferson's words about "genius from rubbish" with a fresh appreciation for what he was seeing: education could be a key to social mobility and to establishing a solid groundwork for establishing and preserving the new republic.

In short, one must bear in mind that the perch from which we approach Jefferson's words is that of a citizenry that has benefited from access to public education for more than 200 years, built on the ideas Jefferson promoted in this excerpt from education bills he wrote in the revised Code of Virginia (1782):

Lay off every county into small districts of five or six miles square, called hundreds, and in each of them to establish a school for teaching reading, writing, and arithmetic. The tutor to be supported by the hundred, and every person in it entitled to send their children three years gratis, and as much longer as they please, paying for it. These schools to be under a visitor who is annually to choose the boy of best genius in the school, of those whose parents are too poor to give them further education, and to send him forward to one of the grammar schools. . . . Of the boys thus sent in any one year, trial is to be made at the grammar schools one or two years, and the best of the whole selected. . . . By this means twenty of the best geniuses will be raked from the rubbish annually, and will be instructed at the public expense. . . . At the end of six years instruction . . . half, who are to be chosen for the superiority of their parts and disposition, are to be sent and continued in their study three years in the study of such sciences as they choose. . . . The ultimate result of the whole scheme of education would be the teaching of the children of all the State reading, writing, and common arithmetic, turning out ten annually of superior genius, well taught in Greek, Latin, geography, and the higher branches of arithmetic, turning out ten annually, of still superior parts, who, to those branches of learning, shall have added such branches of the sciences as their genius shall have led them to; the further furnishing to the wealthier part of the people convenient schools at which their children may be educated at their own expense.[11]

Jefferson's intended result in providing this tiered public education appears to have been that those males deemed worthy of what amounted to the highest level of education in the fields of study of their choice would further advance knowledge in such fields. While I realize that Jefferson's plan completely overlooks social mobility via education for the likes of me—a woman from blue-collar, laboring roots—I admire what he was trying to do with his staggered system that at its base offered a free education "to all." While Jefferson's plan made room for a white female to be offered the basic, three-year education,[12] it did not include education for Blacks.

A final issue with Jefferson's model of public education, one that might be overlooked in the distraction of the Jeffersonian model as mainly serving white males is that the free education is centered on the poor. Notice that Jefferson advocates that "the wealthier part of the people" educate their children "at their own expense."

OPENING THE SCHOOLHOUSE DOORS TO ALL CHILDREN

As the concept of public education progressed into the "common" school movement in the mid-1800s, the idea that public ("free") schools could and should be available to truly *all* students, regardless of class, ethnicity, or gender, was not easily accepted.[13] A critical factor in the promotion of common schools was the 1837 establishment of the nation's first state board of education in Massachusetts. According to the *Encyclopedia of Education*, the rise of the common school movement across the United States had as its primary goals solidifying a nation of law-abiding, harmonious-living citizens:

> To a large extent, the spread of common schools was an institutional response to the threat of social fragmentation and to a fear of moral and cultural decay.

Reformers of various types—ministers, politicians, Utopians, Transcendentalists, workingmen, and early feminists—saw in schools, or at least in education, a way to ameliorate the disturbing social vices that were increasingly associated with swelling urban centers. Schools were seen as a means of turning Americans—whether "native" or "foreign born," rural or urban—into patriotic and law-abiding citizens, thereby achieving the Jeffersonian goal of securing the republic.[14]

Upon the 1837 establishment of a Massachusetts state board of education, Massachusetts legislator Horace Mann was immediately appointed secretary, a position in which he served until 1848 and his election to the U.S. House of Representatives to fill a vacancy created by the death of John Quincy Adams.[15] Credited as the "father of American public education,"[16] Mann viewed publicly available education as necessary for the establishment and maintenance of a stable, peaceful society. As such, he traveled Massachusetts with a message similar to that of Pennsylvania statesman Benjamin Rush from 50 years earlier: Wealthier citizens needed to invest in the education of their less-fortunate neighbors in order to ensure their own security in a stable society. For each year that Mann held the post of Massachusetts secretary of education, he published an annual report. In his 12th report (1848), Mann wrote about education as being "the great equalizer" necessary to prevent the separation of citizens into fixed groupings of the privileged and "servile":

> Now, surely, nothing but Universal Education can counter-work this tendency to the domination of capital and the servility of labor. If one class possesses all the wealth and the education, while the residue of society is ignorant and poor, it matters not by what name the relation between them may be called; the latter, in fact and in truth, will be the servile to the former. But if education be equally diffused, it will draw property after it, by the strongest of all attractions, for such a thing never did happen, and never can happen, as that an intelligent and practical body of men should be permanently poor. . . .
>
> Education, then, beyond all other devices of human origin, is the great equalizer of the conditions of men—the balance-wheel of the social machinery.[17]

Mann's goal with the common school was to bring the classes together to learn. He was also concerned about the physical condition of schools, the curriculum, length of the school year and of a student's whole common school education, and the qualifications of teachers and their pay. In 1838, Mann established the semi-monthly periodical, *The Common School Journal*, in which he addressed these and other issues related to his vision of "equalizing" education.[18] This periodical is one means through which Mann, who also wrote several books on education, influenced public education in Massachusetts and across the nation.

Even as Mann worked to establish public schools in Massachusetts, others across the new nation were advancing similar messages about the need to support some system of public education, including Henry Barnard in Connecticut and Rhode Island, Samuel Lewis and Calvin Stowe in Ohio, and New York–born Catharine Beecher, who advocated for the education of women, including higher education. Beecher desired more than just "ornamental" education for females[19] and founded schools of higher education for women in Hartford, Connecticut; Cincinnati, Ohio; and other locales in the Midwest. She is credited with transforming the teaching profession as suitable for respectable women, thus shifting teaching from a male profession to a predominately female profession.[20]

By the mid- to late 1800s, state adoption of some form of public education had become the norm.[21] The Department of Education Act of 1867 created a federal department of education, but it was not until 1980 that the U.S. Department of Education became a Cabinet-level department.[22] Even with these advances, all children were not offered the same public education: or offered public education at all. Girls were primarily excluded from high school and college, and African Americans, if offered the opportunity to be educated at all, were often required to attend separate schools. Education of deaf and blind children was also limited.[23] In 1855, Massachusetts abolished segregation based on "race, color, or religious opinion."[24] Unfortunately, the South would not end racial desegregation until 99 years later with the *Brown v. Board of Education* decision. The heart of the *Brown* decision—that "education is a right which must be made available to all on equal terms"—rang true in 1954 when it was delivered, and it rings true today. The U.S. Supreme Court raised and answered a critical question, "Does segregation of children in public schools solely on the basis of race, even though the physical facilities and other 'tangible' factors may be equal, deprive the children of the minority group of equal educational opportunities? We believe that it does."[25]

The struggle to truly offer equal educational opportunity continues to be hard fought. The legal racial integration of American public schools "on paper" was a major triumph in the history of the American public school. However, the transference of paper to reality did not automatically happen with the 1954 Supreme Court's *Brown v. Board of Education* decision. I know so from personal experience. Even though I did not begin public school in St. Bernard Parish, Louisiana, until 1972, I was enrolled in a system that chose to resist complete integration of its schools. The federal government stepped in with fiscal leverage offered via the comprehensive education funding bill, the Elementary and Secondary Education Act of 1965, and states had to racially integrate in order to be eligible for ESEA funds. In the year that our local public schools complied with the federal mandate to racially integrate, 1966–67, the district decided to creatively re-segregate, this time according to gender—apparently a common practice in some southern states circa 1960. The excuse offered by the superintendent of the time betrayed a bias that he thought he had concealed: That the boys needed the school with the athletic facility. (I confirmed this as the "official" explanation years later in questioning a then-aging school official.) As such, I attended an all-girls public middle and high school. This form of segregation, sex segregation, continued until 1985, when a lawsuit settled out of court finally resulted in complete integration of the St. Bernard Parish (Louisiana) Public Schools in 1988.[26]

Another issue regarding education eligibility to which our nation had not paid suitable attention until my early years as a public school student was the education of its citizens with special needs. The federal government once again stepped in with Section 504 of the Rehabilitation Act of 1973, the last of three pieces of federal legislation that made discrimination based on race (the Title IV Act of 1964), gender (Title IX of the Education Amendments of 1972), and disability illegal in American public schools. Though the Constitution does not provide for federally run education, it does protect the civil rights of American citizens, particularly under its 13th and 14th Amendments.[27] Thus, in attempting to guarantee civil rights regarding public education, the U.S. Department of Education became a promoter and enforcer of such civil rights.[28] However, with the 2001 reauthorization of ESEA—in the form of No Child Left Behind (NCLB), with its mandates driven by test scores over state education decisions—the federal role in education shifted from civil rights guarantor to arguably unconstitutional, overstepping micromanager of state education affairs in the name of competing globally. More to come on this NCLB federal overstep in subsequent chapters.

This brief history of American public education might be summarized as follows: Our founding fathers expressed lofty ideals concerning the role of education as a public good, an equalizer promoting social harmony, even though the historical center of attention for public schools tended to be on White males. The families of wealthier White males could afford to provide an education, so the initial focus of public education was on poorer White males and poorer White females to a lesser degree. Advances in educating the general populous of White females and extending education to African American children came at a slower pace, and educating African American children entailed inherent discrimination in separating them from White students in schools paradoxically declared to be "separate but equal." This form of discrimination was not eliminated in practice in certain areas of the country until the late in the previous century. Ensuring public education for children with disabilities was also slow in coming, but by 1973, it had arrived, again through enforcement of a federal mandate.

This history brings me to 2015, when, as a traditional public school teacher, I teach all who arrive at my door, regardless of race, gender, and ability and regardless of the school calendar. Whether their arrival is convenient or disruptive to my teaching schedule, I meet all students where they are academically and work to move them forward as they grow as human beings—all in keeping with the messy beauty of American public education.

CHAPTER 3

School Choice as a Means to Preserve Racial Desegregation

St. Bernard Parish is part of the Greater New Orleans area, a place in which racial integration is still not common and where "White flight" is an ingrained practice when African American families move into a predominately White, middle-class neighborhood. I was raised where residential segregation was the norm. In fact, I had become so accustomed to such segregation that when I moved to northern Georgia in the early 1990s, I was surprised to find that the middle-class neighborhood in which I lived was racially integrated. I had not lived in an integrated neighborhood until I left southern Louisiana in my mid-20s.

There are two general types of segregation: *de jure*, which means as a matter of law, and *de facto*, which is a matter of fact. Some people consider neighborhood segregation to be completely *de facto*, but there are ways to enforce segregated neighborhoods so that the segregation is not merely due to the choices of would-be homeowners.[1] For example, banks can refuse to loan money for certain individuals to purchase homes in certain neighborhoods, and homeowners associations can refuse to approve prospective buyers based on their own biases. Growing up in St. Bernard Parish, I heard more than one White person tell me over the years that a Black family moving into a White neighborhood would bring property values down. It is sad for me to write this and to think of the opportunities denied to Black families—and to the White families who were allowed to persist in their own racial isolation.

Individual choice alone may not be enough to confront complex systems of prejudice that enforce residential segregation. Moreover, choice can be leveraged as a tool to actually enforce segregation, which turned out to be true with the issue of school choice in America as civil rights issues were coming to a head in the 1950s and 1960s.

In southern Louisiana, resistance to federal mandates to integrate schools died hard. In this regard, Louisiana was not alone. Politicians in states across the South sought creative means by which they might preserve all-White schools. When I read that school choice is being termed "a civil rights issue" in the 21st century,[2] I find the irony profound given that school choice was a tool used in certain states to intentionally defy federal deseg-regation mandates in the latter 20th century. To understand this tactic, one must become acquainted with Virginia politician Harry Byrd, a segregation-ist concept known as "massive resistance," and a concurrent U.S. legisla-tive Southern Caucus formal position on resisting the federal mandate to integrate schools, known as the Southern Manifesto. As one will read, the attitude across the South was that school choice provided a handy tool for attempting to preserve racial segregation in America's public schools.

Let us examine some Southern states' attempts to fight integration, and let us begin with Virginia politician Harry Byrd and his "massive resistance."

MASSIVE RESISTANCE

Harry F. Byrd, Sr., was a powerful man in Virginia politics. A Democrat, Byrd served in the state senate from 1924 to 1926 and as governor from 1926 to 1930. He then became a U.S. senator from 1933 to 1965.[3] He was also the founder and leader of a political machine that dominated Virginia politics for 4 decades (1920s through 1960s), the Byrd Organization (com-monly known as "the Organization").[4] The Organization's strength was in the control it held over Virginia's rural areas. Byrd used his Organization to stymie efforts to integrate Virginia's schools following the *Brown v. Board of Education* decision in 1954.[5]

The governor of Virginia in 1954, Thomas Stanley, was a member of the Organization. Stanley appointed a Commission on Public Education—all 32 of its members were White Democrats—headed by state senator Garland "Peck" Gray, which became known as the "Gray Commission." In a November 1955 report submitted to Governor Stanley, the Gray Commission stated:

> The Commission believes that separate facilities in our public schools are in the best interest of both races, educationally and otherwise, and that compulsory integration should be resisted by all proper means in our power.[6,7]

In an effort to bypass the 1955 Supreme Court mandate that state courts require school districts to "make a prompt and reasonable start toward full compliance with the [1954] ruling,"[8] the Gray Commission devised what became known as the Gray Plan. In short, the Gray Plan involved the repeal of compulsory education laws in order to allow for school closure as a last resort to prevent desegregation. It also allowed for state-supervised student assignment to schools and tuition grants to allow public school students to attend private schools.

Regarding Virginia's Gray Plan as the result of a regional effort and not just a state effort to resist school desegregation, Byrd offered the following as part of his formal endorsement of the Gray Plan and the use of public money to fund private schools: "Ten other states are confronted with the same acute problem. These states are all seeking a way to preserve their schools, and it is possible that some form of action can be accepted as a pattern for all."[9]

In similar vein, on February 24, 1956, in a press release clarifying his position that he believed southern states should purposely unite and resist the federal mandate to desegregate, Byrd first used the term "massive resistance" for such an undertaking:

> If we can organize the Southern States to massive resistance of this order, I think that in time the rest of the country will realize that racial integration is not going to be accepted in the South. . . . The South has perfectly legal means of appeal from the Supreme Court's order.[10]

Under the advisement of the Gray Commission that he appointed, Governor Stanley called the state legislature into a special session in August 1956, as author Douglas Reed notes, "to devise a legislative response to the prospect of court-ordered desegregation."[11] The resulting legislation based on the Gray Plan (confusingly called the Stanley Plan once passed) included both school closure and vouchers to private schools as options:

> The result [of Virginia's 1956 special legislative session] was a package of laws designed to both thwart and delay desegregation and to shut down public education in any school district in which desegregation was imminent. First, the state assumed control of the placement of students in particular schools, under a statewide pupil placement board. Any transfers of students required the approval of the state board, thereby preventing any local school board from undertaking voluntary desegregation. In addition, the legislature approved a new plan for private school tuition grants and required the governor to seize and close any Virginia public school that confronted imminent desegregation because of a court order. The legislature also gave the governor authority to suspend state aid to any school that voluntarily desegregated.[12]

Using public money to fund private school tuition required an amendment to the Virginia constitution. In forethought, the Gray Commission called for such an amendment, which was passed in March 1956, 5 months prior to the special legislative session.[13]

The Stanley Plan caused incredible disruption to public education in Virginia. Another Byrd Organization member, Attorney General James Almond, Jr., succeeded Stanley as governor in 1958. In response to lawsuits filed by the NAACP, federal courts ordered that Virginia public schools in Charlottesville and Norfolk and Warren and Arlington counties be integrated. Local authorities appealed the decisions, and they attempted to delay the beginning of the school year. Following the delayed openings in September 1958, Almond ordered the schools closed.[14] This action prompted White citizens statewide to appeal to the governor on behalf of preservation of the public schools,[15] and some filed suit in federal court. On January 19, 1959, the Virginia Supreme Court of Appeals overturned the school closure law in *Harrison v. Day*,[16] even as a federal court condemned school closure under the "equal protection" afforded by the 14th Amendment in *James v. Almond*.[17]

In *Harrison v. Day*, the Virginia Supreme Court of Appeals found that the Virginia General Assembly *could* apportion public funds for students to attend "nonsectarian private schools"; however, the court declared that according to the Virginia Constitution, the state *must* "maintain a system of public free schools throughout the state." In short, the General Assembly was not allowed to take funding from the public schools and reallocate it to fund private school vouchers—which is what the General Assembly was doing under its Appropriation Act of 1958.[18]

Following the 1959 court decisions of *James v. Almond* and *Harrison v. Day*, Almond eased up on Byrd's "massive resistance." He did not do a complete turn-around but yielded moderately to the combined pressures of White parents supporting public schools as well as businessmen who confronted him with the effects that school closure was having on the economy. Once the January 19, 1959, court decisions came down, Almond called the legislature into special session and unexpectedly offered a measure to repeal Virginia's school closure laws—which meant he was backing down on his formerly inflexible desegregation stance, much to Byrd's ire.[19]

Then came the Perrow Plan.

Almond's intention was only to offer mild support for desegregation by embracing the concept of "school choice." In 1959, Almond appointed a commission chaired by Virginia senator Mosby Perrow; 19 of its 40 members had previously served on the Gray Commission.[20] In general, the tenor of this commission followed that of Almond—mild support for desegregation, which meant support for token desegregation. Following a 25-day session, Virginia's General Assembly approved the following: an optional provision that school placement decisions be made at the local level; "scholarships" for students to attend private, nonsectarian schools (previous language related to issues of race had been stricken from the new legislation); and reinstatement of compulsory school attendance, which localities had the option of enforcing. As historian Christopher Bonastia observes:

> On the whole, the Perrow plan recaptured the thrust of the Gray plan, emphasizing "freedom of choice" for localities and for students, who would have the option of attending unsegregated public schools (at least in theory), or private schools, most likely segregated.[21]

Under the Perrow Plan, "freedom of choice" was a way to place the onus for integration on African Americans.[22] That is, White citizens needed to do nothing except exist in their all-White schools. If African American students wanted to attend a historically White school, they could try to enroll by, say, applying to the state's Pupil Placement Board (local school placement was "optional"), which would make decisions to uphold Almond's attitude of token integration. In sum, the real "choice" belonged to a state board that only pretended to be amenable to desegregation in order to superficially comply with federal law.

In 1961, the General Assembly bolstered its support for back-door segregation by passing legislation increasing "scholarship" funding, allowing localities to earmark "educational purpose" funds for private schools, and providing for personal and real-estate tax deductions up to 25% in the name of supporting private schools.[23]

The idea of school choice as being rooted in the preservation of "White supremacy" in Virginia's public schools is undeniable. What is equally important to note is that the resistance to integration in schools also contributed to further establishment of desegregated residential areas in Virginia. As noted by James Hershman, Jr., in the *Encyclopedia Virginia*:

> Massive Resistance and its aftermath left a deep and lasting negative imprint on Virginia's system of public education and race relations in the second half of the twentieth century. By delaying effective desegregation until late in the 1960s, during which a decade and a half of extensive, racially segregated suburban development had occurred, it permitted the perpetuation of mostly segregated schools in the state's major metropolitan areas. In several rural counties, it provided time for substantial numbers of white students to withdraw to private, usually all-white, academies. The commitment to integrated public schooling was delayed and, in many cases, undercut.[24]

RESISTANCE IN OTHER SOUTHERN STATES

Virginia was not alone in its push to fight the 1954 federal mandate to integrate public schools. During the same time that Virginia was enacting its Stanley Plan in August 1954, North Carolina Governor William Umstead created his own advisory committee on education under the direction of Rocky Mount farmer and businessman Thomas Pearsall. Committee membership comprised six White and three Black citizens, and the committee advised against integration. The resulting Pupil Assignment Act of 1955 was a creative means of reinforcing desegregation while not calling is as such.

Governor Umstead died in November 1954 and was succeeded by Governor Luther Hodges, who created a seven-member, all-White Pearsall Committee. In what was known as the Pearsall Plan, the committee advised

the North Carolina General Assembly to alter compulsory school attendance as a means of excusing students from attending desegregated public
schools. The committee also recommended that the state fund tuition grants
for students to choose to attend private schools so as to avoid attending integrated public schools. The Pearsall Plan was not declared unconstitutional
until 1969.[25]

In resistance to follow the 1954 Supreme Court mandate to integrate,
Mississippi lawmakers also "adopted tactics intended to forestall and per-
manently delay integration."[26] As author John Hale notes, Mississippi was
able to openly defy even beginning integration of public schools for 10 years,
until 1964.[27] In fact, on May 17, 1961—the seventh anniversary of the
Brown v. Board of Education decision—the Jackson, Mississippi, Citizens
Council publicly celebrated its success in resisting the federal mandate to
integrate Mississippi's public schools. As Hale records, at the event, Citizens
Council president John Wright, declared, "Every white Mississippian can
be justly proud that our state has held the line against race-mixers in the
face of highly organized and well-financed efforts to force our people to
integrate."[28]

In March 1964, U.S. District Judge Sidney Mize ordered school districts in Biloxi and Jackson and Leake County to submit plans for public
school integration that would be effective July 1964. The integration was
to systematically transpire one grade at a time. The Citizens Council pressured lawmakers to close schools rather than to integrate. However, an all-
White women's organization, Mississippians for Public Education, openly
confronted the Citizens Council regarding school closure.[29] Meanwhile,
Mississippi legislators were aware of the 1964 U.S. Supreme Court decision
against Prince Edward County, Virginia, which had completely shut down
its public school system and created private schools for White children—
paid for by tuition grants and tax credits—while offering no such option
to the county's African American children.[30] Mississippi lawmakers decided
to create a tuition grant program that would not be stricken down in any
court. Their final plan involved $165 per student in state funds and $35 per
student in local funds for students to attend nonsectarian private schools;
public schools were also kept open with the agreement that the schools
would be integrated one grade at a time, beginning with first grade. Over
the next several years, from 1964 to 1968, the number of private schools
more than quadrupled, from fewer than 10 in 1964 to more than 40 in
1968. As author Jon Hale notes, "In areas of relative wealth like the cities in
the Delta, where there were strong segregationist tendencies amidst a large
black population, private academies—directly affiliated with the Citizens'
Council—would thrive and symbolize the deep resistance to federal integration orders."[31]

In keeping with an obvious plan to massively resist integration, other
southern states played "let's not call it segregation, though it is" games.

For example, in Louisiana in 1961, Governor Jimmie Davis called the legislature into a special session that resulted in passage of Act 2, which allowed public schools to declare themselves "private"—a semantic change alone—in order to escape the federal integration requirement now faced by the state's "public" schools. Act 2 also allowed districts that chose to close schools to use public funds to provide lunch, transportation, and financial grants for children to attend private schools. Louisiana's Act 2 of 1961 resulted in the lawsuit, *Hall v. St. Helena Parish*, in which the U.S. District Court of Baton Rouge ruled in favor of the plaintiffs:

> The statute in suit violates the equal protection clause on two counts. Most immediately, it is a transparent artifice designed to deny the plaintiffs their declared constitutional right to attend desegregated public schools. More generally, the Act is assailable because its application in one parish, while the state provides public schools elsewhere, would unfairly discriminate against the residents of that parish, irrespective of race.[32]

The justices also called out Louisiana legislators for their being "at pains to use language disguising [Act 2's] real purpose."[33] The Louisiana legislature's persistence in using grants-in-aid as a means of preserving segregation—Act 147 of 1962—resulted in a 1966 lawsuit, *Poindexter v. Louisiana Financial Assistance Commission*. The plaintiffs' complaint was as follows:

> The plaintiffs, Negro public school children in New Orleans and their parents, bring this class action. . . . The theory of the complaint is that private schools largely supported by state grants are in reality a segregated public school system. The complaint asserts that this system is "only a continuation of the original scheme of, and a part of the public school system, designed and administered to maintain and perpetuate the separation of pupils by race and color." The Negro children allege that tuition grants are unavailable to them unless they attend segregated private schools; they were refused admission to three schools allegedly because of their race. This imposes upon them, they say, an unconstitutional condition. They have a choice of refusing tuition grants or accepting them for use within a segregated system.[34]

On January 15, 1968, the U.S. District Court of Baton Rouge declared Act 147 of 1962 unconstitutional, noting that "the purpose and natural or reasonable effect of this law are to continue segregated education in Louisiana by providing state funds for the establishment and support of segregated, privately operated schools for white children."[35]

The Southern state efforts to send white children to private schools as a means of dodging integration continued with Alabama Governor George Wallace. In an effort to prevent the integration of Tuskegee High School,

Wallace promised that a newly declared "private" school only enrolling White students, Macon Academy, would be legislatively funded by grants-in-aid, as would other private schools, in place of funding specific public schools. According to *Lee v. Macon County Board of Education* (1964), these particular grants-in-aid were declared unconstitutional since they were being used to advance segregation in public schools.[36]

Meanwhile, in South Carolina, the legislature passed its own version of scholarship grants to enable public school students to attend private schools, Act 297 of 1963. In May 1965, the U.S. District Court of Columbia issued restraining orders concerning payments made via Act 297 until the issue could be heard in court as per a class action suit filed against the South Carolina Board of Education. On May 31, 1968, the U.S. District Court of Columbia declared Act 297 of 1963 unconstitutional because the legislation "clearly reveals that the purpose, motive and effect of the Act is to unconstitutionally circumvent the requirement first enunciated in *Brown v. Board of Education of Topeka*."[37]

Thus, what is clear about tuition grants, scholarships, or grants-in-aid, and the history of American public education is that these were tools used to preserve segregation. There it is: The usage of choice for separating school children into those who are "desirable" and those who are not. Though it seems that most Southern states were ready participants in resisting the federal requirement to integrate their public education systems, Senator Byrd's sentiment of "massive resistance" was even formally declared in a U.S. legislative document commonly known as the "Southern Manifesto."[38]

The Manifesto states that the U.S. Supreme Court has perpetrated "encroachment" on the rights of states, in violation of the U.S. Constitution, and accuses the federal government of having placed states in "the explosive and dangerous condition created by this [*Brown v. Board of Education*] decision and inflamed by outside meddlers."[39] The closing of this brief document includes the following "commendation" and "pledge": "We pledge ourselves to use all lawful means to bring about a reversal of this decision which is contrary to the Constitution and to prevent the use of force in its implementation."[40]

"By any lawful means" included creating tuition vouchers and scholarships and reinventing public schools as private schools to allow White students the choice to avoid attending integrated public schools.

Nineteen senators and 77 representatives from Alabama, Arkansas, Florida, Georgia, Louisiana, Mississippi, North Carolina, South Carolina, Tennessee, Texas, and Virginia—all Democrats except for one—signed the Manifesto.[41]

From these states, 3 senators and 26 representatives refused to sign. No senators from Tennessee signed, including Al Gore, Sr., and Lyndon Johnson, who as president would later put pressure on states to integrate schools or be deprived of federal funding associated with the Elementary and Secondary Education Act (ESEA) of 1965. Most representatives from Texas also refused to sign. However, all legislators from Alabama, Arkansas, Georgia, Louisiana, Mississippi, South Carolina, and Virginia chose to sign the Manifesto.[42]

Despite the fact that Byrd played no key role in composing the Southern Manifesto, he certainly supported the formal drafting of a position that he and those in his Byrd Organization were already enacting in Virginia, including the Manifesto's purported "by any legal means" route of using tuition grants to keep the races separate in Virginia's schools. This practice was emulated by officials across the southern states.

BRINGING IT HOME—LITERALLY

This chapter began with reference to my own experiences in southern Louisiana, in St. Bernard Parish, a predominately White, neighboring parish to Orleans Parish. That St. Bernard extended from New Orleans is histori- cally evident: The 1814 Battle of New Orleans was fought in St. Bernard, and we have the military cemetery to prove it. St. Bernard Parish and the neighboring Orleans Parish were embroiled in another type of battle in the 1960s, joining other school districts across the South in an attempt to thwart mandated school integration.

This era in St. Bernard Parish history does not inspire pride.

Orleans Parish schools have an established history of separate but cer- tainly not equal. In the 1940s and 1950s, despite the fact that enrollment of African American children was growing faster than White enrollment, the Orleans Parish School Board (OPSB) refused to construct new schools for African American children. At one point, OPSB superintendent Lionel Bourgeois planned to offer the buildings of low-enrollment White schools to use as a means of addressing increasing African American enrollment, but White parents protested. So, African American children were offered portable classrooms in place of much-needed permanent buildings. The NAACP and the African American community sued in 1952 for what the U.S. Supreme Court would end up supporting in 1954—the unconstitution- ality of "separate but equal." However, despite even the *Brown v. Board of Education* decision, OPSB refused to integrate its schools. The Louisiana legislature even shut down the NAACP in Louisiana. Local political boss and White Citizens Council member Leander Perez[43] "encouraged white parents in New Orleans to establish cooperatives at their children's schools, paving the way to converting the schools from public to private."[44] The efforts of Perez and others to prevent desegregation of the public schools in Orleans Parish would not last long; on May 16, 1960, District Court Judge J. Skelly Wright ordered the OPSB schools to be desegregated one grade at a time, beginning in September 1960 with the first grade.[45] OPSB appealed to Judge

Wright to limit the order, noting that desegregation of the entire first grade in September 1960 would be overwhelming since the district anticipated the enrollment of 11,000 first graders. On another front, Louisiana Governor Jimmie Davis tried to thwart Wright's desegregation order by assuming control of OPSB schools in August 1960. Davis's attempt was quashed 10 days later by the district court. However, "impressed with the good faith and sincerity of the [Orleans Parish] board,"[46] Wright allowed instead for a voluntary integration, with parents volunteering via Louisiana's Pupil Placement Act,[47] and he postponed the integration from September to November 14, 1960.

In his determination to preserve segregation in Orleans Parish schools, Governor Davis called an unprecedented five special legislative sessions to prevent Wright's order from being carried out. The Louisiana legislature was creative: It tried seizing OPSB finances; forbidding banks from lending money to OPSB; canceling the agreement with the bank the state used for OPSB payroll; declaring November 14, 1960, a school holiday; privately addressing OPSB board members; repealing the legislation that created OPSB; dismissing the OPSB attorney, and twice creating a replacement board for OPSB. These and other related legislative actions designed to prevent integration of Orleans Parish schools did not stand in federal court.[48]

The 1962 *Bush v. Orleans Parish School Board* case notes record the events that transpired when Wright's deadline arrived:

> One hundred and thirty-four Negro children applied for admission to 'white' public schools in New Orleans. November 14, 1960, four little Negro girls were admitted to two white schools. Small as this may seem in terms of effective desegregation, this was the first time since the founding of the public school system in New Orleans in 1877 that Negro children have attended classes with white children. The effect of this profound change in social customs produced demonstrations, picketing, stone-throwing, and turmoil that continued for months; all white parents withdrew their children from one of the schools and all but a handful of parents withdrew their children from the other school. These are facts of life difficult for the ordinary layman to ignore.[49]

Over the next 2 years, it became clear that OPSB desegregation was a token effort only, with African American student choice of school attendance purposely limited so as to maintain general racial segregation.

The four African American children integrated into traditionally White OPSB schools in 1960 were sent to two schools, Franz and McDonogh 19, in the New Orleans downtown area known as the Ninth Ward, an area from which Whites began to move in the 1950s into neighboring St. Bernard Parish. Whites remaining in the Ninth Ward complained in parents meetings in the summer of 1960 of such issues as "being deprived of freedom" by not being able to determine to have their children "associate with whom they want"—a euphemism for desiring racial segregation to remain in place. Both daily newspapers, the *Times-Picayune* and the *States-Item*, endorsed segregation in editorials. In 1960, White mothers stood outside of the two Ninth Ward schools to wait to yell particularly at White parents who tried to bring their children to these two integrated schools.

School Choice

Backing this intimidation effort was all of the force of the Citizens Councils and their ability to bully, threaten, and interfere with a White desegregationist's livelihood.

Almost all White parents of students who were initially enrolled at Franz and McDonogh 19 quickly withdrew their children from school. And they sought a place to enroll their children. A White place.

Like neighboring St. Bernard Parish. Like the Arabi Annex School.

The first time I heard about the Ninth Ward Elementary School was in 2012. I was talking with one of my former middle school teachers about her career. She told me, "You know, my first teaching job was in 1961 at the Annex. Superintendent Joe Davies asked me if I would be fine teaching in a converted warehouse."

I had never heard of such a school. "It was in Arabi, near the parish line. White parents from Orleans sent their children to attend school in St. Bernard. There was also a voucher school opened on Japonica Street for White students in the Ninth Ward. White parents would go get their voucher money and bring it each month to the Japonica Street school."

I was amazed. This was news to me.

It turns out that White supremacist political boss Leander Perez had quite the hold over St. Bernard Parish politics in 1960. Growing up, I had heard adults comment in passing about Perez and his political clout, but without specifics. Within weeks of the White boycott of the two integrated Ninth Ward elementary schools, St. Bernard schools accepted fleeing Ninth Ward students in grades 5 and 6 into two St. Bernard elementary schools. But more space was needed for remaining Ninth Ward White students. Therefore, organized Whites leased an empty building that once housed a motor rebuilding plant in St. Bernard near the St. Bernard–Orleans parish line, and Perez paid to have the building converted into a school.[50]

The resulting Arabi Elementary Annex in St. Bernard opened its doors to White Ninth Ward students on December 8, 1960. St. Bernard Superintendent Joseph Davies intended that the Arabi Annex would serve all White students formerly enrolled at the Ninth Ward's Franz and McDonogh 19 elementary schools except for kindergarten, which was not yet available in St. Bernard. But this dual-parish, anti-integration effort did not last for even one full school year. Under threat from the U.S. Department of Justice led by Attorney General Robert Kennedy, even local political kingpin Leander Perez sent the White students from Ninth Ward back across the parish line before the 1960–61 school year came to an end.[51]

At the same time that Ninth Ward students were enrolling in the Arabi Annex, parents organized to plan their own private school for White students only in Orleans Parish, which ended up being housed in a building on Japonica Street. This school, the Ninth Ward Elementary School, allowed for the continuation of racial segregation even after the St. Bernard effort ended. The 1960 Louisiana legislature approved tuition grants to be made available beginning in 1961. Ninth Ward Elementary School was wholly financed by these tuition grants. Furthermore, all Louisiana schools funded via tuition grants were segregated and remained so until the tuition program was officially declared unconstitutional in January 1968.[52]

In the final year of Louisiana's tuition grants program—1966–1967—White parents received $4,920,120. African American parents received $338,760.[53] Such is the history of school choice.

CHAPTER 4

Milton Friedman and His Unrealistic School Choice

Economist Milton Friedman is considered the "father of school choice" for his advocacy of school vouchers for universal private education in his 1955 paper, *The Role of Government in Education.*[1] The publication of this paper coincided with school choice initiatives across the South intended to preserve racial segregation.

Friedman himself was not a Southerner. He was born in 1912 in Brooklyn, New York, to Jewish immigrant parents. He graduated from Rutgers University in 1932 with a degree in mathematics and economics and then attended the University of Chicago to complete his masters in economics in 1933. Friedman went to Washington, D.C., in 1935 to work in connection with Franklin Roosevelt's New Deal. It is during this period that Friedman began formulating his ideas regarding how the economy worked. However, though he and his future wife, Rose, spent time in Washington working on the New Deal, neither held a position that influenced policy.[2] Roosevelt based the New Deal on the then-popular Keynesian economics model[3] of "market fluctuation," which advocated increased government spending, lowered taxes, and controlled interest rates to alleviate economic depression. In contrast, Friedman believed that the Great Depression resulted from the Federal Reserve allowing the money supply to shrink, a concept known as "money contraction."[4] Still, during his time with the U.S. Department of the Treasury from 1941 to 1943, Friedman advocated the Keynesian-styled concept of taxation[5] as a means of funding the World War II effort, specifically via payroll withholding. In a June 1995 *Reason* magazine interview, Friedman recalled his decision to introduce withholding as a means of financing World War II: "I think it's a great mistake for peacetime, but in 1941–43, all of us were concentrating on the war. I have no apologies for it, but I really wish we hadn't found it necessary and I wish there were some way of abolishing withholding now."[6]

In 1943, Friedman joined Columbia University's Division of War Research as a mathematical statistician. He completed his PhD in economics in 1946 and taught for one year at the University of Minnesota before joining the faculty of the University of Chicago in 1946 as a professor of economic theory. In 1976, Friedman was awarded the Nobel Prize in Economics.[7]

In his 1995 interview with *Reason* magazine, Friedman identified himself as "a Republican with a capital 'R' and a libertarian with a small 'l.'"[8] Ideologically, he believed in zero-government, but realistically, Friedman did not see this as possible. He viewed government as becoming too big following the onset of the Great Depression in 1929, including mandates for compulsory education:

> If in the absence of compulsory education, only 50 percent would be literate, then I can regard it as appropriate.
>
> Some issues are open and shut. . . . But education is not open and shut. In *Capitalism and Freedom* we came out on the side of favoring compulsory schooling and in *Free To Choose* we came out against it. . . . I see the voucher as a step in moving away from a government system to a private system. Now maybe I'm wrong, maybe it wouldn't have that effect, but that's the reason I favor it.[9]

In 1996, Friedman and his wife, Rose, started the Friedman Foundation "to advance a system of K-12 education in which all parents, regardless of race, origin, or family income, are free to choose a learning environment that is best for their children."[10]

While theoretically his model would seem to have some strengths, Friedman did not acknowledge that "free to choose" could be co-opted as a means to perpetuate school segregation and exploited for profiteering by would-be "edupreneurs." School choice might be another Friedman ideal that cannot be realized, just like zero-government.

THE ROLE OF GOVERNMENT IN EDUCATION

Even as Friedman published his 1955 essay, school choice was being exploited in the South, and state and local governments were complicit in the act. It took the federal government and district courts decades to successfully curb the southern, white-supremacist intention to offer choice to preserve racial segregation. Still, in his 1955 essay, *The Role of Government in Education*, Friedman sees government as having a vital role as a referee— and one not susceptible to any agenda of its own—not even one that is profit-based:

> In what follows, I shall assume a society that takes freedom of the individual, or more realistically the family, as its ultimate objective, and seeks to further this objective by relying primarily on voluntary exchange among individuals

for the organization of economic activity. In such a free private enterprise exchange economy, government's primary role is to preserve the rules of the game by enforcing contracts, preventing coercion, and keeping markets free. Beyond this, there are only three major grounds on which government intervention is to be justified. One is "natural monopoly" or similar market imperfection which makes effective competition (and therefore thoroughly voluntary exchange) impossible. A second is the existence of substantial "neighborhood effects," i.e., the action of one individual imposes significant costs on other individuals for which it is not feasible to make him compensate them or yields significant gains to them for which it is not feasible to make them compensate him—circumstances that again make voluntary exchange impossible. The third derives from an ambiguity in the ultimate objective rather than from the difficulty of achieving it by voluntary exchange, namely, paternalistic concern for children and other irresponsible individuals.[11]

Although Friedman assumes that the education system should reflect the ideal of a "free private enterprise exchange economy," he notes that he expects the government "to impose on parents without further action" the requirement that "each child receive a minimum amount of education of a specified kind." Those words beg for government bureaucracy. That stipulation that "each child receive a minimum amount of education" assumes that society accepts all members as equal, a naïve assumption given the extreme measures undertaken in an attempt to preserve school segregation in the South.

Friedman further writes of the necessity of the government subsidizing not only a basic education but more advanced levels as well. Toward this end, he assumes that the hashing out of details can happen without exploitation via "accepted political channels." He further adds that the governmental requirements of compulsory education and the financing of such education can be separated. In other words, the government can just hand money over to parents, instructing them on basic educational requirements, and the apparently capable and trustworthy free market will take it from there:

> Governments could require a minimum level of education which they could finance by giving parents vouchers redeemable for a specified maximum sum per child per year if spent on "approved" educational services.
>
> Parents would then be free to spend this sum and any additional sum on purchasing educational services from an "approved" institution of their own choice. The educational services could be rendered by private enterprises operated for profit, or by non-profit institutions of various kinds. The role of the government would be limited to assuring that the schools met certain minimum standards such as the inclusion of a minimum common content in their

programs, much as it now inspects restaurants to assure that they maintain minimum sanitary standards.[12]

In this same paper, Friedman notes that as an economist, he is there to "clarify the issues to be judged by the community." Nevertheless, in his supposed "clarity," Friedman does not leave room for the possibility that government officials could become involved in complicated political and fiscal school choice arrangements that would favor a free market at the expense of the quality of education rendered or even the "choice" of the parent.

In short, Friedman failed to reasonably account for the 21st-century reality that the entity with the most choice is often not the parent but the profit-seeking, educational venture potentially peppered with conflicting fiscal interests. In many cases, these ventures are subjected to less of a quality check than are restaurants in the same neighborhood. As noted in subsequent chapters, the proliferation of financial shadiness and scandals now commonly associated with school choice has been widely reported.[13]

Friedman's simplistic solution regarding the market ensuring quality schools is that parents could merely remove their children from one school and enroll in another. But it is not that simple. School choice fosters its own bureaucracy. For example, the all-charter Recovery School District (RSD) in New Orleans has a detailed application process for parents to choose schools, the Walton-Foundation-Funded OneApp. I wrote a blog post based on my experience navigating the third-round OneApp in 2013.[14] The application was extensive and laden with errors, including errors concerning which schools were still available to be selected. The relatively few preferred schools were quickly chosen, with most parents forced to choose almost exclusively from a list of non-school-board-run charters graded as D or F schools. (The issue of choosing from predominately D and F schools had not changed by the 2014–15 school year.)[15] What parents could not do was assume that their child could attend the neighborhood school. Nor could families change their children's schools at will. They had to wait for the next year, for the next convoluted OneApp process.

I learned in January 2015 that some schools also required a supplementary application to accompany the OneApp, an application process that included attending special meetings).[16] Children of parents who were unaware of additional requirements—or who did not or could not persevere in completing yet another application and associated meetings—were not considered in the student selection process.

The use of a supplemental application that is not well publicized is a back-door means of the school choosing its own students. Such a practice complements the findings of a 2012 Educational Research Alliance study involving principals of New Orleans schools, in which ten admitted using tactics to manipulate student enrollment. As the study's author, Huriya Jabbar, notes in his report:

> One-third of schools in the study (N = 30; n = 10) reported using selection strategies. These schools used a combination of targeted marketing and unofficial referrals in order to fill seats with more desirable students. Some schools chose not to declare open seats, preferring to have vacant seats rather than attract students who might lower school test scores. *The combined pressure to enroll a greater number of students and raise test scores to meet state targets seems to have created perverse incentives, encouraging the practice of screening and selecting students.*[17]

Friedman's idea of the market as a disinterested player in the game of choice simply is not consistent with practice. Moreover, in the case of the lack of true parental choice in New Orleans schools, students could actually be assigned to attend voucher schools as a last-resort "choice." Voucher schools are those approved by the state for students to choose to attend using public funds. That voucher school selection would be included as a last-resort parental choice in school selection is a bit shady given that it can be used by the state to boost the appearance of parents' desiring the state-run voucher program. Other students were assigned separate schools even though they were all siblings living in the same house and close enough in age to attend the same school. Still other families were forced to choose another school because the one their children had attended had been closed down by the state.[18]

Choice in practice is not the well-oiled machine that Friedman espoused.

In the end, it is not the Orleans Parish parents who decide to open or close so-called choice schools. It is officially the state, the entity that approves, retains, and closes schools. It is also unofficially manipulated by some school administrators, as previously noted. And in Louisiana, the state does not even regularly audit the quality of choice of either charter or voucher schools.[19] So, when I read the following words of Friedman from 1955, I experience a complete disconnect between what he writes and the reality of school choice in New Orleans:

> Here [in education], as in other fields, competitive private enterprise is likely to be far more efficient in meeting consumer demands than either nationalized enterprises or enterprises run to serve other purposes. . . .
>
> The only additional complication is the possibly greater opportunity for abuse because of the greater freedom to decide where to educate children. Supposed difficulty of administration is a standard defense of the status quo

against any proposed changes; in this particular case, it is an even weaker defense than usual because existing arrangements must master not only the major problems raised by the proposed arrangements but also the additional problems raised by the administration of the schools as a governmental function.[20]

To give Friedman credit, he did not believe that choice could work well so long as compulsory education existed:

> Perhaps a somewhat greater degree of freedom to choose schools could be made available also in a governmentally administered system, but it is hard to see how it could be carried very far in view of the obligation to provide every child with a place.[21]

Here we have the idea that for the market to be at its best, it needs to be free from any obligation to educate all children. By extension, parents need to be free of the requirement to see to their own children's education, and they need to be willing to accept that no agency will guarantee that their children are educated in cases in which the market fails to offer any reliable, suitable, and safe choice.

NOT GREED, BUT SOCIAL RESPONSIBILITY

Given its drive for profits above all else, the free market can be a self-serving place. In an article published in *The New York Times* in September 1970, "The Social Responsibility of Business Is to Increase Its Profits,"[22] Friedman argues that actions undertaken by a corporate executive in the name of "social responsibility" undermine the service the executive is supposed to undertake: to increase profits for shareholders, reduce the cost of a product for customers, or decrease wages for employees. Though he gives token heed to the possibility that some entities are not profit-driven (he includes schools in this group), Friedman maintains that the corporate employee belongs to shareholders, customers, or fellow employees, and the tenor of its title and most of the article content suggests that most companies are profit-driven. Strangely, he fails to discuss the company as its own entity and does not address the possibility that a social service entity such as a school could possibly be run by those with the ulterior motive of garnering financial profits.

In keeping with Friedman's 1955 ideas regarding potential exploitation and abuse related to school choice as non-issues, he notes a similar idea in his 1970 article, but with a twist that the "exploitation" of the corporate employee's "doing good" instead of focusing on profits will take care of itself.

Reflecting on Friedman's 1970 assertion that increasing profits is the expected, single goal of the corporate executive, *Forbes* contributor and former World Bank executive Steve Denning notes:

> The shareholder value theory thus failed even on its own narrow terms: making money. The proponents of shareholder value and stock-based executive compensation hoped that their theories would focus executives on improving the real performance of their companies and thus increasing shareholder value over time. Yet, precisely the opposite occurred. . . . Since 1976, executive compensation has exploded while corporate performance declined.[23]

When the market becomes "freer," it does not regulate itself. On the contrary, CEOs tend to serve themselves. Denning continues with the market reality of the euphemism, "maximizing shareholder value":

> The supposed management dynamic of maximizing shareholder value was to make money, by whatever means are available. Self-interest reigned supreme. The logic was continued in the perversely enlightening book, *Hardball* (2004), by George Stalk, Jr. and Rob Lachenauer. . . . In an effort to win, they (firms) go up to the very edge of illegality or if they go over the line, get off with civil penalties that appear large in absolute terms but meager in relation to the illicit gains that are made.
>
> In such a world, it is therefore hardly surprising, says Roger Martin in his book, *Fixing the Game*, that the corporate world is plagued by continuing scandals. . . . Banks and others have been gaming the system, both with practices that were shady but not strictly illegal and then with practices that were criminal.[24]

In keeping with the abuses of the free market, underregulated school choice also has established itself as more than capable to game its own system. In May 2014, two organizations, the Center for Popular Democracy (CFPD) and Integrity in Education (IIE), produced a report, *Charter School Vulnerabilities to Waste, Fraud and Abuse*, detailing charter school fiscal mismanagement in 15 states. The following summarizes their work:

> "Charter School Vulnerabilities to Waste, Fraud And Abuse," authored by the Center for Popular Democracy and Integrity in Education, echoes a warning from the U.S. Department of Education's Office of the Inspector General. The report draws upon news reports, criminal complaints and more to detail how, in just 15 of the 42 states that have charter schools, charter operators have used school funds illegally to buy personal luxuries for themselves, support their other businesses, and more. The report also includes recommendations for policymakers on how they can address the problem of rampant fraud, waste and

abuse in the charter school industry. Both organizations recommend pausing charter expansion until these problems are addressed. . . .

The problem is pervasive; our search, despite being limited to fewer than half of the states with charter schools, found over $100 million in public tax funds lost to waste, fraud, and abuse.[25]

The states included in the CFPD/IIE study included Arizona, California, Colorado, Florida, Hawaii, Illinois, Louisiana, Minnesota, New Jersey, New York, Ohio, Pennsylvania, Texas, and Wisconsin, and the District of Columbia. The $100 million in lost tax dollars involve monies spent in state and/or federal prosecution of the fraud as well as the public money directly lost to fraudulent activity perpetrated by charter operators and/or staff. The general categories of fraud set out in the report include charter operators (1) using public money for personal gain; (2) using money to finance the operator's other businesses; (3) mismanaging money in such a way as to endanger or potentially endanger students; (4) failing to provide services for monies received; (5) falsifying enrollment records to increase incoming funding, and (6) generally mismanaging both funding and schools. Of these six categories, the researchers found that charter operators using funding for personal gain was the most common form of fraud.

This 11-page general report includes recommendations for charter oversight (e.g., requiring charter governing boards to be elected, with those serving on such boards required to live in the general area in which the school is located; requiring charter governing board members and operators to file full financial disclosure statements, including declaring potential conflicts of interest; and amending state laws so that charter schools are held to the same transparency requirements). Moreover, an additional 38 pages include appendices detailing the specific fraudulent acts and the public costs of prosecuting such acts in cases in which prosecution has occurred.

The CFPD/IIE report offers the following breakdown for the total taxpayer money—in excess of $100 million—and the manner in which the fraud was discovered or the state of prosecution:

- $51,146,094.65, federal prosecution of charter official/staff completed.
- $33,400,000, state agency audit finds violation of federal law by charter official/staff.
- $30,575,143.76, state agency audit finds violation of state law by charter official/staff.
- $1,161,887.93, state agency audit finds violation of federal and state law by charter official/staff.
- $19,550,489, charter official/staff is indicted by a federal grand jury.

- $150,000, charter official/staff criminal prosecution in progress.
- $20,000, charter official/staff is arrested and admitted to fraud.
- *Total: $136,003,615.34.*[26]

Parental choice does not perpetuate honesty among charter operators.

VOUCHERS: THE CHOICE BELONGS TO WHOM?

In his 1955 conceptualization of school choice, Friedman advocated a system whereby parents receive vouchers and can choose from among a variety of schools for their children to attend, including those run for profit, those run by nonprofits, and even some managed by government. Friedman assumed that parents would choose schools based on the quality of the education offered. However, such is not guaranteed in the United States or abroad.

Sweden

In Sweden, a country in which education vouchers have been readily available since the early 1990s, it appears that an important means for private schools to attract voucher students involves grade inflation. That is, a school appears more attractive if students perceive that it is easier to make better grades on teacher-graded tests. As *National Review* contributor Tino Sanandaji observes,

> Grade inflation has indeed become a major problem. Private schools have an incentive to give their pupils more lenient grades in order to attract more applicants. Competition for students has given public schools similar perverse incentives. . . .
>
> Swedish universities are not allowed to adjust for grade inflation and have to take grades set by schools as given. This gives schools strong incentive to set grades excessively high. Students find out which schools that are lenient and take their voucher money there. Grade inflation was predictable and indeed predicted by several economists, but the problem was ignored by the center-right government.[27]

The Swedish system suffers from a lack of established and effective regulation to prevent voucher-seeking private schools from maximizing their profit potential. As Sanandaji notes:

> There has also been an element of crony capitalism in Swedish privatizations of schools and other services: Public assets have been sold below their market price. The business lobby acted shortsightedly and used its influence

to thwart demands for more control and regulation. Fisman also brings up a scandal where a private-equity firm operating schools abruptly closed down their operations, causing chaos for 10,000 pupils. Regulation is now tighter, and some of this abuse has been stopped, but the fact that the center-right government only acted after national scandals has nevertheless damaged their credibility.[28]

Interestingly, even though vouchers to attend private schools are readily available to all Swedish students, as of 2014, only 14% of Swedish parents of 15-year-old students elected to use vouchers. Apparently not trusting such entities over the public system, one-third of Sweden's municipalities do not even have private schools. In Sweden, private schools are more likely to be located in cities.[29]

Another issue related to vouchers in Sweden, one already discussed in these pages, is their use as a means to school segregation. Despite the efforts of the Swedish government to institute the voucher system in a way that offers all students choice, two subgroups—Swedish children whose parents are more educated and Swedish nationals—are more likely to use vouchers than their counterparts. As Sweden's Institute for Evaluation of Labour Market and Education Policy (IFAU) researchers Anders Böhlmark, Helena Holmlund, and Mikael Lindahl note in their 2015 working paper, *School Choice and Segregation: Evidence from Sweden*:

> In regions where school choice has become more prevalent, school segregation between immigrants and natives, and between pupils with high/low parental education, has increased over and above what we should expect given neighbourhood sorting. The estimates indicating a positive association between school choice and segregation between immigrants and natives are robust throughout a number of empirical specifications. . . .
>
> Segregation in general is higher in urban municipalities, and these are also the municipalities where school choice has grown the most. . . .
>
> We cannot fully rule out that confounders are driving our results, but we believe that the evidence is in favour of a causal interpretation of the association between parental choice and school segregation between immigrants and natives, as well as between pupils of immigrant/Swedish background.[30]

Böhlmark and colleagues note that Sweden is "still a low-to-medium segregated country" when compared to other countries (e.g., Canada, the United Kingdom, and the United States). Surely one major contributing factor to higher rates of segregation in the United States than in Sweden involves America's centuries of ingrained racial inequity. The authors also make the point that even though school choice is available to all students across Sweden, many municipalities refuse to participate, thereby keeping increased school segregation in Sweden in check.

Chile

The only way that Friedman's theory of school choice could work is if opportunities for system gaming were nonexistent. His theory assumes that schools in the school choice system will be regulated by parental choice and that integrated schools are an expected byproduct of parental choice focused on academic excellence. Unfortunately, school choice in practice often serves as a vehicle for exploitation.

Perhaps the best illustration of Friedman-style economics gone awry involves the country of Chile. Between 1957 and 1970, approximately 100 university students from Chile studied economics at the University of Chicago, where their perspectives were shaped by Friedman. These Chilean students came to be known collectively as "the Chicago Boys." This group influenced Chilean General Augusto Pinochet, who seized power of the Chilean government in a coup in 1973. Once Pinochet was in power, the Chicago Boys became his principal economic advisors.[31]

As one might expect, they advised Pinochet to follow Friedman's ideas on school choice. Friedman himself visited Chile in 1975 and, at Pinochet's request, offered suggestions for Chile's economy.[32] Given that Pinochet had seized control of Chile by force, one might logically expect that the Chilean reality of Friedman's school choice ideal might go astray. Indeed, prior to Friedman's visit, in June 1974, Pinochet established himself as dictator of Chile.[33] In the midst of this upheaval comes Friedman's suggestion that Chile should decentralize its schools.

Dictatorial "decentralization" is nothing more than cosmetic. It should come as no surprise that local governments answered to a centralized government. Ironically, the situation of Chilean education under Pinochet is reminiscent of the dual educational systems created in the 21st-century United States in areas in which traditional public schools are required to compete with underregulated private and quasi-public charter schools for taxpayer funding. In Chile's case, such competition came from private schools that were allowed to charge tuition in addition to receiving government voucher funding.[34] In times in which the Chilean government decided not to pay voucher money to schools and instead divert it to other issues, private schools could still charge tuition, whereas public schools could not. Still, the public schools survived because the government apparently assumed responsibility for the effect its erratic voucher funding had on public schools by subsidizing public schools in financial crisis.[35]

Friedman's school choice model assumes that all schools equally compete for voucher money. It does not consider the possibility that private interests or other private funding (e.g., tuition) might afford some schools an advantage in the choice competition. It also holds compulsory education as a detriment to the success brought about by market-driven competition. In Chile, as in the United States, public schools could not reject students as private schools could.

Friedman's model also assumes that parents would not demur to an authoritarian government.[36]

Friedman's school choice model is utopian. Chilean education reality is not.

In 1995, the Chilean government introduced into its education system yet another component not accounted for in Friedman's choice theory, a test-based competition known as the System of Merit Awards to Schools (SNED), which includes financial merit awards to both schools and teachers based on student test scores.[37] Given the freedom of private schools to cultivate a preferential student body via student selection, it is no wonder that test results strongly coincide with socioeconomic status,[38] with financial rewards flowing to schools in less need than public schools.

Even though, as of 2010, Chile has democratic leadership in place,[39] the reality of school choice continues to rest more with schools than with parents. As researchers Veronica Lopez, Romina Madrid, and Vincente Sisto observe in their article, "Red Light" in Chile: Parents Participating as Consumers of Education Under Global Neoliberal Policies":

> In order to compete, many private subsidized schools have implemented selection processes to exclude those who might have a negative impact on tests scores or that would "drive quality down." Given this practice, it is the school that chooses the family and not the other way around! Schools are choosing parents through stringent selection processes and voiding enrollment if the student does not "adapt to the school." The "chosen few" are those with high economic, cultural, and social capital. . . .
>
> Municipal schools, on the other hand, do not select their students. They cater to all students, including those rejected by private entrepreneurs, students from low-income families. . . .
>
> Thus despite the benefits of freedom to choose proclaimed by Friedman's (1955) market theory, research in Chile has shown that the main consequences of three decades of implementation of this model in education have been the segmentation of the educational system and a modest track record of achievements in terms of [overall] learning outcomes. . . .
>
> The [school] selection process does not operate using the expected academic-driven rationale.[40]

Yet another example of choice working to the advantage of the school, not the student. Yet another example of school choice as resulting in segregation.

Certainly not Friedman-styled, school choice utopia.

Milwaukee

The oldest and largest voucher program in the United States, Milwaukee, Wisconsin, has had its program in place since 1990. Students were allowed to choose to attend private schools using public funding. Initially considered an experiment with only 340 students participating, the Milwaukee Parent Choice Program was expanded in 1995 to include religious schools. By the 2000–2001 school year, roughly 9,200 Milwaukee students were using school vouchers to attend 103 private schools.[41] By 2015, the numbers had risen to 26,000 students at 112 private schools.

Gauging the success of the Milwaukee voucher program has become somewhat of a game. For example, an "independent" research investigator of the Milwaukee voucher program is Patrick Wolf of the University of Arkansas Department of Educational Reform, which is funded by the Walton Foundation.[42] The Walton Foundation is a major supporter of school choice, which introduces a major conflict of interest that makes Wolf less than independent. In a 2012 study conducted by Wolf and others, *Student Attainment and the Milwaukee Parental Choice Program: A Final Follow-Up Analysis*,[43] researchers claim that voucher "exposure" contributed to students being "somewhat more likely" to graduate high school and enroll in four-year postsecondary institutions. However, what is clear from reading the study is that most students in the sample (56%) were no longer enrolled in the voucher program by their senior year. (At one point, the number reported was 75%, but the researchers changed it after the study had been published.)[44] Yet these students were counted as voucher students because they had been "exposed" to vouchers—as though a voucher is a medication or a disease.

In short, the study by Wolf and colleagues offered no evidence to substantiate the assertion that the use of school vouchers had improved public education in Milwaukee. The lackluster results of this study appear to be supported by equally lackluster results on Wisconsin state tests in 2013–2014, not only for voucher use in Milwaukee but statewide. In reports in which students results were reported for all students statewide, in Milwaukee, and in Racine, and then with voucher students removed statewide, in Milwaukee, and in Racine, respectively, scores often did not change, and if they did, the resulting average test score rose with the removal of voucher students.[45]

When it comes to state test scores, the Milwaukee voucher program appears to keep up with students who chose not to participate, at best.

And despite these disappointing results, public money continues to be funneled to private schools via vouchers. Moreover, the money flow is not regulated. As Milwaukee's *Journal Sentinel* education writer Alan Borsuk noted in 2012:

> MPS (Milwaukee Public Schools) schools have elaborate accountability systems and tons of information is available about each school. . . .
>
> Milwaukee charter schools also are required to report quite a bit of information publicly. . . .
>
> Voucher schools, however, report to pretty much no one. They are accredited by organizations, but accreditation is kind of a big-picture look at whether a place fits the definition of a school. It is not really an accountability system. In practical terms, it's really hard for anyone to tell a voucher school to shape up or lose your money, if the school meets a variety of regulations. A very limited amount of information on voucher schools is public record. . . .
>
> One of the core principles of the voucher movement was that parental choice would provide accountability because parents would choose only good schools. Frankly, that hasn't played out well at quite a few specific schools.[46]

The legislative session of 2015 appeared to be the one that would yield a bill detailing how Wisconsin's voucher schools might be held accountable to the public. Unfortunately, no such legislation was passed, despite Governor Scott Walker's declared intention to expand Wisconsin's school voucher program. In an *Urban Milwaukee* piece, Senate Democratic leader Jennifer Schilling observes in April 2015:

> Over the past decade, more than fifty taxpayer-subsidized private schools have been kicked out of the voucher program for issues ranging from financial mismanagement and fraud to student health and safety concerns. Under Senate Bill 3, taxpayer-subsidized voucher schools would be required to hire licensed teachers, conduct staff background checks, meet state graduation standards and be located in Wisconsin.[47]

The likes of Senate Bill 3 are long overdue in Wisconsin. Indeed, another issue that should be addressed concerns where to draw the line for publicly funded private schools that are able to hide behind private school status when choosing to selectively respect student rights. Milwaukee journalist Barbara Miner captures the public–private tension present when the state funds a program beyond its ability to regulate the program:

> Limits have been lifted on the percentage of voucher students in a school. As a result, every single student in a Milwaukee voucher school can receive a publicly funded voucher, yet the school is still defined as "private." Last year, most of

the schools enrolled predominantly voucher students; 27 schools were 100% voucher students. . . .

The problem is most clear when one looks at Wisconsin law that prohibits discrimination against students in public schools—a law that voucher schools can ignore. . . .

Nor are we talking insignificant amounts of money. Since vouchers began in Wisconsin, more than $1.8 billion in public dollars has been given to private voucher schools. This year alone, the three voucher programs in Wisconsin will receive $209 million in taxpayer funding. . . .

Conservatives have used the rhetoric of "choice" to mask the legislatively sanctioned discrimination within the voucher program. . . .

The fundamental question is why schools that are completely dependent on public tax dollars get to define themselves as private and play by vastly different rules than public schools.[48]

In sum, what Wisconsin has is a 25-year-old urban school voucher program that has not produced student outcomes that surpass those of its public schools but that is not regulated. As a result, this system and allows for unchecked fraud and discrimination—even as it stands to be expanded.

Cleveland and Washington, D.C.

Cleveland, Ohio, also has a school voucher program, instituted beginning with the 1996–1997 school year. Though the program allowed parents to choose to send their children to either private schools or public schools in an adjacent district, only private schools participated, most of which are religious schools.[49] The program was soon challenged in court for allowing state funds to be spent on religious education, thereby potentially violating the Establishment Clause. The program was suspended in 1998 and declared unconstitutional in 1999–2000 in both federal and circuit courts. However, in 2002, the U.S. Supreme Court reversed the decision by a 5 to 4 vote.[50] In 2015, the maximum amount allowed for a K–8 voucher was $4,250, and for high school, $5,700.[51]

What is interesting about the Cleveland voucher program is that does not appear to be steeped in corruption. That is, no stream of scandalous stories is readily associated with the private schools that accept vouchers from Cleveland students. What is equally noteworthy is there appears to be no mechanism in place for systematic oversight of the Cleveland private schools accepting vouchers. The state approves the schools, and students attending the voucher schools must take state tests,[52] but there is no means for discerning what the publicly funded voucher is specifically funding. In short, no audit of public funds sent with the student to the private school is required. Once the private school receives the public money, the money trail ends.

Concerning academic outcomes, the educational benefits of Cleveland's voucher program appear to be mixed at best. Based on 2012–2014 state testing results posted on the Ohio Department of Education website,[53] students attending private schools using vouchers outscore their public school counterparts in reading. However, the opposite tends to be true for math. For grades in which science scores are available, the results are mixed.[54]

Thus, even though Cleveland has had a school voucher program for almost two decades, such choice has yet to demonstrate it is clearly and overwhelmingly superior to its public education system counterpart.

One more. The school voucher system in Washington, D.C., has the distinction of being the first federally funded school voucher program. Known as the DC Opportunity Scholarship Program, school vouchers in DC were the result of legislation under President George W. Bush, the DC School Choice Incentive Act of 2003.[55] Written in so-called "accountability" language reminiscent of No Child Left Behind (NCLB), the purpose of the program was to Save Children from Failing Schools until such schools improved:

> The purpose of this Act is to provide low-income parents residing in the District of Columbia, particularly parents of students who attend elementary schools or secondary schools identified for improvement, corrective action, or restructuring under section 1116 of the Elementary and Secondary Education Act of 1965 (20 U.S.C. 6316), with expanded opportunities for enrolling their children in other schools in the District of Columbia, at least until the public schools in the District of Columbia have adequately addressed shortfalls in health, safety, and security, and the students in the District of Columbia public schools are testing in mathematics and reading at or above the national average.[56]

The legislation provided for grants of up to $8,000 for students in grades K–8 and up to $12,000 for students in high school, with amounts to be adjusted for inflation. Schools receiving voucher money had to be located in DC and had to agree to oversight, including site visits and providing information on accreditation. Of course, given the atmosphere of accountability based on test scores, participating voucher schools were required to comply with federal testing mandates.

A 2008 *Washington Post* article reported the number of DC students participating in the voucher program at 1,903 in grades K–12 and attending 54 private voucher schools for a cost of roughly $12 million.[57] In 2009, President Barack Obama planned to phase out the DC voucher program, allowing the then-enrolled 1,713 students to finish but not allowing new students to enroll.[58] In 2010, the DC voucher program was continued under new legislation, the Scholarships for Opportunity and Results Act (SOAR).[59] A September 2013 Government Accountability Office (GAO) report had the number of DC students receiving vouchers at almost 5,000 for a total cost of $152 million since program inception.[60]

A 2007 GAO audit of the DC voucher program found inadequate oversight from the administrative agent, the Washington Scholarship Fund:

> In 2007, we reviewed OSP and found a need for increased accountability from the program administrator. Specifically, we found that the administrator at the time of our review—the Washington Scholarship Fund—did not have the capacity to oversee participating private schools and administer a growing scholarship program funded with federal dollars. We also found that because of inadequate accountability mechanisms, the program administrator could not provide key information to low-income families about school performance, quality indicators.
>
> In 2010, the Washington Scholarship Fund withdrew as the administrator of OSP and the Department of Education (Education) transferred the grant to run the program to the DC Children and Youth Investment Trust Corporation (the Trust).[61]

As it turns out, the 2013 GAO audit found that the Trust did not sufficiently, efficiently, and correctly communicate information to the public regarding the application process and about the DC voucher schools themselves, including accreditation status, the amount of voucher money needed for attendance at some schools, additional fees, and the expectation of parental involvement in school activities.

Another problem identified as hampering school choice was parental notification that their children had received vouchers after application deadlines had passed for many schools. This left parents to choose from among schools that had not closed the application process or that were willing to allow students to enter despite their missing the application deadline.

The Trust was also criticized for monitoring voucher school compliance in part by relying on self-reporting from the voucher schools. Even when it conducted site visits, the Trust do not bother examining school documents to verify voucher schools' self-reported compliance on issues such as accreditation status and financial solvency, including the degree to which the school was dependent on voucher money to keep its doors open. The Trust

did not even have adequate procedures in place for addressing noncompli-
ance if it did happen to discover such information, nor did it adequately
document its own expenses.[62]

In short, the DC voucher program was hardly managed at all.

The market was in charge of itself, a runaway vehicle recklessly running
over the supposed empowerment of Friedman-credited parental choice.

CHAPTER 5

The Origin of the Charter School

I remember the first time I learned that someone I knew was connected to a charter school. It was 1995, and I had been teaching at an alternative school in northern Georgia. It was a small school; I was the entire English department. Every time I received a new student, it was because that student had either been expelled from another school or strongly encouraged to leave. I applied for and accepted the position because a colleague I knew and trusted had become principal.

Teaching at and operating this alternative school required much energy. Since the school had no assistant principal, I filled in as a substitute administrator when the principal was absent, mostly in the role of disciplinarian. Given the intensity of mental and emotional effort and time commitment needed to operate the school, and given the travel distance to the school (60 miles one way from the town in which both my principal and I resided), I was not surprised to learn at the end of that first year that my friend resigned his position as principal to accept another administrative position in a "regular" school close to home. In discussing my principal's decision with another colleague, I remember her commenting distrustfully, "Yes, but the school he will be working at is a charter school."

I knew the school. It had a good reputation, so far as I had heard. I knew very little about the charter school concept at that time. I did know that they were not run by a local school board and instead operated via their own negotiated agreement, their charter. However, this colleague's passing comment was the first time I had experienced anyone offering a negative sentiment regarding charter schools. In 1995 in Georgia, there was no campaign to grade teachers and schools using student test scores. There was no media exposure about "bad" teachers in Georgia needing to be "held accountable." In fact, in the district in which I taught from 1995 to 1998, teachers were given a series of raises, 6% each year for 4 consecutive years, as a result of Georgia lottery revenue provided for school funding as promised.

In sum, there was not yet a "failing public school" atmosphere in Georgia and no goaded competition between traditional public schools and privately run, publicly funded charters that were touted as the means of ensuring some supposedly threatened U.S. global competitiveness. There was no educational business push to take over traditional Georgia public schools as a self-serving, opportunistic means of dipping into taxpayer money with little to no oversight.

Nevertheless, I will not forget that moment in 1995 and the air of distrust surrounding the idea of a school being a charter school and how foreign such distrust was to me those 20 years ago.

THE CHARTER SCHOOL CONCEPT

The idea of the charter school originated with University of Massachusetts Amherst retired School of Education professor, Ray Budde. Originally from St. Louis, Budde attended St. Louis University, from which he graduated in 1943. After serving in the U.S. Navy during World War II, Budde returned to Illinois and earned his MBA. He then moved to East Lansing, Michigan, where he taught and later became an administrator. While in Michigan, Budde earned a doctorate in education from Michigan State University in 1959.[1]

In 1966, Budde joined the faculty of the University of Massachusetts Amherst School of Education, where he taught until 1973. Following his time as a university professor, Budde served as the director of the Upton, Massachusetts, Blackstone Valley Educational Collaborative until 1985.[2]

It was just after Budde left the university that he presented his idea for what he called a "charter school" in a 1974 educational conference paper at the annual meeting of the Society for General Systems Research.[3] In 1988, Budde published the article "Education by Charter: Restructuring Our School Districts" for the Regional Laboratory for Educational Improvement in Andover, Massachusetts. In his paper, Budde offers a fictitious example of how a superintendent might go about converting a traditionally board-run school district, Hometown Public Schools, into a district run by use of a chartering agreement system. In this example, the superintendent proposes a "Decade Plan for School Improvement for the Hometown Public Schools." To understand Budde's original intention, one must suspend the modern idea of charter schools run by charter operators outside of the school district. In contrast, Budde's idea involves teacher teams within the district producing their own ideas for schools.

Here is Budde's 10-year "vision for the public schools of Hometown":

> **Year One:** Encourage up to three pilot teams of teachers to develop three- to five-year plans for the school board to approve. These plans—I call them "Educational Charters"—would include items such as: rationale and scope of their teaching and curriculum; description of the developmental and learning needs of their pupils; strategies for helping pupils acquire lifelong learning skills;

how career plans and professional growth activities are linked
with curriculum and program needs; materials, media to be used
(including computer applications); and the manner in which inside/
outside program evaluation will take place.

Years Two and Three: Depending on when the applications for
charters are completed and approved, the pilot teams would go into
the first of their three- to five-year plans. One team might be ready
by the start of school in [one year]; the others might not be ready
until the following year.

Year Four: Presuming that the pilot teams were being successful
and that there were an increasing number of teams of teachers
wanting to develop charters, I would see the need for an intensive
institute/workshop to address needs such as: How does the school
board change its pattern of operation so that it can spend an
increasing amount of time on curriculum matters? How should the
ever-expanding amount of knowledge be categorized for school
purposes? What K–12 functions should be institutionalized to
support educational charters during their planning and operational
stages? Participants in this institute/workshop would include:
school board; professional staff; parents, community resource
persons, and others who have helped in starting Education by
Charters; representatives from the secondary schools/colleges
accrediting agency; and selected experts depending on the questions
to be addressed. (State "school improvement funds" could be
tapped to cover the cost of such an institute/workshop.)

Year Five: Under the school district curriculum structure worked out
at the institute/workshop, additional teams of teachers would be
encouraged to apply for charters. Detailed plans for new K–12
functions (including budget amounts) would be developed so that
these functions would become operational in July [of the coming
school year].

Year Six: The newly designed functions to support educational
charters would be implemented. The early charters would be
expiring and teams would have to decide whether to let the charter
terminate or to apply for a new or revised charter. It is hoped that
by the end of this school year 75% of education in Hometown
would be conducted under educational charters.

Years Seven through Nine: The new organization for the Hometown
Public Schools (based on Education by Charter) would now
be in full operation. During Year Eight, the Hometown High
School would host its ten-year accreditation visitation team. The
accrediting agency will have already approved the reorganization of
the curriculum of the high school. The high school will be evaluated
on the basis of its performance within the new curriculum structure.

Year Ten: A second intensive institute/workshop would be held to
evaluate the impact of the reorganization of the school district.
Out of this evaluation would come the seeds and shape of the
second decade plan for the Hometown Public Schools. The second
decade plan would start on July 1 [of the coming school year] and
end June 30 [ten years later].[4]

Notice that Budde's plan leaves no room for teacher or district disenfran-
chisement, or for outside interests to form their own charters and assume
control of the district in the name of choice. His plan also is absent of potential fiscal exploitation.

In his scenario, Budde envisions the charter as a means of reaching
"the untapped, unused capabilities of people," including "the vast reserve
of energy and learning power within bored and unstimulated pupils"; "the
richness and creativity inside the heads and hearts of teachers locked into
an outdated curriculum, using bland, outdated textbooks—locked into an
instructional system which they had no part in making and which they have
no power to change"; "the communication and group process skills of principals which are poorly used because they are saddled with the impossible,
know-it-all, generalized role of educational leader"; "the unfulfilled aspirations of parents who stand outside the system and who see the initial enthusiasm of their children turn to 'Ugh—school!' as the weight of 'schooling'
takes its effect"; and "the dried up energy of a librarian with a vision of
connecting books, materials, and computer data banks with learning experiences having to settle for 'teaching the kids how to use the library'"
(page 39).

In sum, Budde proposed his charter school idea as a means of revolu-
tionizing public education from the inside out, by way of those invested in
the system—not by career-climbing, profit-seeking education business and
policy people descending on a district, imposing their own bureaucracy, and
in the end, being the ones with the power and means to be intentionally
positioned to "choose."

Budde's report continues the scenario with a follow-up information session between Superintendent Wright and the Hometown School
Board. In this addendum, Budde suggests that school superintendents
should move on after a decade, having exhausted their creativity. Another
suggestion involves teachers receiving "three- to five-year mandates (and
funds) for instruction directly from the school board—with no one between the teachers and the school board"[5] and cutting out all other levels
of bureaucracy, including principals, superintendents, and even curriculum
directors.

Under Budde's blueprint, the only way principals and curriculum
directors could participate in decision making (i.e., be included on the
teacher-directed charter teams) would be if they are also currently in

the classroom. Other stakeholders, such as parents and those from post-secondary institutions, could be on the teams.

Budde also proposes that planning via the charter committee would have to happen outside of the school day. His fictional Superintendent Wright states, "Teaching should be a full-time, full-year professional job," and continues by saying that charter team meetings should occur when school is not in session, including weekends, evenings, and vacations. Even though Budde calls for additional compensation for an increased teacher workload, his paper does not address the potential for teacher burnout. However, it does advocate for increased clerical assistance for teachers.

The charter team as envisioned by Budde would have the power to negotiate with the school board over resource allocation and hiring replacement staff, when necessary. The charter teams could also offer options to parents for different ways a subject might be taught, thereby introducing the element of competition and empowering parents to become more involved in public education via the ability to choose programs offered by different schools in the district.

In Budde's charter-team conception, if parents do not choose to enroll students based on the ideas of one charter team, the teachers might lose the charter but not their jobs. Thus, high-stakes outcomes leading to potential gaming the chartering system would be reduced. Teachers could simply try again with a new teaching idea and by forming a new team and applying to the school board for a new charter if they wish.

A final observation is that Budde wanted to pilot his charter idea and not recklessly proceed to overzealous full implementation. His 110-page report was an effort to expose readers to many of the details involved in his vision about how teachers might become the empowered center of the local-board-led public education process. Nevertheless, he clearly realized that his ideas on paper and implemented in real districts were not one and the same. He did, however, believe that some sort of school district restructuring needed to happen for efforts to "upgrade" American education to succeed.[6]

AFT PRESIDENT ALBERT SHANKER
AND THE SCHOOL-WITHIN-A-SCHOOL

Also in 1988, American Federation of Teachers (AFT) President Albert Shanker[7] presented Budde's idea for charter teams to the National Press Club. In his speech, Shanker acknowledged the need for states to pass legislation regarding moving from the "soft" public education of the 1960s and 1970s to one based upon standards and regulations, such as the length of the school day. However, Shanker then noted that it was time for public education professionals "to come up with their own [reforms] and, indeed, with better answers than would be imposed upon them from those not actually involved in the field."[8]

Shanker argued that "the first wave of reforms" attempting to address criticisms of U.S. education in the 1983 Reagan Administration report, *A Nation at Risk*, could not meet the needs of a varied student body:

> We're doing more and maybe a little better of the same things we've always done. We're back at one end of the pendulum swing this country seems always to move in. Now we have tight standards—and that's very good for the kids who are able to fit the traditional system, but it tends to say to all the other kids: "Don't go on, because you're not going to make it." And then we say, "That's no good, because we're pushing too many out." So we soften up the standards, and then we say, "That's good, because we're keeping a lot of kids in school." But then the kids who used to learn a lot aren't learning so much, because they know they can get a free ride."
>
> We are now moving back to higher standards, but we always seem to be moving back and forth between easy and tough, hard and soft. Very few people are asking, "Can we do something that's different? Can we move out of this pendulum swing, neither end of which is very good for anybody?"[9]

Shanker continued by stating that the current education reform response suited the approximately 20% of students who were academically capable and just needed to be challenged to meet their potential, but it did not suit the needs of the remaining 80% of students. He added, "We don't have flexibility; we don't adjust."[10]

Shanker saw the "second wave of reform"—the one aimed at meeting the needs of the remaining 80% of students—as having already begun via healthy collective bargaining relationships. But more was needed, Shanker maintained, in the form of a proposal for "a new type of school."[11] Enter Budde's idea of teacher-directed charter teams, slightly modified.

Shanker continued:

> This union now needs to seek ways that will enable any group of teachers . . . in any building—and any group of parents to opt for a different type of school.
>
> How would this work? The school district and the teacher union would develop a procedure that would encourage any group of six or more teachers to submit a proposal to create a new school. Do not think of a school as a building, and you can see how it works. Consider six or seven or twelve teachers in a school who say, "We've got an idea. We've got a way of reaching the kids that are not being reached by what the school is doing."

> That group of teachers could set up a school within a school which ulti-
> mately, if the procedure works and it's accepted, would be a totally autonomous
> school within the district.[12]

Shanker's conception of a "school within a school" extends Budde's idea
by allowing the charter team to become a school in its own right, not just
on a team focusing on a particular teaching style for a certain subject.
Shanker also introduced the idea that the union might be involved in charter
approval, not just the school board.

Even though Shanker did not want to lock the idea for a school within
a school into an exact mold, or "master plan," he did offer ideas of qualities
that might be effective in such school proposals:

> I would approve such a proposal if it included a plan for faculty decision mak-
> ing, for participative management; team teaching; a way for a teaching team to
> govern itself. . . .
>
> I would also include the following: How would you design a school that
> would eliminate most of the harmful aspects of schools at the present time? We
> know that everybody learns at his or her own rate, but schools are organized so
> the kids better learn at the rate the teacher is talking. . . .
>
> Can we come up with a plan that does not require kids to do something
> that most adults can't do, which is to sit still for five or six hours a day listening
> to someone talk? . . . Kids who are able to do it later become college graduates.
> That's the greatest educational requirement that we have.
>
> What about a plan that says that learning mathematics or social studies is
> more than repeating and regurgitating back things on standardized examinations,
> that we're going to have a school that also develops creativity and other aspects
> of intelligence? Because the kids who do the best on these tests are not necessarily
> people who later on in life make the greatest contributions to society. . . .
>
> I would also ask the teachers who submit a plan to show that the group of
> kids that they're taking in reflects the composition of the entire school. That is,
> we are not talking about a school where all the advantaged kids or all the white
> kids or any other group is segregated to one group. The school would have to
> reflect the whole group.[13]

In his conceptualization of this new type of school, Shanker defined "choice"
in such a way that both parent and teacher would be empowered—not some
outside entity descending on a school:

> This would be a school of choice; that is, no teacher would be forced to be in
> this subunit, and neither would any parent be compelled to send a child to this
> school. It would be a way for parents and teachers to cooperate with each other,
> to build a new structure.[14]

Regarding funding, Shanker advocated that the charter school operate using "the same money that other schools do." Though he alludes to "cost savings" associated with more manageable, small-group teacher accountability, Shanker did not detail the potential budgeting burden of a district's financing an additional school and how such might affect funding for existing schools. Shanker did expect additional funding from the federal government, state government, philanthropy and/or business; however, such funding was supposed to be for technology and networking expenses (e.g., additional teacher professional development and collaboration meetings).

Shanker believed in starting small with his teacher-led, school-within-a-school plan because of too much potential resistance from too great a change at once. He did not believe that the new-school concept should be imposed on teachers who had not bought into it, and he recommended that associated educational policy should reflect such support for smaller, innovative teacher groups.

Finally, among the key issues in Shanker's plan were teachers governing themselves, including setting outcome goals and publicizing the results; no stiff classroom atmosphere in which students are expected to be the well-behaved recipients of teacher-dispensed learning; no hyper focus on standardized tests as the supreme evidence of student learning; and no using the school-within-a-school concept to isolate students into biased groupings.

These attributes do not apply to many 21st-century charter schools. In such schools, teachers are not empowered. Students are often trained to parrot "toe the line" compliance in the name of "no excuses" behavior management. Standardized test scores are the end-all determination of school success. And charters often employ procedures to ensure a certain, preferred student demographic.

In short, the 21st-century charter was not what either Budde or Shanker envisioned.

SHANKER, BUDDE, AND THE CHARTER SCHOOL

Shanker's school-within-a-school idea was featured in *The New York Times* on April 1, 1988. Included was the following polite yet neutral reception from the U.S. Secretary of Education's office:

> Responding to Mr. Shanker's remarks, William Kristol, chief of staff and counselor to Education Secretary William J. Bennett, said the department "didn't have problems" with the proposal, but added, "We think there is lots of evidence that traditional methods are working."[15]

In a 1996 *Phi Delta Kappan* article, Budde also noted the quiet reception his idea initially received:

> Back in the early 1970s I developed an outline for a book tentatively titled *Education by Charter: Key to a New Model of School District*. I circulated the outline to a number of my colleagues and friends, some of whom were superintendents and principals, and asked them, "Does this charter concept make any sense? Is it workable? Do you know any school districts that would be willing to give this a try?"
>
> The response: zero. Nothing. Oh, some of my friends thought the idea was "interesting." . . .
>
> It soon became evident that I was pushing something that was simply not going to happen. So I put the idea of "education by charter" on the shelf and went on to other things.[16]

Amid much public discussion on reports such as *A Nation at Risk*, Budde published his book about the teacher-led, charter team concept in 1988. Meanwhile, Shanker did as he proposed in his March 1988 speech to the National Press Club: At the AFT convention in the summer of 1988, he encouraged local unions to support his idea for teacher-led schools-within-a-school. AFT delegates voted to seek a cooperative arrangement whereby local school boards and local unions together would develop a protocol, according to Shanker, "that would enable teams of teachers and others to submit and implement proposals to set up their own autonomous public schools within their school buildings."[17] Reflecting on the favorable reception of this approach at the 1988 AFT convention, Shanker wrote in his July 10, 1988, "Where We Stand" column for *The New York Times*, "The main idea that gripped the delegates was the prospect of having hundreds, even thousands of school teams actively looking for better ways—different methods, technologies, organizations of time and human resources—to produce more learning for more students."[18]

In that same column, Shanker's and Budde's ideas for teacher-led schools came together when Shanker publicly named his version of "school within a school" using Budde's term, *charter*:

> There is a problem in finding a name for these schools. School-within-a-school is technically correct, but that name has two problems. First, it makes people think of the 1960s and 70s alternative schools that thought that they already had all the answers and whose standard was, "do your own thing." But the purpose of the AFT delegates was to help authorize school teams to search for answers and to underscore the importance of high standards for all students. Second, many schools-within-schools were or are treated like traitors or outlaws for daring to move out of the lock-step and do something different. . . . But the AFT delegates

advocated the establishment of a regular policy mechanism that would make innovation an ongoing and valued part of the school community. But what name
could capture all this?

   The best answer so far is "charter schools," a suggestion made by Ray
Budde in "Educating by Charter: Restructuring School Districts". . . . Explorers
got charters to seek new lands and new resources. . . . As Budde notes, the charter concept can also be applied to public education.[19]

Budde's charter teams idea did not involve starting independent schools. Before he wrote the column in which he combined Budde's terminology with
his own ideas to form the new concept of *charter schools*, Shanker did not
consult with Budde. In fact, Budde found out in Juky 1988 when his wife
told him, "Hey, Ray, you're in *The New York Times*!" as she was reading
Shanker's column.[20] In a 1996 *Phi Delta Kappan* article, Budde admits having "mixed feelings" about his charter teams idea being altered to apply to
independent schools-within-schools:

> Starting a brand-new school stirs the creative and adaptive juices of everyone
> involved. Starting a new school requires a deep sense of commitment and hours
> and hours of time. It's a truly unique peak experience, with frequent jour-
> neys down the mountain to valleys of anxiety and frustration. I had to admit
> that there was a much more powerful dynamic at work in chartering a whole
> school than in simply chartering a department or program. If everyone else had
> decided that it was more strategic to charter schools than programs, so be it.[21]

LET THE CHARTER LEGISLATION
(AND CHARTER SCHOOL OPPORTUNISM) BEGIN

Building on the ideas of Budde and Shanker, in the spring of 1988, a committee of the Minnesota Citizens League began developing its version of
charter schools.[22]

   By November 1988, as a means of advising the Minnesota legislature
to enact policies to formally allow for charter schools, the Citizens League
published a proposal that charters become stand-alone schools in their own
buildings and that they meet certain criteria, including those that would
"prevent creation of 'elitist' schools," such as "an affirmative plan for promoting integration by ability level and race"; that student refusals be based
on lack of space, not any intention to "cream" academically able students
unless the purpose of the school was to meet the needs of a specific subset
of students, such as those at academic risk; that schools be prohibited from
charging tuition; and that charter schools be operated by licensed teachers.[23]

   Much of this proposal focused on complex problems associated with
desegregating Minnesota's public schools by race, family income, and the

effect of family income on a child's future academic success. The committee suggested that the Minnesota legislature carefully consider and study
the implications of attempts at desegregating schools via solutions such
as redistricting so as not to exacerbate segregation issues. Moreover, the
Citizens League committee suggested that the legislature allow for the authorizing of charter schools via school board in Minneapolis and St. Paul
beginning in September 1989 and that by 1992, charter authorization
would also be granted via the state department of education. However,
the state department of education would "not play a part in the school's
operation." The chartered group would operate the school, basically on its
honor to follow laws and regulations. Teachers would be funded by the
state but would not be employees of the school district. Teachers would be
free to join unions.[24]

During both the 1989 and 1990 legislative sessions, Minnesota Senator
Ember Reichgott was able to include the charter school idea as part of a
Senate omnibus bill that did not make it out of House committee. In 1991,
with the help of other legislators, Reichgott was successful: The Minnesota
legislature passed the nation's first charter school bill.[25] The bill did not
establish or mandate charter schools; it only allowed them. Former chair of
the University of Minnesota Humphrey Institute Center for School Change
Joe Nathan, who was involved with the Citizens League charter effort in
1988, was a catalyst for encouraging teachers and others to submit proposals for charter schools. In 1992, California passed charter school legislation,
and in 1993, other states did so as well, including Colorado, Massachusetts,
and Wisconsin.[26]

Even as numerous statehouses adopted this legislation, Shanker was
becoming concerned about the potential for charter school operators to
exploit public education dollars. In his July 3, 1994, "Where We Stand"
column, Shanker wrote:

A key idea behind charter schools . . . is that many terrific opportunities to improve public education are squelched by school bureaucracies. Charter school
laws . . . are supposed to allow teachers and others the chance to establish public schools that are largely independent of state and local control. . . . But it's not
so easy to draw the line. . . .

This problem is already obvious in Michigan. . . . The first "school" out
of the gate will be the Noah Webster Academy, . . . a clever scheme to get public money for children who are already being educated by their parents—at
home.

. . . Noah Webster's founder . . . has signed up 700 students—mostly Chris-
tian home schoolers—for a school that is actually a computer network. The
students will continue to study at home the way they do now, but every family
will get a taxpayer-paid computer, printer and modem, and there will be an
optional curriculum. . . .

Noah Webster's founder discovered a tiny, impoverished school district—it has 23 students, one teacher, and a teacher's aide, and it nearly went broke a few years ago. It agreed to sponsor his school [now known as Noah Webster] and give it a 99-year charter, in return for a kickback of about $40,000.[27]

Shanker continues by noting that Noah Webster garnered roughly $4 million in state funding for a so-called school that actually had kids sitting at home in front of a computer. More than 20 years after Shanker wrote this account, and as noted in Chapter 4, similar stories of exploitation associated with charter schools abound.

Shanker was concerned about the need for charter school legislation to be "carefully crafted and controlled" to prevent the raiding of public coffers. He warned that charter schools could not improve public education if such schools were divorced from the districts whose students they were supposed to serve—and all without any public debate or oversight.[28]

Over the next few remaining years of his life (he died in February 1997),[29] Shanker continued to voice his concern about charter schools being perceived as the "panacea" for all ills of American public education. One of his chief concerns was about how charter school success might be gauged, including the false or easy success based on a charter school's ability to draw an academically preferred student body. In December 1994, he wrote:

Given the current enthusiasm for charters, a school that has not yet opened may have more applicants than it has places. If these schools select their students according to criteria like grades, interviews and student and parent interest, they will be able to pick kids who are likely to do well—the way private schools do now. Even in states where the law requires charter schools to use a lottery to decide among applicants, self-selection will undoubtedly give charters highly motivated student bodies. It will not be remarkable if these students achieve at high levels, even if a new school does nothing new or creative.[30]

Shanker came to see charter schools as disappointingly far from his 1988 conception of them as providing the necessary opportunity to increase the quality of education though teacher-invested innovation rooted in measurable outcomes and impervious to corruption. In his December 1996 "Where We Stand" column, Shanker noted that the charter school had become "an oxymoron, a private school that is funded with public money."[31] He illustrated this view with the story of a Washington, D.C., charter school that was approved by a board that had no idea about the credentials of the charter school leader, no details on the financial state of the school, and no appreciable understanding of the proposed curriculum. The charter school leader had been charged with assault with a deadly weapon in 1986, and the school security guard (the school leader's nephew) had been convicted of armed robbery and assault with a deadly weapon in 1978, armed robbery in 1984, possession of cocaine in 1989, and attempted unauthorized use of a motor vehicle in 1995.[32] Pointing to this example, Shanker commented about "exactly why such things as charter schools and school voucher programs cannot succeed in the end":

> A pluralistic society cannot sustain a scheme in which the citizenry pays for a school but has no influence over how the school is run. . . . Public money is shared money, and it is to be used for the furtherance of shared values, in the interest of *e pluribus unum*. Charter schools and their like are definitely antithetical to this promise.[33]

Even as Shanker had clearly soured on the idea of charter schools by 1996, Budde's view was more favorable. He viewed the charter schools as a potential catalyst for positive change. Writing in 1996, he observed:

> Policy makers and citizen groups in Minnesota pushed the charter concept in another direction and, in a real sense, were the ones responsible for starting the nationwide charter school movement. Ted Kolderie explained the intent of the charter school idea . . . :
>
>> The essential idea is worth re-stating: It is to offer change-oriented educators or others the opportunity to go either to the local school board or to some other public body for a contract under which they would set up an autonomous (and therefore performance-based) public school which students could choose to attend without charge. The intent is not simply to produce a few new and hopefully better schools. It is to create dynamics that will cause the main-line system to change so as to improve education for all students. . . .
>>
>> It suddenly dawned on me . . . that we have a once-in-many-generations—opportunity. . . . Scholars of school district decentralization report that more than half of the larger districts in the country are trying out some form of [site based management, or SBM] . . . .
>> Perhaps the charter concept can be useful in strengthening this movement to decentralize medium-sized to large school districts. . . . I thought about how I might be able to link chartering schools with SBM.[34]

Whereas in his 1996 *Phi Delta Kappan* piece cited previously, Budde considered the freeing aspects of SBM, in the issues raised in subsequent chapters of this book, regarding the utility of SBM in education, he does not broach the topic of the very real potential for fiscal mismanagement and exploitation of students in an under-managed system—and especially a high-stakes system with few controls in which school survival depends on student test scores. In short, Budde apparently did not anticipate the serious potential for charter operator corruption when decentralization translated into a lack of accountability to the public for how public money was being spent—and the potential to game a system in which charter authorizers were proving to be a vulnerable link.

CHAPTER 6

Who Wants Charters?

Support for charter schools among politicians and within the educational community has shifted significantly since the first charter school legislation was approved in Minnesota in 1991—as have the structure and degree of oversight on these schools envisioned by early proponents. By 2015, according to the Education Commission of the States website, 42 states, the District of Columbia, and Puerto Rico all had charter school laws. Of these, 33 states had charter authorizing bodies, yet only 15 states and Washington, D.C., had standards for charter authorizers and the requirement that charter authorizers annually produce formal reports regarding the charter schools they oversee. Furthermore, only 11 states and the District of Columbia specify performance criteria to determine whether a charter should be continued or revoked.[1]

CHARTER SCHOOLS:
BIPARTISAN WITH A CONSERVATIVE STREAK

Who wants charter schools? In Minnesota, Democratic Senator Ember Reichgott[2] was the first to author and successfully pass charter school legislation. The governor who signed Minnesota's charter school legislation into law in 1991, Arne Carlson, Sr., was a Democrat until the early 1960s, when he switched to the Republican Party. Interestingly, Carlson has the distinction of being the first Republican governor in Minnesota to be denied his party's endorsement for reelection.[3]

In 1992, California became the second state to pass charter school legislation. Authored by Democratic Senator Gary Hart, SB 1448 allowed for 100 teacher-created charter schools.[4] California's charter school bill was signed into law by Republican Governor Pete Wilson.[5]

Based on the history of charter school legislation in Minnesota and California, it seems that in some states, the birth of charter school legislation occurred in an atmosphere of bipartisan support. The same appears to be true for Colorado, which passed its charter school law in 1993. In a 2013 article featuring former Colorado Lieutenant Governor Barbara O'Brien, who was instrumental in advocating for charter schools in the state, *Colorado*

Chalkbeat writer Ben DeGrow observes the bipartisan support for charter legislation there:

> After the sudden passing of charter champion Rep. John Irwin (R-Loveland) in December 1992, O'Brien and then-Sen. Bill Owens invited Rep. Peggy Kerns to assume the crucial role of House sponsor, at which she succeeded admirably.
>
> Maybe it was more in the spirit of the times, but O'Brien noted that support for SB 93-183, the original charter school bill, brought together an unprecedented "diverse coalition." True bipartisanship is evident throughout the story.[6]

Cooperative, bipartisan support for charter school legislation appears to have occurred in some other states that adopted such legislation in the 1990s. However, "bipartisan support" for passage of New York's charter school law in 1998[7] was much more coercive. New York Republican Governor George Pataki[8] wanted the charter law and used the threat of a veto on a legislative pay raise to corner New York's predominately Democratic Assembly into supporting charter school legislation that it obviously did not want. And given the strongly expressed concerns of the president of American Federation of Teachers (see Chapter 5) about the direction of charter schools, it is unsurprising that the New York State United Teachers (NYSUT) opposed Pataki's charter school plan. In an ironic twist, the idea for charter schools as conceived and once promoted by a former New York union president was now staunchly opposed by NYSUT, which by 1998 was concerned that New York's charter school plan would lead to nonunionized schools. Pataki attempted to placate the union by including language that required unionization of New York charter schools enrolling more than 250 students. Still, NYSUT leadership was clearly displeased by the veto threat Pataki leveled against legislators by connecting charter school law passage with a legislative pay raise.[9]

What is also ironic about the passage of the 1998 charter school legislation in New York is that charter schools in theory are designed to empower both teachers and parents. However, as *The New York Times* reporter Clifford Levy notes, public input had taken a back seat to political prowess and maneuvering behind closed doors:

> Mr. Pataki has long supported the autonomous schools, known as charter schools, asserting that children and educators have a better chance of thriving if they are freed from local educational bureaucracies that he says can stifle innovation. New York would become the 34th state with charter schools, a favorite of conservatives, and Mr. Pataki is expected to promote the plan as he seeks to broaden his national reputation after easily capturing a second term.
>
> "The creation of charter schools represents the single greatest improvement in education in state history," he said in a statement after the bill had been endorsed by legislative leaders.

The plan calls for one of the most far-reaching changes in New York public education in decades, but as is customary in Albany, it was approved with little if any debate or input from the public. Pataki aides and legislative leaders worked out the last details in private talks Thursday night, and lawmakers barely had time to peruse the bill before voting.[10]

It is notable that by 1998, support for charter schools was already being termed "a favorite of conservatives." Based on the clouded history of charter school legislation in New York, it was clear that claims of teacher and parent empowerment could be easily converted into a tool for serving one's political aspirations. Nevertheless, bipartisan support for charter schools continued: President Bill Clinton became the first president to sign federal legislation supporting charter schools, the Charter School Expansion Act of 1998. In his remarks on October 22, 1998, regarding the Act, Clinton thanked Congress for its bipartisan support for the bill:

> Today I am pleased to sign into law H.R. 2616, the "Charter School Expansion Act of 1998." This bill will help foster the development of high-quality charter schools, consistent with my goal of having 3,000 charter schools operating by early in the next century, and will help lead to improvements in public education more generally. I am particularly gratified by the bipartisan manner in which this bill passed the House and Senate.[11]

Clinton stressed the need to be sure that charter schools had "clear and measurable performance objectives" and were "held accountable to the same high standards expected of all public schools." However, even as he spoke of accountability, Clinton added that the bill he just signed would allow states to receive federal money based on the rather lax criteria that the state's charters be reviewed "at least once every five years."[12] Such lenient criteria for review hardly qualify as being held accountable.

Though the first federal-level charter school legislation was signed into law under a Democratic president, the contention that charter schools are favored by conservatives also holds true. Behind the conservative push for charter schools was the free-market, deregulated, business ideology promoted by Republican President Ronald Reagan.[13] Thus, it is not surprising that Republican governors like Michigan's John Engler[14] viewed the charter school as a means of "deregulating" public education. As Michigan State University 2011 doctoral candidate James Goenner observed in his historical study of Michigan charter schools:

> When charter schools. . . began to appear as a non-voucher approach for fostering educational choice and competition, policymakers became very interested. From a public policy standpoint, charter schools gave political leaders a viable market-based reform strategy that they could use to advocate for choice and

competition *within* public education. Further, with charter schools being public schools, political leaders were able to mitigate the privatization and undermining public education arguments used against them by voucher opponents.[15]

The fact that Engler added a bit of marketing drama to his October 5, 1993, charter school promotional speech helped the Michigan legislators in attendance to rally around the charter school cause. As Iowa State University professor Christopher Lubienski notes in the book, *What's Public about Charter Schools?*:

> On Tuesday, October 5, 1993, Michigan Governor John Engler stood in front of an assembly of state legislators with a 20-gauge sawed-off shotgun and voiced his support for school choice. Engler brandished the gun, "confiscated from a student, to dramatize school violence and promote his plan to allow parents more leeway in choosing the schools their children attend".... According to the armed governor...:
>
>> The total funding level of schools will be determined by how many students they can retain or attract. The schools that deliver will succeed. The schools that don't will not. No longer will there be a monopoly of mediocrity in this state... because our kids deserve better.
>
>> The unusual spectacle did not end there. Engler asked a 9-year-old student, Rory, to stand up from his reserved seat in the gallery. Rory's family wanted to transfer him from their small rural school district to one with a gifted program, but their request was denied by the home district seeking to retain per-pupil funds. "It was a small district," according to Rory's father, and "children are dollar signs in their system."
>
>> The connection between Rory's plight and the shotgun was telling. Engler was portraying a public school system in a deep state of crisis due to its governance structures—in the governor's words, "Public education is a monopoly, and monopolies don't work." This point of view holds that public schools fail in promoting academic excellence just as they fail to promote character and values because they rely on a captured clientele. Shielded from competition, they have no incentive to respond to the preferences of parents. Engler declared: "It's because of experiences like yours, Rory, that we need real change. This plan's for you."[16]

On December 24, 1993, the Michigan legislature passed its charter schools act; on July 14, 1994, Engler signed the act into law.[17] However, nothing in the statute could guarantee that no charter school student would bring a sawed-off shotgun to school or that little Rory would be guaranteed a seat in a charter school for gifted students. And we can add the idea that basing schools on free-market, business ideals would somehow prevent children from being "dollar signs in their system," as Rory's father spoke about district-run schools, to our growing list of choice-school ironies.

Advocating for choice within public education via charters turned out to be a stickier business in Michigan than the statement reveals on its surface. When AFT President Albert Shanker proposed his version of charter schools, he clearly envisioned teachers and unions as partners in creating these autonomous schools, along with other entities, including those from the business sector, and he did not endorse charter schools as a deregulated, market-driven replacement for traditional public schools. Nor did Shanker conceive of charter school teachers as being nonunion. But this is the direction that the market-based charter sector was headed. Even in Michigan in 1994, the Michigan Education Association (MEA) expressed concern when its members realized that a charter school established by Saginaw Valley State University (SVSU) was to be in competition with local districts for both funding and potentially the best students academically. As MEA Regional Executive Director David Sabedra noted in a May 26, 1994, letter to SVSU President Eric Gilbertson:

> The loss of even one student to a charter school authorized by the University will have significant financial impact on local districts. This financial loss will seriously impede their ability to deliver quality education programs to those students remaining in the district. Additionally, should the University charter or authorize the charter of the Osconda Institute for Math and Science, districts will lose their best and brightest students to an elite institution causing a decline in district-wide national norm performance tests, as well as deprive remaining students of the positive role model these brighter students provide.[18]

Sabedra's words convey two major concerns of local school districts when forced to compete with charter schools: loss of funding and potential loss of the best academic students. However, in the minds of conservative governors and others espousing the ability of the free market to remedy the ills of American public education, inserting such competition into what they call the traditional, board-run, public school "monopoly" is exactly the plan— and in no other single piece of major legislation does that plan come to light than in the No Child Left Behind Act (NCLB) of 2001, which was the brainchild of a conservative Republican governor who became president, Texan George W. Bush.

NO CHILD LEFT BEHIND: PROPOSING CHARTERS AS A SOLUTION

It was Bush's NCLB that introduced charter schools into the Elementary and Secondary Education Act (ESEA) of 1965 and, by extension, to both Title I funding "accountability" and in their own right as part of Title V, "Promoting Informed Parental Choice and Innovative Programs."[19] Regarding NCLB accountability and the role of charter schools in this plan, education historian

Diane Ravitch offers the following summary in her book, *Death and Life of the Great American School System*:

> NCLB was complex and contained many programs. Its accountability plan included these features:
>
> 1. All states were expected to choose their own tests, adopt three performance levels... and decide for themselves how to define "proficient."
> 2. All public schools receiving federal funding were required to test all students in grades three through eight annually and once in high school in reading and mathematics....
> 3. All states were required to establish timelines showing how 100 percent of their students would reach proficiency in reading and mathematics by 2013–2014.
> 4. Any school that did not make adequate progress (AYP)... would be labeled a school in need of improvement (SINI). It would face a series of increasingly onerous sanctions. In the first year of failing to make AYP, the school would be put on notice. In the second year, it would be required to offer all of its students the right to transfer to a successful school, with transportation paid from the district's allotment of federal funds. In the third year, the school would be required to offer free tuition to low-income students.... In the fourth year, the school would be required to take "corrective action," which might mean curriculum changes, staff changes, or a longer school day or year. [In the fifth year, a school] would be required to "restructure."
> 5. Schools that were required to restructure had five options: convert to a charter school; replace the principal and staff; relinquish control to private management; turn over control... to the state, or "any other major restructuring of the school's governance."[20]

Through NCLB—a conservative piece of legislation that garnered the bipartisan support necessary for its late-2001 passage[21] but not for its 2007 reauthorization[22]—President Bush attempted to punish American public education into "100 percent proficiency in reading and math" perfection, and he used the potential conversion of traditional, district-run schools to charter schools as a component of that punishment. Moreover, Bush's NCLB also included provisions for states to receive ESEA Title V funding as an incentive to "increase national understanding of the charter school model" by

1. providing financial assistance for the planning, program design, and initial implementation of charter schools;
2. evaluating the effects of such schools, including the effects on students, student academic achievement, staff, and parents;
3. expanding the number of high-quality charter schools available to students across the Nation; and

4. encouraging the States to provide support to charter schools for facilities
   financing in an amount more nearly commensurate to the amount the
   States have typically provided for traditional public schools.[23]

In other words, according to NCLB language, the public would "understand" charter schools more if there were more of them. And the federal
funding was there to "encourage" the expansion of "high-quality" charter
schools—where "high quality" meant charter schools "that are held accountable in the terms of the schools' charters for meeting clear and measurable objectives for the educational progress of the students attending
the schools."[24] In turn, these "clear and measurable objectives" were to be
tied to "how the program will enable all students to meet challenging State
student academic achievement standards."[25] At the same time, NCLB promoted charter school fiscal deregulation: "The State ensures that each charter school has a high degree of autonomy over the charter school's budgets
and expenditures."[26]

Bush's NCLB assumed that charter schools would provide a necessary solution for "failing" public schools. Indeed, the document includes
no details regarding the possible failure of the charter schools, including no
stipulation that a failed charter be "restructured" by returning the school's
operation to the local district in which the school was located.

RACING TO THE TOP VIA A CHARTER CASH COMPETITION

Even though NCLB was not reauthorized in 2007, the Democratic president
who succeeded Bush, Barack Obama, supported the NCLB core compo-
nents of states being "held accountable" via test scores and the potential
conversion of "failing schools" to charter schools. Obama's 2009 centerpiece of education legislation, Race to the Top (RTTT), introduced state
"competition" for $4.3 billion in American Reinvestment and Recovery Act
(ARRA) funding, part of which involved promoting a national expansion of
charter schools.[27]

Obama selected Chicago crony and former CEO of Chicago Public
Schools (CPS) Arne Duncan to be U.S. Secretary of Education. As part of a
"listening and learning tour" preceding the official announcement of RTTT,
Duncan spoke about charter schools in a June 2009 speech at the National
Alliance for Public Charter Schools:

> The charter movement is one of the most profound changes in American educa-
> tion, bringing new options to underserved communities and introducing com-
> petition and innovation into the education system. . . .
>   So, I'm a big supporter of these successful charter schools and so is the
> president. That's why one of our top priorities is a $52 million increase in

charter school funding in the 2010 budget. We also want to change the law and allow federally funded charters to replicate.

But the CREDO (Center for Research on Education Outcomes at Stanford University) report last week was a wake–up call, even if you dispute some of its conclusions. The charter movement is putting itself at risk by allowing too many second-rate and third-rate schools to exist. Your goal should be quality, not quantity. Charter authorizers need to do a better job of holding schools accountable— and the charter schools need to support them—loudly and sincerely. . . .

I want to salute the California Charter Schools Association, which recently announced an accountability proposal that links charter renewal to student achievement and growth. We should watch this closely and see if it can become a model for other states.

We also need to work together to help people better understand charters. Many people equate charters with privatization and part of the problem is that charter schools overtly separate themselves from the surrounding district. This is why opponents often say that charters take money away from public schools, but that's misleading. Charters are public schools, serving our kids with our money. Instead of standing apart, charters should be partnering with districts, sharing lessons, and sharing credit. Charters are supposed to be laboratories of innovation that we can all learn from.[28]

In his speech, Duncan states that equating charters with privatization of schools is a problem. However, as is clear in the language of NCLB, charter schools are a potential replacement for "failing," traditional, local-board-run, neighborhood public schools. They are not held to the same regulations as traditional public schools; they can be chartered to serve special populations, as opposed to teaching all students; and they are of a hybrid, public-private nature by virtue of their being able to draw on private funding. In Duncan's words, charter authorizers can maintain "too many second-rate and third-rate schools." And the public funding for a charter school does take money from the district—and if it mismanages that money and closes mid-year, students are still entitled to a public education and must be offered such an education somewhere, whether the misspent funding can be recovered or not.

Duncan also notes that the charter movement "introduces competition." Still, he says charter schools should "partner with districts." In market-based thinking, these two ideas are not compatible. If the charter is competing with the traditional school district for students and for funding, why should the charter share its "innovative" ideas with the district? In a true competition, there is only one first place.

Duncan continues his speech by noting that charter schools are not "inherently anti-union." He then references Shanker as "an early supporter."[29] Duncan does note why Shanker withdrew support and became an opponent. By 1996, Shanker was concerned with shady charter school authorization and practices, which had become a much broader problem by the time Duncan spoke in 2009.

In that speech, Duncan stated, "Many charters today are unionized."[30] However, in a charter school survey published in 2014, the Center for Educational Reform (CER) stated, "The overwhelming majority of charter schools have been non-union since the early days of the charter movement," with unionized charter schools tending to be in states that require unionization. Moreover, CER reported that between 2009 and 2012, the proportion of unionized charter schools dropped from 12% to 7% even as charter school growth continues, with the greatest growth in jurisdictions with multiple independent authorizers, greater opportunity to expand, and high autonomy. Though the CER report notes that teachers are more likely to be held to "skills-based and performance-based contracts" coupled with a longer school day—both at the discretion of the charter school administration—CER includes no information on how such requirements affect teacher attrition and, by extension, school stability. Instead, CER views the lack of unions as positive for the charter schools:

> The percentage of charter schools implementing skill-based and performance-based staff contracts has increased by eight percentage points for the former and 18 percentage points for the latter. This is a positive trend that shows that when given the freedom, charter schools take hold of their own staffing authority and create a salary system based on skills and performance, and reject the fixed salary levels that have been comfortably adhered to and influenced by teachers unions to ensure uniformity across all public schools.[31]

There is a trade-off not acknowledged by CER: The union is an advocate for teachers, to offer teachers a voice in confronting real or potential administrative abuses, including erratic firings, undependable salary, unhealthy work hours, and unrealistic job duties. As a unionized teacher, I know when my workday ends and when my private life begins, and vice versa. And my students benefit because my union-negotiated and union-protected work parameters help ensure that I do not burn out professionally, thus contributing to a stable school environment conducive to teaching and learning.

There are charter school teachers who desire to have their rights protected via union membership, and as one might imagine, there are charter school leaders who want to put a sure end to any teacher talk of unionizing. In June 2015, at the National Charter Schools conference in New Orleans, several charter school teachers publicly confronted an administrator as he participated in a panel discussion and said he endorsed the "best practice" of building relationships with teachers—even as he wrongfully dismissed them for planning to unionize.[32] The case went before the National Labor Relations Board (NLRB), and in October 2014, NLRB Regional Director

Allen Binstock found that I CAN administrators engaged in coercive and re-taliatory behavior against employees desiring to unionize, including refusing certain employees teaching contracts for the 2014–15 school year.[33]

In a negotiation that followed the October 2014 hearing, I CAN ad-ministration agreed to pay its fired teachers $69,000 in lost wages, among other judgments, including reinstating the wrongfully dismissed teachers and posting in prominent areas a notice of teachers' rights.[34] I CAN ad-ministrators told *Plain Dealer* reporter Patrick O'Donnell they do not want unions. While their public admission is a surprise, their stance is not. The 21st-century charter school follows a top-down model, not the teacher-em-powering collaboration that Ray Budde or Albert Shanker first envisioned. Instead, the charter school administration holds the power, and the teachers do as they are told:

> Both [I Can founders Marshall Emerson and Jason Stragand] said they do not want their teaching staffs to be unionized.
>
> "It would really cripple our principals and administrative staff. It could dramatically change the model. It could drastically change what we do," Emerson said.
>
> The founders said I Can has Saturday morning classes, allows principals to decide each year which teachers to bring back, has a longer school year than traditional schools—220 days instead of 180, has teachers more involved in adjusting lessons to the new Common Core standards, and does not always schedule teacher planning time as strictly as in a unionized school.
>
> Stragand said the extra effort is key to making the schools work.[35]

"The key to making the schools work" is for I CAN administration to wield the power over a disenfranchised teaching faculty—hence the desire to unionize:

> Fired teacher Kathryn Brown and union organizer Mason Pesek, who still teaches at Northeast Ohio College Preparatory School, said they want a union at the schools because teachers don't feel valued.
>
> They said teachers work long hours and are expected to meet high expecta-tions, but have little say in how the school is run.
>
> Both said that I Can has a particular model it wants everyone to follow.
>
> "They have a rigid approach for how you're supposed to do things," said Brown. "The I Can network believes that administration and a teaching tem-plate are all you need for education. That's the big flaw and why I got involved in unionization. A school is not just administration."[36]

In the 21st-century charter school model, profits matter, and in the case of reform driven by student test performance, high scores are necessary for charter school profitability. Thus, unions—with their advocacy for higher pay and better benefits for teachers—only interfere with the smooth ex-ecution of the top-down, profit-driven model. Given the charter sector's administrative-empowering, anti-union bent, it should come as no wonder that the chief philanthropic organization supporting school choice in the United States, including the shaping of policy in conjunction with school choice, is the Walton Family Foundation.

WHAT THE WALTONS WANT

If one examines the Walton Family Foundation's spending, it does not take long to realize that what the Waltons hold dear is a deregulated, free market. The Waltons despise unionization, and the family, through its foundation, spends heavily to promote school choice in the form of vouchers and charter schools. In my book, *A Chronicle of Echoes*, I detail the degree to which the Waltons push the limits of free enterprise: The family's retail chain, Walmart, has been cited for violating child labor laws and for bribing Mexican officials to speed up building permits; it employed prison labor to build a distribution center to avoid paying living wages to local construction workers, and the company has used forced prison labor to grow produce. Moreover, though Walmart operates 4,000 stores across the nation, the mega-chain has the distinction of an amazing absence of unionized workers. Many Walmart employees must rely on public programs for health care coverage, because they do not receive those benefits through their employer.[37]

In 2012, the Walton Family Foundation spent more than $158 million on education reforms, which included those that shaped public policy and promoted school choice via both existing charter schools and new charter schools. In 2013, that total increased to more than $164 million,[38] and in 2014, to more than $200 million.[39] The Waltons openly note that their school reform strategy includes financial support for organizations advocating for school choice in the form of vouchers, charters, and open enrollment.[40]

The Walton Foundation does not contribute to teachers unions.

A 2014 *Inside Philanthropy* article details a number of Walton school choice investments and offers advice to organizations considering applying for Walton Family Foundation charter school funding:

> In the area of development, Walton is a major funder of the Charter School Growth Fund. . . . The foundation's public policy focus also counts plenty of high-profile charter groups, including the California Charter Schools Association [for $15 million to expand charters in Los Angeles] and the Alliance for School Choice. . . .
>
> As evidenced by its grantmaking, the Walton Family Foundation likes to go pretty big. . . . KIPP [the Knowledge Is Power Program] is one of the largest—if

not the largest—charter school networks or organizations in the United States [and funded by Walton for $25.5 million]. . . .

California is home to 12 of the largest school districts in the country, so you can see why Walton went with the California Charter Schools Association. . . .

[A] number of [Walton Foundation] grants [go] to statewide charter school associations, such as the Arizona Charter Schools Association and the DC Public Charter School Board. . . .

[The Walton Family Foundation] expects results and. . . expects a return on its investment. . . . Another factor. . . is that Walton judges charter schools, associations, and organizations by the company they keep. Those that belong to large charter school organizations such as KIPP or Building Excellent Schools may have a better chance of receiving Walton funding than those that do not.[41]

The Walton Foundation invests millions into school choice, and it prefers to invest in charter chains and in large school districts. Doing so is a solid strategy for scaling charter school presence. In a Walton Foundation document entitled "Creating Opportunity So Individuals and Communities Can Live Better in Today's World," the Walton Foundation offers the following as part of its "vision" on education reform:

Our core strategy is to infuse competitive pressure into the nation's K–12 education system by increasing the quantity and quality of school choices available to parents, especially in low-income communities. When all families are empowered to choose from among several quality school options, all schools will be fully motivated to provide the best possible education. Better school performance leads, in turn, to higher student achievement, lower dropout rates and greater numbers of students entering and completing college.[42]

According to the union-shunning Waltons, competitive pressure combined with focusing on strategic locations will produce results—which the billionaire Waltons "intend to show":

The foundation focuses on a select number of investment sites, where we intend to show that parental choice can inspire meaningful improvements in the education system and higher academic achievement for all students. The foundation's investment sites are: Albany, Atlanta, Boston, Chicago, Denver, Detroit, Harlem (NY), Indianapolis, Los Angeles, Memphis, Milwaukee, Minneapolis, New Orleans, Newark (NJ), Phoenix and Washington, D.C.[43]

As part of its intention to show that choice works—and putting the influencing weight of its fortune behind its words—the Arkansas-based Waltons have even established their own Department of Education Reform at the University of Arkansas.[44] Furthermore, in March 2015, the Waltons put their billions and resulting influence behind the proposed state takeover of the Little Rock School District via a piece of legislation, Arkansas HB 1733. As Max Brantley of the *Arkansas Times* blog reports:

> [HB 1733 is] monumental legislation that would make all school teachers and administrators fire-at-will employees without due process rights. It would destroy one of the two last remaining teacher union contracts in Arkansas. It allows for the permanent end of democratic control of a school district or those portions of it privatized. It would capture property tax millage voted by taxpayers for specific purposes, including buildings, and give them to private operators. It would allow seizure of buildings for private operators at no cost. . . .
>
> This bill is the work of the Walton Family Foundation. People the Walton money supports—lobbyists Gary Newton of Arkansas Learns, Scott Smith of the Arkansas Public School Research Foundation, Kathy Smith of the Walton Family Foundation and Laurie Lee of Arkansas Parents for School Choice—are the leading lobbyists. Smith has been quoted by others as saying he's the primary author (his organization gets $3 million a year from the Waltons). . . .
>
> The goal is to make the Little Rock School District a laboratory for the pet education aims of the Waltons, who own the University of Arkansas, particularly the department ginning out propaganda in behalf of this bill.[45]

As it turns out, public outcry against HB 1733 prompted the bill's sponsor, Representative Bruce Cozart, to pull the bill and not reintroduce it for the remainder of the 2015 legislative session. Cozart admitted to Brantley that Scott Smith of the Arkansas Public School Research Council (a Walton-financed organization) brought him the bill, which Cozart filed, as Brantley reports, "without much thought." Cozart began to hear from superintendents, who saw that the bill could make it possible for an entire district to be taken over from the local school boards if even a single school was in "academic distress." Cozart admitted that the bill "needs a complete rewrite."[46]

Former Little Rock school board member Jim Ross told Brantley, "We hear there was pressure from the Walton family who are tired of the bad press."[47] Ross was a plaintiff in a lawsuit filed in February 2015 to prevent state takeover of an entire district. The lawsuit argued that state takeover of a local school district violates the Arkansas constitution.[48] Two days after Cozart pulled HB 1733, on March 19, 2015, the lawsuit was put on hold.[49]

In their efforts to combat bad press, the Waltons will have to face the organization In the Public Interest (IPI), which has a formal petition requesting the Walton Family Foundation to hold accountable the charter schools it funds.[50] The petition drive is connected with a report IPI produced in conjunction with the American Federation of Teachers (AFT), entitled *Cashing in on Kids: Brought to you by Wal-Mart? How the Walton*

Family Foundation's Ideological Pursuit Is Damaging Charter Schooling.[51] In the report, IPI and AFT accuse the Waltons of an education privatization agenda that

> has taken the U.S. charter school movement away from education quality in favor of a strategy focused only on growth. Under the guise of "choice" to improve schools for low-income children, WFF (Walton Family Foundation) has supported the unregulated growth of a privatized education industry— quantity over quality, and "freedom" over regulation. It's been lucrative for some, but a disaster for many of the nation's most vulnerable students and school districts.[52]

In detailing the Walton contribution to privatizing American public education, IPI and AFT note that the Waltons' "flagship" education reform is the school voucher, which allows for public money to flow to private schools, and that Walton funding for vouchers has been "instrumental" in promoting such a reform:

> The nation's first publicly funded voucher program was launched in Milwaukee in 1990. That same year, John Walton helped create the Alliance for School Choice, a national umbrella group for statebased voucher advocacy organizations (many of which are funded by the WFF). . . .
>
> In 2013, the Walton Family Foundation announced that it would provide $6 million to the Alliance for School Choice to double the number of students in the U.S. attending private schools with publicly funded vouchers.[53]

IPI and AFT clearly oppose the Walton money flowing to organizations promoting school vouchers. However, the IPI and AFT complaint also concerns the Center for Popular Democracy (CPE) and Integrity in Education (IIE)'s 2014 report of their 15-state examination of charter fraud, previously detailed in Chapter 4. IPI and AFT take issue with the presence of Walton funding allegedly enabling such fraud, including the foundation allegedly funding recipients fighting for unlimited charter schools and Walton lobbyists purposely opposing charter school regulation:

> Fundamental to the Waltons' belief in an unfettered market is opposition to any limits on the number of charter schools allowed in a given state or district. In the early years of chartering, many state legislatures placed caps on growth as a way to maintain control over the quality of the schools. WFF grantees have doggedly opposed these caps. . . .
>
> After its funding for charter start-ups, the Walton Family Foundation's second largest education program area is for shaping public policy.
>
> The foundation has spent nearly $280 million since 2009 to support advocacy organizations in more than 30 states. . . .

The original intent of "flexibility" for charter schools was to allow experimentation with education practices. For the Walton family, any regulation is an impediment to growth. Hence, Walton-funded advocacy groups oppose initiatives requiring charter school governing boards to comply with state conflict-of-interest or contracting rules, for example, or even rules requiring that governing board meetings be open to the public.

Free-market charter school advocates are quick to refer to charters as "public schools" in discussions about funding levels and access to public facilities. But in almost every other instance, WFF-funded lobbyists have argued strenuously that charter school governing boards are private corporations not subject to the same regulations that govern traditional public schools. Examples of this doublespeak abound. . . .

In 2014, the Center for Popular Democracy and Integrity in Education released the results of a media survey of charter school fraud, waste and abuse in just 15 states (43 states have active charter school laws). The groups found more than $100 million in fraud (later updated to over $200 million). Many of the schools and entities caught up in the scandals, or with documented examples of profiteering off the charter industry, have been funded by the WFF.[54]

At the end of their report, which includes numerous examples of the Walton role in promoting the endgame of education privatization, the IPI and AFT explain that the petition—located at the opening of the report under the heading "Tell the Walton Foundation to Support Oversight and Accountability Agenda"—is the "first step" in "changing the Walton Foundation":

Supporters of public schools designed to serve *all* children must not only work to change how politicians and policymakers view charter schools. We also must change the Walton Family Foundation, which has driven the current market-based reform agenda over the past 20 years. This report, and the accompanying petition, are a first step in making change at the Walton Family Foundation.[55]

The degree to which the Walton Family Foundation bends to this IPI and AFT criticism remains to be seen.

THE AMERICAN LEGISLATIVE EXCHANGE COUNCIL

Another chief supporter of charter schools is the American Legislative Exchange Council (ALEC), which describes itself as follows:

The American Legislative Exchange Council works to advance limited government, free markets, and federalism at the state level through a nonpartisan public-private partnership of America's state legislators, members of the private sector and the general public.[56]

I wrote a chapter about ALEC in my book, *A Chronicle of Echoes: Who's Who in the Implosion of American Public Education.* The very conservative ALEC was formed in 1973 in Chicago and received its nonprofit status in 1977. Its founders included Illinois representative Henry Hyde, "Moral Majority" founder Paul Weyrich, and 1968 Reagan campaigner Lou Barnett. Other formative ALEC members included a powerful group of future governors or Congressional delegates: John Engler, Terry Brandstad, Robert Kasten, Tommy Thompson, and John Kasich.[57]

In short, ALEC is a group that operated primarily in secret until 2011, when the Center for Media and Democracy (CMD) began publicizing ALEC in its "ALEC Exposed" writings.[58] Then, in April 2012, the public interest group Common Cause filed a whistleblower complaint against ALEC with the IRS for ALEC's allegedly being little more than a lobbying front group[59] in which corporate members paid thousands of membership dollars for opportunities to court legislators (who paid $100 per year) in an effort to promote ALEC-approved, conservative legislation in statehouses around the country. ALEC sponsors conventions in popular vacation spots and offers corporate-funded "scholarships" for legislators, who are encouraged to bring their families. These conventions allow corporations the venue in which to influence legislators to return home and promote legislation that has a nod of approval from ALEC corporate membership.[60]

When the Common Cause story on ALEC broke in spring of 2012, a number of ALEC corporations severed ties with the organization.

One of them was Walmart.[61]

ALEC develops and approves legislation via its "task forces." Beginning in 1986, ALEC divided itself into several task forces to "develop policy covering virtually every responsibility of state government."[62] This idea is modeled after the 1981 Reagan-created task force, the National Task Force on Federalism, in which ALEC members were deeply involved. A chief purpose of the ALEC task force is to bring corporate and legislative members together to develop and approve "model legislation" that legislators might take back to their states, fill in the blanks to personalize, and promote as their own. The official approval happens in task force meetings at ALEC conventions.[63]

One of the ALEC task forces is its Education Task Force. In September 2007, ALEC's Educational Task Force members approved the Next Generation Charter Schools Act as official ALEC model legislation.[64] In addition to the Next Generation Charter Schools Act, by 2015, ALEC advertised two other pieces of model legislation related to charter schools: the Charter School Growth and Quality Act[65] and the Indiana Education Reform Package.[66]

In its model legislation, ALEC tells legislators what to include to personalize the legislation. For example, the Next Generation Charter Schools
Act includes the following:

> The State of [state] recognizes establishment of charter schools as necessary
> to improving the opportunities of all families to choose the public school that
> meets the needs of their children. . . .
>
> The Charter School Act of [year] as approved by this body has provided
> students in our state with high-quality public school choices while advancing
> overall academic excellence[1] and helping to close the achievement gap. . . .
>
> "School district" means each school district now or hereafter legally orga-
> nized as a body corporate pursuant to [insert state statute].[67]

As for help with that proof of charters in "advancing overall academic excellence," the model legislation includes this endnote regarding where a legislator might find answers:

> [1]. Insert supporting references of studies of charter school achievement and/or
> test-score/achievement comparisons. See www.edreform.com for information
> about current studies.[68]

Of course, there is always the possibility that a legislator will not complete his
or her homework, which happened to Florida State Representative Rachel
Burgin in 2012, when she neglected to remove the ALEC mission-statement
headliner from a corporate anti-tax bill she submitted as her own. Burgin
quickly withdrew the bill, removed the ALEC headliner, and resubmitted it
under a new bill number.[69]

In its suggestion to legislators regarding where they might go in order
to locate "supporting references of charter school achievement," ALEC suggests the website, edreform.com, which is the home page for the Center for
Education Reform (CER). If one peruses the affiliations of CER's board of
directors,[70] one might notice that a number of these individuals are involved
in education ventures and that others are simply hedge funders.

The 21st-century charter school movement, with its center of education
privatization and "freeing the market," has hedge funders involved in supporting charter schools—and financially bolstering politicians willing to ag-
gressively promote charter schools. Thus, this chapter will close with a brief
examination of how hedge funders are advancing the charter school cause.

HEDGE FUNDERS AND THE CHARTER SCHOOL INVESTMENT

Where there is a hedge-fund interest, there is the opportunity to make
money. The hedge fund interest in charter schools is no exception—even if

the opportunity for profits is on the creative side and includes added perks. As Hofstra University teacher and *Huffington Post* blogger Alan Singer notes in his May 2014 post entitled "Why Hedge Funds Love Charter Schools":

> Obscure laws can have a very big impact on social policy, including obscure changes in the United States federal tax code. The 2001 Consolidated Appropriations Act, passed by Congress and signed into law by President Bill Clinton, included provisions from the Community Renewal Tax Relief Act of 2000. The law provided tax incentives for seven years to businesses that locate and hire residents in economically depressed urban and rural areas. The tax credits were reauthorized for 2008–2009, 2010–2011, and 2012–2013.
>
> As a result of this change to the tax code, banks and equity funds that invest in charter schools in underserved areas can take advantage of a very generous tax credit. They are permitted to combine this tax credit with other tax breaks while they also collect interest on any money they lend out. According to one analyst, the credit allows them to double the money they invested in seven years. Another interesting side note is that foreign investors who put a minimum of $500,000 in charter school companies are eligible to purchase immigration visas for themselves and family members under a federal program called EB-5.[71]

Given the profit potential of charter schools—including the potential for those generous tax credits and immigration visas—a March 2015 *Business Insider* article entitled "The Walmart Family Is Teaching Hedge Funds How to Profit from Publicly Funded Schools" makes perfect sense to any who are familiar with the Walton interest in replacing local-board-run public schools with a free market of charters:

> Charter Schools are drawing promoters from a place you might not think of: Walmart.
>
> The Walton Family Foundation—the philanthropic group run by the Walmart family—sponsored a symposium at the Harvard Club for investors interested in the charter school sector, last week.
>
> The event, hosted in Manhattan, was called "Bonds and Blackboards: Investing in Charter Schools," and was cosponsored by the Bill & Melinda Gates Foundation.
>
> With the explicit intent of helping investors "Learn and understand the value of investing in charter schools and best practices for assessing their credit," the event featured experts on charter school investing. . . .
>
> Hedge funds and other private businesses are particularly interested in the growth and success of charter schools. The growth of charter networks around the US offer new revenue streams for investing, and the sector is quickly growing. Funding for charter schools is further incentivized by generous tax credits for investments to charter schools in underserved areas.[72]

Not only can hedge funders benefit from tax credits, they can feel safe doing so:

> "It's a very stable business, very recession resistant, it's a high demand product. There are 400,000 kids on waiting lists for charter schools. . . the industry is growing about 12–14% a year."[73]

But really, it's all for the *kids*. . . or not. *Nation* reporter George Joseph writes about the millions of dollars in hedge fund money flowing into New York and to the aid of Democratic Governor Andrew Cuomo, who in his 2014 reelection campaign vowed to break the "monopoly" of public education.[74] In his March 2015 article "9 Billionaires Are About to Remake New York's Public Schools—And Here's Their Story," Joseph notes:

> Though Families for Excellent Schools presents itself as a grassroots parent education reform organization, four of its five original board members are Wall Street titans like Bryan Lawrence and Paul Appelbaum, who made their millions in the hedge fund and private equity worlds respectively. Families for Excellent Schools' known donors include corporate foundation groups like the Walton Family Foundation ($700,000) and the Broad Foundation ($200,000), but these donations account for only a tiny fraction of Families for Excellent Schools' overall revenue. . . .
>
> Families for Excellent Schools is largely funded by . . . nine hedge-fund billionaires. . . .
>
> Through savvy investments in lavish protests, hedge-fund managers have paid for a full-blown social movement, thus conferring legitimacy on proposals that stand to benefit hedge-fund managers much more than New York state's chronically underfunded public school system.[75]

The hedge funder interest in assisting a Democratic governor with realizing his dreams is not restricted to New York. Connecticut's Democratic Governor Dannel Malloy has also received financial support from hedge funders who just also happen to be interested in charter schools. As *Hartford Courant* reporter Jenny Wilson notes in May 2015:

> Several Wall Street billionaires who have invested heavily in the expansion of charter schools contributed more than $200,000 to Democrats in the 2013–14 election cycle, helping Gov. Dannel P. Malloy secure re-election.
>
> The campaign contributors earned their fortunes as hedge fund managers and private equity investors before earning reputations as "education philanthropists." They have helped bankroll charter school movements throughout the country, spending to influence elections and to support advocacy movements.

Malloy opened this year's legislative session with a budget proposal that included $4.6 million in funding to open two new privately managed charter schools, and an additional $17 million for new charter school seats in the next two years. Funding for local school districts would remain flat.[76]

Wilson continues by noting that on the campaign trail in the fall of 2014, Malloy did not say much about school choice; indeed, his Republican opponent, Tom Foley, was the one who included school choice as part of his campaign. But for some reason, the hedge funders backed Malloy, and, for some reason, Malloy decided to include the opening of two new charter schools in Connecticut's 2012 budget negotiations.[77]

Who wants charters? Far too many folks whose motivations should concern the American public.

CHAPTER 7

The Charter Take-Away from the Neighborhood Public School

When American Federation of Teachers President Albert Shanker introduced his idea of the autonomous charter school to the National Press Club in 1988, he could not have anticipated that charter schools would be promoted as a free-market-favored *replacement* for the neighborhood public school. He could not have foreseen that powerful, anti-union funders like the Waltons would spend millions to promote a deregulated version of choice that empowers financial investors and politicians to benefit from charter school conversion. Shanker did not anticipate the possibility that regulated, board-run schools would be put in competition with less-regulated, autonomous charter schools that would receive per-pupil public funding that could be squandered without oversight, leaving students to seek an education elsewhere—which might mean returning to a local, now-underfunded public school. In the years before his death in 1997, Shanker began to witness these abuses and wrote passionately about their impact on American education (see Chapter 6).

Consider this very real scenario of two schools, one regulated by a local board of citizens elected from the community and another less regulated (or not regulated) by an entity that need not even be in the same state. Is there any question that the greater potential for fiscal abuse rests with the less-regulated school? Any revenue taken from the more-regulated school and given to the less-regulated school runs a risk of being squandered, even as the loss of such funding contributes to the destabilization of the regulated school.

An American education system available to all citizens in their formative years will be undone via underregulated fund siphoning of school choice narrowed by test score criteria. Competition must have a loser. In the general scheme, American compulsory education will be that loser.

Those in favor of the free-marketization of public education advance the idea that competition will take care of all and will induce the traditional public school to become better in order to survive. Given America's obsession with test scores, "better" is almost exclusively defined by standardized test results, and likely only those in English language arts (ELA) and math. Thus, the schools with the higher test scores win, and the others lose, which could well mean the losing schools are closed and replaced by charter schools—or if these losing schools are already charter schools, they might be replaced by other charter schools.

In 21st-century American public education, conversion from a local-board-run, neighborhood school to a charter school is almost certainly a one-way voyage, though I did find an exception. As the *Philadelphia Inquirer* reports in June 2008, six Philadelphia charter schools were returned to the local district after they "failed to deliver higher test scores than district schools did, despite costly interventions."[1] Four of the six belonged to Edison Schools, a for-profit chain that achieved some politically engineered favor despite its established reputation for failure: In 2003, Florida Governor Jeb Bush and the Florida legislature decided to spend $182 million in Florida teacher pension money to bail out Edison Schools.[2] Still, Bush's twisted preference for Edison could not save it from its woes; in 2012–2013, one of the few remaining schools run by Edison (then Edison Learning) went bust in Kansas City, Missouri, leaving teachers to discover on their final payday that they would be receiving no compensation due to litigation between Edison and its sponsor, the University of Missouri, Kansas City, over Edison's default on the school's bond payments. In November 2012, the university pulled its sponsorship of the Edison school due to fiscal mismanagement and poor test score outcomes in three of the previous four years.[3] The failed school, Derrick Thomas Academy, was "locked behind a heavy black gate" at the end of the 2012–2013 school year.[4] Even though a transition administration helped run the school for the remainder of the 2012–2013 school year, the 950 students in attendance had to find another school to attend in 2013–2014.

One of the guarantees of school choice: collateral damage.

THE 21ST-CENTURY CHARTER THREAT, TEST SCORES, AND POVERTY

In Chapter 4, I noted that the first time I had heard of someone I knew as planning to be employed at a charter school was in 1995, during my time as a classroom teacher in Georgia. The next time the idea of charter schools would touch my professional life was in November 2011. By then, I had been teaching high school English for several years in St. Tammany Parish, Louisiana, a district comprised of 55 schools serving more than 38,000 students, with just under half of its students receiving free or reduced-price lunches.[5] In November 2011, the recent state board election yielded a board membership that was friendly to "reforms" driven by test scores, including vouchers, charter schools, and the employment of temporary Teach for America (TFA) teachers.

Among teachers, administrators, and public officials in my parish and other school districts, there was talk of the push to convert school-board-run schools into privately managed charter schools. At the time, my colleagues and I did not know exactly what to expect. We did not know under what conditions a private entity might be allowed to assume control over our school, but we did know that charter operators had the freedom to fire teachers, and we had heard about schools where conversion to a charter school meant all faculty were fired and had to reapply for their jobs. In the previous month, schools across our state had just received their first letter grade scores; 44% of Louisiana's schools were graded as D or F according to the criteria then in place[6] (the grading scheme has changed frequently over several years, but a chief component is always student test scores).

I soon learned that schools graded as F could be taken over by the state and converted to charter schools—and I knew that faculty in schools graded as D were anxious.[7] Some might say, "If they did their job, those teachers would not be in a school rated a D. They should be anxious." However, research has shown that there is a clear relationship between student academic performance and poverty—and a school's letter grade and its socioeconomics.[8]

As a classroom teacher, I do not control the socioeconomic composition of my school. Nevertheless, the financial circumstances of students' families are strongly related to school performance as measured by test scores, and schools declared to be "failing" could be handed over to a charter operator, which could receive a state allotment of public funding and significant autonomy in which to operate. But here is the bottom line: If the reason for a low school letter grade is strongly related to socioeconomics, then the charter operator will likely, at best, produce the same results with the same students as the school did when it was under district control. Or, the charter operator will have to figure out a way to influence either the socioeconomic composition of the student body or the test-scoring outcomes that largely constitute school letter grade formulations.

In sum, a system in which socioeconomics strongly influences high-stakes testing outcomes begs to be gamed, and the deregulation that so often accompanies school choice makes the possibility of gaming that much stronger. That is not to say that such gaming cannot happen in a traditional board-run system: The 2009 Atlanta Public Schools cheating scandal proves that it can.[9] Indeed, the high stakes nature of reform based on test scores invites cheating and allows for board-run schools to fall victim to socioeconomics, to be mislabeled as failing, and to be taken over by often-underregulated, free market charter schools.

The relationship between poverty and test scores is real.

Generally, the greater the proportion of students on free and reduced lunch at a school, the lower the school letter grade (which is largely based on student performance on standardized tests). Research in a number of states supports this socioeconomic–test score connection. For example, in their 2014 report entitled, *The Relationship Between School Poverty and Student Achievement in* Maine, researchers at the Maine Education Research Policy Institute offered the following summation:

> Without question, the evidence examined in this study indicates that levels of school poverty and average student achievement are related. The magnitude of the relationship varies, and other factors are related to poverty and achievement, *but the single best predictor of performance is school poverty level.* [Emphasis added.][10]

Researchers in Maine are not alone in their conclusion regarding poverty and test scores. In their analysis *Addressing the Impact of Poverty on Student Achievement*, researchers Edward Fiske and Helen Ladd concluded the following regarding North Carolina's school letter grade system, which is based on test scores:

> The most striking pattern that emerged from the letter grades from the NC Department of Public Instruction was the near-perfect correlation between letter grades and economic disadvantage. The News & Observer reported that 80 percent of schools where at least four-fifths of children qualify for the federal free or reduced lunch received a D or F grade, whereas 90 percent of schools with fewer than one in five students on the subsidized lunch program received As or Bs.
>
> This pattern comes as no surprise.
>
> The fact that, on average, students from disadvantaged households perform less well in school than peers from more advantaged backgrounds has been documented at all levels of education.[11]

In yet another state, Arizona, researchers at the Center for Student Achievement lamented the fact that their 2012 finding of a strong negative correlation between school letter grades and school poverty levels was ignored by policy makers and that their 2013 and 2014 analysis of Arizona's school letter grades revealed the same, grade-based-on-poverty problem:

> In 2012, the Center for Student Achievement released *School Ratings: Improving The Data In Data-Driven Decision Making* where we examined the relationship between Arizona's A–F school letter grades and the level of poverty in a school. We found that a school's letter grade is highly and negatively correlated with the percentage of its students who qualify for free and reduced priced lunch. In other words, schools with high percentages of poor students received lower letter grades, on average, than schools with more affluent students. This relationship is due, in great part, to the way in which Student Growth Percentiles (SGPs) are used in the accountability formula. . . .

After broadly communicating these concerns to state-level policy makers, which resulted in no changes to this portion of the A–F formula, we wondered if this was still the case in 2013 and 2014. As we expected, schools continued to earn most of their letter grade from the percentage of students who are proficient on AIMS (composite points). As the percentage of poor students in a school increases, the percentage passing continued to decrease. . . .[12]

The issue of school letter grades as measuring student socioeconomics was a problem even in Florida, where the idea of grading schools using an A–F letter grade system originated in 1997. In a detailed study of factors associated with school letter grades in Duval County, Florida, based upon Florida Comprehensive Assessment Test (FCAT) scores for 4th- and 5th-grade students who took the test in the 1999–2000 school year, researchers from the University of North Florida and Jacksonville University found that schools with a higher proportion of students on free and reduced lunch were less likely to receive a school grade of A.[13] Still, Florida's letter grades were used as the basis for awarding schools extra money per student ($100 per full-time student for A schools) or decreased funding for F schools (from which students could transfer and have their funding follow).

But there is something else important regarding Florida and school letter grades: In December 2010, the free-market-promoting American Legislative Exchange Council (ALEC, see Chapter 6) approved model legislation based on Florida's school letter grading system. ALEC's endorsement calls Florida's system "an elegant but powerful formula," noting that "people instantly and intuitively understand letter grades, and this system served as the lynchpin for [Florida's other educational] reforms [which include a strong charter school law]."[14] The fact that several states now use school letter grading systems is expected, given that ALEC features school grading as part of its free-market education agenda.

Allow me to bring this point home: Soon after ALEC featured Florida's system for school letter grades as part of its model legislation in education at its Washington, D.C., conference in December 2010,[15] Louisiana began grading schools using letter grades. The following year, at ALEC's summer meeting in New Orleans in August 2011, Louisiana Governor Bobby Jindal was a featured speaker and also received the Thomas Jefferson Award, ALEC's "highest honor" for "exemplary work and dedication to common-sense, limited government principles."[16] Of course, since ALEC's influence moves far beyond education to encompass issues such as health care, fiscal responsibility, environmental policy, and public safety, one might assume that Jindal's service to ALEC extends beyond education. But it certainly includes it.

Back to those school letter grades and what they really measure: A 2012 report from Louisiana-based Cowen Institute included the following statement regarding the relationship between socioeconomics and Louisiana's school letter grades: "Schools that serve high proportions of economically disadvantaged students tend to demonstrate lower academic achievement than schools with fewer economically disadvantaged students."[17]

Keeping in mind those anxious Louisiana teachers in classrooms at D-rated schools, as of 2015, no school in my district, St. Tammany Parish, has been taken over by a charter operator because of being declared failing. However, this concern is shared by teachers in traditional public school districts across the country. Traditional public schools are declared to be failing. The neighborhood school is closed and is replaced by a quasi-public-charter—a school that receives public funding but is controlled by a for-profit or non-profit organization that does not answer to an elected public school board and may not even be required to serve the entire student population of the former neighborhood school that it purportedly replaced.

CHARTER SCHOOLS: FUNDING ABSENT ACCOUNTABILITY

Via charter school lack of accountability, it is often the charter operator is often afforded greater ability to choose in the school choice model than are parents and students. And based on the ever-increasing number of stories of charter school fiscal mismanagement, that choice is often self-serving. Indicative of the greater autonomy afforded to charter schools, for example, Success Academies Schools in New York City was allowed by Manhattan Supreme Court Judge Thomas Breslin to dodge an audit by New York State Comptroller Thomas DiNapoli. In New York State, the state comptroller is not allowed to audit any charter school even though these schools receive state money because charter schools are hybrid, public-private entities, which allows them to hide behind their private status when such a label benefits them.

The New York justice declared "hands-off" of any state audit of charter school finances because charter schools, he declared, are not "units of the state."[18] Such a declaration begs the question: If charter schools are not "units of the state," why should they receive state funding?

As to the underregulated federal funding of charter schools, the Center for Media and Democracy's (CMD) PR Watch reported in May 2015 on the federal government's intent to increase charter funding by 48% in 2016—without any adequate mechanism in place even for its past funding of charter schools, which totaled $3.3 billion over the past two decades.[19] The report goes on to note:

> Despite the huge sums spent so far, the federal government maintains no comprehensive list of the charter schools that have received and spent these funds or even a full list of the private or quasi-public entities that have been approved by states to "authorize" charters that receive federal funds. And despite drawing

repeated criticism from the Office of the Inspector General for suspected waste and inadequate financial controls within the federal Charter Schools Program—designed to create, expand, and replicate charter schools—the U.S. Department of Education (ED) is poised to increase its funding by 48% in FY 2016.[20]

A CMD review of U.S. Department of Education (USDOE) internal audits identified "numerous reports" from state-level education officials regarding an inability to account for federal charter school funding. Moreover, USDOE chose to award federal money for charter schools to states the department knew had no process in place for monitoring the funding. Instead, USDOE apparently made grants based upon some accountability-elusive "flexibility" that states allowed their charter school operators, the report charges. CMD concludes:

> As a result of lax oversight on the federal level, combined with many state laws that hide charter finances from the public eye, taxpayers are left in the dark about how much federal money each charter school has received and what has been wasted or spent to enrich charter school administrators and for-profit corporations who get lucrative outsourcing contracts from charters, behind closed doors.[21]

Perhaps some charter schools are hiding private funding from public view, and perhaps some of the funding attributed to traditional public schools is actually funding that those public schools must spend for auxiliary costs associated with charter school attendance. In their February 2015 review of the *Separating Fact from Fiction* report by the National Alliance for Public Charter Schools (NAPCS), researchers for the National Education Policy Center (NEPC) focused on 21 charter school claims:

> When comparing public funding of charter schools with that of district schools, it is critical that the portion of "pass-through" funds to charter schools from school districts be subtracted. Otherwise, the district revenues are erroneously and vastly inflated. For instance, if a public school district has the responsibility of providing transportation of charter school students, then the taxpayer funding for that transportation should be attributed to the charter schools, not the public school district. But sloppy calculations do not do this.
>
> Further, it is necessary to account for private dollars devoted to charter schools that are not publicly reported. This private funding is almost non-existent for some charter schools, but it is very large for others. A study of KIPP found that KIPP schools were actually receiving $800 more per pupil in public sources of revenue than local school districts. Further, while KIPP schools reported no private revenues in the federal district finance dataset, a review of IRS 990 tax forms revealed that KIPP schools were receiving an average of $5,700 per pupil in private sources of revenue in 2008.

Nevertheless, there is indeed a widespread research consensus that charter schools receive less public funding per pupil than surrounding district schools. This is largely explained by charter schools spending less on special education, student support services, transportation, and food services.[22]

The NEPC researchers conclude that charter schools could receive more funding if they were to serve the same student subpopulations as public schools and also offer the same programs:

> Charter schools can receive a lot more public resources if they wish. Yet, they can only receive additional (categorical) funding if—for example—they serve more children with moderate or severe disabilities and if they start offering programs such as vocational technical programs that would qualify them for targeted funding.[23]

The NECP report continues by noting that charter schools tend to be "more segregative than local school districts" on a number of factors, including "race, class, measured achievement, special education status (particularly when severity of disability is considered), and English-language-learner status." Furthermore, regarding teaching special needs students, the NECP researchers note that few charter schools focus on students with disabilities (approximately 60 nationwide); most charter schools serve between 0% and 7% of students with disabilities, most of whom have mild disabilities. In contrast, the 2011 national average proportion of students with disabilities for traditional, district-run schools was 13%.[24]

Though the NEPC notes that charter schools could receive increased taxpayer funding if they served the same populations, it appears to be possible for some charter schools to receive funding for special populations without actually serving such students. For example, in Louisiana, a glitch in the per-student funding formula (known as the Minimum Foundation Program, or MFP)[25] allows regular education students transferring from a traditional public school to a charter school to receive an average per-student funding allotment—where the average student expenditure includes money earmarked for special education. For example, if I have a little school—say, with three students, two in regular education and one requiring special education—the state might allot $10,000 per regular education student and $15,000 per special ed student. Therefore, I would receive from the state $45,000 for my school of three students. Now, let's assume that one of my regular education students transfers to a charter school. In this case, the state sends with that student the average per-pupil funding for one of my students, or $45,000/3 = $15,000. As a result, the charter school receives an extra $5,000 for this regular education student, and that $5,000 is taken from funding for a special education student the charter does not serve.

The Louisiana MFP funding glitch is an issue for a student transferring to any school, traditional public school or charter. However, the issue is exacerbated by the reality that Louisiana charters serve disproportionately fewer special education students than do traditional public schools. Neither the 2015 Louisiana legislature nor the state board of education has rectified this funding issue even though information generated by the state department of education noted specific dollar amounts that certain New Orleans charter schools are receiving in overpayment. In fact, the pro-charter state education department presented the overpayment as money that the charters would "lose" if the funding overpayment actually followed the special education students for whom the money was dedicated in the first place.[26]

The NECP observation about charters having the ability to expand available state funding leads to a second issue of supposed charter school funding inequity: the appeal of the charter school to organizations like the Walton Family Foundation, which is known for its attitude to aim for a cheap bottom line on employee benefits. An October 2013 article in *The New York Times* reported that New York charter schools were cheaper than traditional public schools by more than $3,000 per student because teachers in traditional public schools are unionized and have better employee benefit plans. In addition, charter schools have not been around as long as the traditional public schools have, so the higher salaries paid to more experienced teachers in public schools in comparison to less-experienced teachers at charter schools might also account for some of the disparity in not only salaries but also benefits.[27] Moreover, there is the issue of teacher turnover at charter schools. In an August 2010 study of Wisconsin charter school teacher attrition, the Center on Reinventing Public Education (CRPE) found that charter schools tend to hire younger, less-experienced teachers and to place them in schools serving poorer children in urban settings. Such teachers are more likely to leave. CRPE also cites 1999–2001 findings from a U.S. Department of Education teacher survey; one particularly notable finding is that the most common reason charter school teachers indicated for exiting teaching was to pursue another career. Thus, if the charter school teacher's mindset on entering the classroom is that teaching is only a temporary career move, then the charter school is not incurring the same health benefits and pension costs for such temporary employees.[28] The result is an unstable school system—but a cheaper one for the charter school manager.

ISSUES OF FUNDING PARITY AND EVALUATIONS OF QUALITY

Related to issues of accountability and funding, a fair question arises on an assumption in the April 2014 University of Arkansas charter funding report that charter schools *should* receive the same per-pupil allotment as traditional public schools. In a world of market-driven competition, the goal is to drive down costs while increasing profits. Translating this into the competition between charter schools and traditional public schools, the competitive goal should be that charters produce better test scores than traditional public schools for less money.[29] However, charter schools do not consistently outperform public schools. In fact, the narrative has shifted from one of charters outperforming traditional public schools to charter schools performing on par with traditional public schools,[30] and some research does not even support a general "breaking even" narrative. According to a 2013 analysis of data from 27 states by the Center for Research on Education Outcomes (CREDO), there is some evidence of an "upward trajectory" of charter school performance in ELA and math scores for grades 3 through 8; however, a comparison of the 2013 CREDO results in the 16 states that also participated in its 2009 study produced mixed results (note that CREDO separated charter schools in these 16 states into two subcategories: continuing schools and new schools):

> In reading, the 2009 charter school impact on learning gains was significantly lower than their TPS (traditional public school) comparison by about seven days of learning per year. In 2013, the charter impact on student learning in reading is positive and significant. It amounts to about seven days of additional learning for charter students compared to the average TPS student. Looking at just the continuing schools in 2013, students at these same charter schools had about seven more days of learning than their TPS counterparts in reading. Results for charter students in new schools mirror the 2009 findings: students at new schools have significantly lower learning gains in reading than their TPS peers.
>
> The 2009 and 2013 charter school impacts on math learning gains are significantly lower than their respective TPS counterparts. . . . The difference for charter students in 2009 was 22 fewer days of learning, while in 2013 the deficit has shrunk to about seven fewer days of learning, indicating a relative improvement over time. For continuing schools, charter school students learn significantly less in math than their TPS peers. The new charter school results in math follow the pattern seen for reading—the performance of the new charter schools mirrors the 2009 results.[31]

Stanford University–based CREDO is the major researcher on charter school outcomes. However, its research is largely restricted to grades 3 through 8. How charter schools fare in grades 9 through 12 has not been the subject of any established national study. Moreover, the CREDO study is singularly focused on test score outcomes. It does not account for other monetary and nonmonetary costs associated with charter school presence in a community, including the loss of community schools to the sense of community; the effect of charter-school churn on community stability and student mental and emotional well-being; the impact of narrowing curricular offerings due to an excessive focus on raising standardized test scores on a well-rounded education, and the impact of the lack of charter school regulation on the potential taxpayer revenue lost to a competing traditional public school system.

Another important truth regarding CREDO comparisons of charter school to traditional public school performance is that the research center does not include in its charter-to-traditional-school comparisons traditional public schools that send fewer than five students to charters. CREDO does not clearly publicize such restriction and allows readers to assume that CREDO compares charters to the general population of traditional public schools. The reality is that all traditional public schools that send no students to charter schools are unexplainably omitted from CREDO research.[32]

Yet another notable bias of CREDO research is that it excludes charter school dropouts. That is, if a student drops out of a charter school, CREDO drops the student from its study, which could artificially boost charter school performance.[33]

In short, CREDO research has some serious limitations.

Regarding the lack of a national study on high school charters, let me note that such a study would need to account for the issue of unaccounted-for students, creatively termed "opportunity youth."[34] Such an issue is a reality in New Orleans, where approximately 89% of schools attended by the public school population are charter schools. The state-run, 60-school New Orleans Recovery School District (RSD) is completely a charter school district as of fall 2014, while the local-board-run, 22-school Orleans Parish School Board (OPSB) only has five direct-run, district schools.[35] As NPR reported in April 2015, these students disappear from school and are also unaccounted for in the job market:

> The latest euphemism is "opportunity youth." Whatever you call them, these are young people ages 16 to 24 who are neither regularly in school, nor regularly working. There are 5 1/2 million of them in the United States.
>
> These are the kids who are chronically truant, run away, get expelled, drop out, run afoul of the law. Some get pregnant. Others face mental health issues, learning disabilities, homelessness, trauma or abuse. Sometimes, it's all of the above.[36]

New Orleans ranks 3rd out of 10 major cities for the estimated percentage of opportunity youth, with 18.2% of 16- to 24-year-olds not in school and not formally employed, behind first-ranked Memphis (21.6%) and Las Vegas (19.6%).[37] In terms of actual numbers in New Orleans, the Youth Transition Funders Group (YTFG) cites the 2010 U.S. Census as documenting 14,000 opportunity youth, with the number skyrocketing to more than 30,000 by 2012.[38] This is astounding. This notable proportion of youth not in school or working is a community issue, and any charter school "success" trend research on grades 9 through 12 needs to account for this crucial sub-population and should consider how the loss of stable community schools impacts this urban challenge. Indeed, the NPR article observes as much:

> Many critics of the all-charter school system here [in New Orleans] ask: Does the decentralized school system itself contribute to young people's disconnection?. . .
> When youth get into trouble, whether it's a serious crime or even a single arrest for loitering or truancy, it's a big risk factor for their future. Getting them back on track requires sophisticated coordination among schools, social agencies, and law enforcement.[39]

If New Orleans' school system, dominated by charters, is evaluated as a success, how does that evaluation account for the tens of thousands of 16- to 24-year-olds who have apparently fallen through the educational cracks?

The community stress evident in the disconnected lives of these young people touches on another issue that charter schools must confront in their bid to outdo the traditional school model: student attrition. The 21st-century charter school, with results measured solely on the basis of test scores, is built on the business model of "disruptive innovation." However, giving an issue a catchy name does not expunge its problematic nature. One of the disruptions associated with charter choice is the fact that students who might have even entered into a lottery for charter school entrance need not enter any lottery to exit. Such students go somewhere else, possibly to another charter. However, part of charter freedom involves not accepting students at times inconvenient for the charter school. In contrast, there is no such restriction on traditional public schools: Whenever the student arrives, no matter how inconvenient such arrival is for the student or teacher, the student is enrolled.

WAITLIST ILLUSIONS

One of the selling points for increasing the number of charter schools (thereby increasing the number of seats) is the number of students waiting for charter school admission. Indeed, in a May 2014 report, NEPC details a number of problems with a 2013 estimate that 920,007 students are waiting for charter school admission, as noted in the NAPCS report sensationally titled *National Charter School Waitlist Numbers Approach One Million*.[40] When the public reads that almost 1 million students are waiting for a seat at a charter school, the public deserves to know, first of all, that many students apply to multiple charter schools. After stating its sensational million-student waitlist in the title of its 2013 report, NAPCS offers a "conservative estimate" disclaimer about multiple applications and reduces its million by almost half:

Families often apply to multiple charter schools hoping to increase their odds. This year's survey also includes an estimated calculation of the number of individual students on waitlists. This estimate shows that at a minimum, more than 520,000 total individual students—many of whom are on multiple charter school waitlists in the hopes of increasing the chance of getting into at least one—are on waitlists across the country.[41]

Even the less-spectacular half-million lacks credible substantiation, contends NEPC:

> Even the NAPCS 520,000 estimate is problematic. For most jurisdictions, it is derived from unaudited and unauditable numbers reported to NAPCS through a survey it administers annually. The survey apparently asks for the number of applications received, as well as the number of available seats. The waiting list numbers are then calculated as applications minus seats.
>
> There is no state or federal indicator that is called "waitlist." Instead, this is a statistic developed by NAPCS and others who hope to advance the argument that, "With such demand, it is up to our elected officials to remove the facilities and funding barriers that exist to ensure that every child has the option to attend a high-quality public charter school" [as stated by] Nina Rees, NAPCS president and CEO.[42]

Not only is there no federal statistic collected called "waitlist," but the charter schools themselves have no protocol for tracking waitlist numbers. As a result, some schools that keep waitlists do so cumulatively, which means that waitlisted students actually offered a seat in one school might still be on a cumulative waitlist for another school. Even students later offered seats in the named school might not be removed from the waitlist for the school even though the wait is over. Such issues inflate waitlist numbers.[43]

Another misleading issue concerning waitlists involves the limited number of "oversubscribed" charter schools. That is, not many charter schools lack the capacity to enroll all students who apply. As NEPC notes, a 2010 *Mathematica*/Institute of Education Sciences (IES) study on charter schools that are oversubscribed and require a lottery ended up with a sample of 36 charter schools. Initially, 77 charter schools agreed to participate in the *Mathematica*/IES study but were ineligible due to their having no waitlist following having an admissions lottery.[44]

One charter chain that capitalizes publicly on the lottery is Eva Mostkowitz's Success Academies in New York. If one wants to market demand for charter schools, one should not simply send letters to the parents of prospective students to make them aware of acceptance or nonacceptance into the charter school for which they applied. Such a subdued procedure would help those who were not accepted to avoid public exposure as "losers." The charter school operator hoping to capitalize on the sensationalism of declaring some students "winners" of coveted charter school seats would miss a great opportunity to publicly exploit the disappointment of children who did not "win." In 2010, the public lottery for acceptance into Moskowitz's Harlem Success Academy was featured in a film directed by Madeline Sackler, simply entitled *The Lottery* (which is actually creepy if one is familiar with the 1948 Shirley Jackson horror story by the same name). Here is an excerpt of the description of the film, as noted on the back cover of the DVD case:

> In a country where 58% of African American 4th graders are functionally illiterate, *The Lottery* follows four families who have entered their children in a charter school lottery in hope of a better future. Out of thousands of hopefuls, only a small minority will win.[45]

The film captures the joy of the "winners" and the sadness of the "losers," but it only does so in one highly publicized moment. The film does not return years later to see how many "winners" remained Harlem Success Academy students. Mostkowitz's school loses students—a lot of students. In June 2014, Harlem Success Academy 1 graduated its first eighth-grade class. The class started first grade in 2006 with 73 students; however, by the time of that eighth-grade graduation in 2014, only 32 students remained.[46] Moreover, Moskowitz must not be too worried about those who were not accepted in previous lotteries, for the schools refuse to "backfill" in all grade levels—to allow new students to enroll in place of those who have left. This idea touches on an NEPC criticism of charter school waitlists: Charter schools do not accept students at all grade levels, but they might "waitlist" a student even though that student has zero chance of admission for not entering at a preferred grade level.[47]

Moskowitz will not backfill emptied seats at her schools beyond 4th grade. According to Geoff Decker of *Chalkbeat New York*, Moskowitz responded in a WNYC radio interview that her decision not to backfill in higher grades was really a district issue: If the district would send her better prepared students, she would backfill:

> If they backfilled older grades, she said, the incoming students' lower relative academic preparation would adversely affect the schools' other students.
>
> "We have an obligation to the parents in middle and high school, and the kids in middle and high school, that until the district schools are able to do a better job, it's not really fair for the seventh grader or high school student to have to be educated with a child who's reading at a second or third grade level," Moskowitz said.[48]

Moskowitz assumes the extreme in excusing her schools from backfilling higher grades—and simultaneously highlights her inability to selectively admit and her preference for not risking her schools' reputation as a top-test-scoring charter chain by allowing parents to really be the choosers in the game of school choice. In addition, this statement implies that all of her schools' students are on level—the ones that remain at Success Academies, that is. For Moskowitz's students to all be on level, attrition is a given.

Just because Moskowitz has set her rules for backfilling does not mean that school choice advocacy organizations consider the issue closed. A parental choice advocacy group active in New York City, Washington, D.C., and Camden, New Jersey,[49] Democracy Builders, produced a report in 2015 on New York City charters, entitled *No Seat Left Behind*.[50] Regarding the issue of backfill, Democracy Builders had this to offer:

> THE BACKFILL BACKSTORY Initially, charter authorizers allowed operators to replicate financial and enrollment models that constrained student entry to a few specific grades, such as kindergarten or 5th grade. Almost no charters included backfill in their enrollment process. When seats opened up in non-entry grades, they remained unfilled, resulting in the growth of non-entry grade waitlists. Our analysis finds that from 2006–2014 charter schools lost an average of 6% to 11% of their students each year, leaving more than 2,500 seats available in 2014 alone. Despite the tens of thousands of waitlisted families knocking to come in, at most grade levels, the charter sector only permits mobility out.
>
> WHY DON'T ALL CHARTERS BACKFILL? Perverse incentives. The media, philanthropists and some charter authorizers focus relentlessly on schools' "percent proficient." Schools that maintain or increase their absolute number of proficient students while decreasing their number of total students tested show increases in their percentage proficient each year and are lauded for their achievements. This misdirected praise exacerbates incentives for schools to minimize backfill in order to give the appearance of improving performance.[51]

Once again, choice belongs to the charter school operator, not to the parents wishing to choose the school. And there are those who promote themselves as school choice advocates and who believe this is the way it should be. Consider Fordham Institute President Michael Petrilli's February 2015 response to the Democracy Builders' push for backfilling empty charter seats, a blog post entitled "Backfilling Charter Seats: A Backhanded Way to Kill School Autonomy":

> There are strong instructional arguments for not backfilling. Great schools spend a lot of time building strong cultures. . . . Culture-building is a whole lot harder to do if a school is inducting a new group of students every year in every grade. Furthermore, schools that help their charges make rapid gains in their early years will be forced to spend a lot of time remediating new students who enter midstream. . . .

These are tough questions without one right answer. And in the absence of a clear and compelling right answer, the choice is always best left to individual schools. In fact, that's the whole point of charter schools: to allow educators to escape the Gordian knot of regulations and requirements that have imprisoned traditional public schools. When we force charters to backfill, or adopt uniform discipline policies, or mimic district schools' approach to special education, we turn them into the very things they were intended to replace.[52]

And those "things" charter schools are "intended to replace" are, in the end, neighborhood public schools. What is Petrilli's ultimate solution to the issue of a competition in which schools can choose to selectively backfill or not backfill at all versus the traditional public schools where backfilling is a given?

So here's a proposal: Eva Moskowitz should stop using proficiency rates to argue that her (backfill-free) schools are better than other charter schools, like Democracy Prep. And Democracy Prep should stop using growth scores to argue that its schools are better than district schools. And everyone should get out of everyone else's business. Deal? Now, let's get back to doing the work of educating children.[53]

There it is. Issue solved with armchair-quarterback ease by a man whose experience with K–12 education comes from a think tank. Yet Petrilli's glib solution underscores the fact that in the end, the real choice rests with the charter school operator, not parents.

A more reasoned response to backfilling comes from NEPC's May 2014 report on charter waitlists:

Student mobility is a simple reality for traditional public schools and charter schools alike, particularly those in lower income areas. Throughout the school year, substantial numbers of students leave and new students attempt to enter. Although some charter schools choose to "backfill" (i.e., replace leaving students with new students), many charter schools do not. . . .

Backfilling would also make charter schools more responsive to market pressures, which seems reasonable given that one of the key arguments for charter schools has been that they are market driven and responsive to market accountability. In a functioning market place, when demand from consumers increases, successful producers increase the supply; but popular charter schools are apparently not doing so.[54]

When charter schools choose not to admit students for whom the schools have space, those charters are gaming the school choice system. Their actions communicate to waitlisted students, "We do not want you here."

Another issue worth noting with Moskowitz's high-attrition, limited-backfilling schools concerns the first Harlem Success Academy 1 eighth-grade graduating class: These students scored in the top 1% of students on the New York State math tests in 2013–2014 and in the top 5% in reading. However, as Juan Gonzalez reports in the June 18, 2014, *New York Daily News*, not one of the 27 Harlem Success Academy 1 eighth graders who took New York's Specialized High Schools Admissions Test was admitted into one of New York's elite high schools. Such a result illustrates the issue that passing state tests might not reflect actual, transferrable learning. If scoring remarkably well on state tests truly means that Moskowitz's students both mastered content and improved in their ability to think critically, then such should be reflected by remarkable outcomes on the Specialized High School Admissions Test. Instead, Moskowitz's students, who are all African American/Latino, did not match the usual 12% admission rate of New York's African American and Latino students who take the test, which would have meant two or three of Harlem Success Academy 1's graduates would have been admitted into elite high schools. And that would have been breaking even.[55]

THE CHARTER SCHOOL TAKE-AWAY

Traditional public schools have been placed into competition with charter schools, and it is an unfair competition. The purpose of the traditional public school is to educate all students, both regular and special education, whenever they arrive. The 21st-century, test-score-driven, quasi-public, underregulated charter school has not shown itself to educate students consistently better than the neighborhood public school, yet it is allowed to escape fiscal accountability for the public funds it draws away from the neighborhood school. Furthermore, in the name of autonomy, the charter school gets to choose its students, not the parents or students. In the end, America can have a suitably funded K–12 public education system open to all, or it can have deregulated, competitive charter schools, but it cannot have both.

For-Profit Charters (and Associated For-Profit Education Business Opportunities)

One factor that may seem to complicate the debate over privatizing public education is the status of charter school operators as nonprofit or for-profit organizations. I maintain that so long as nonprofit charters are able to hide behind the designation of "private corporation" in order to avoid accountability for the public funding they receive, then the term *privatized* suits them. Such schools need not be classified as for-profit entities to profit from taxpayer money originally spent on educating students in neighborhood, board-run schools. In addition, autonomous, nonprofit charters are often free to form business partnerships that are clearly intended to benefit business owners, where the business owners could well be the charter school operator, the charter management organization, or members of the charter boards and their families.

Investigative reports on charter school scandals and shady deals abound. A 2013 *Forbes* article, "Charter School Gravy Train Runs Express to Fat City," charged that "charter schools are frequently a way for politicians to reward their cronies."[1] In its 2014 article "Education Newsmaker of the Year: Charter School Scandals, " the Education Opportunity Network noted, "Stories about charter operators being found guilty of embezzling thousands of taxpayer dollars turned into other stories about operators stealing even more thousands of dollars, which turned into even more stories about operators stealing over a million dollars."[2] A 2015 Center for Popular Democracy/Alliance to Reclaim Our Schools report found that charter fraud in 15 states topped $200 million.[3] In sum, many individuals running charter schools—whether for-profit or nonprofit—had every intention of profiting by steering public funds into private coffers. A key difference between these entities might be the more brazen way that for-profit corporations promote their ability to siphon taxpayer dollars away from the public school classroom in the name of investment.

THE BIG BUSINESS OF CHARTER SCHOOLS

The first article I read on the corporate interest in charter schools as an investment opportunity appeared in an August 2012 issue of *The Washington Post*. Written by education columnist Valerie Strauss, the article, pointedly titled "The Big Business of Charter Schools," examines how a real estate investment trust, Entertainment Properties Trust (later EPR Properties), makes money on charter schools by financing school facilities.[4] In 2015, most of EPR's investments were in for-profit Imagine Schools, which is converting to a nonprofit and describes itself as a "multi-state school district" with 70 schools in 12 states and the District of Columbia. According to EPR, out of a total of 61 charter schools, it finances 22 Imagine Schools facilities.[5]

In her 2011 article on EPR, Strauss includes a partial transcript from a CNBC interview with then-EPR President David Brain, who was abruptly relieved of his position in February 2015, the same day that EPR reported that its fourth quarter 2014 net income had dropped over $10 million from the fourth quarter in 2013.[6] Most of EPR's net income (65 percent) as of March 31, 2015, derived from its entertainment properties (megaplex theaters, entertainment retail centers, and family entertainment centers), not from its education investments (charter schools, private schools, and early childhood education).[7]

In the 2011 CNBC interview, Brain is confident in the stability of the charter market because of its backing with taxpayer funds despite the fact that a number of Imagine Schools did not seem to be faring well:

> *Anchor:* . . . Why would I want to add charter schools into my portfolio?
> *Brain:* Well I think it's a very stable business, very recession-resistant. It's a very high-demand product. . . . It's a public payer, the state is the payer on this, uh, category, and uh, if you do business with states with solid treasuries. Then it's a very solid business.
> *Anchor:* Well let me ask you about potential risks, here, to your charter school portfolio, because I understand that three of your nine "Imagine" schools are scheduled to actually lose their charters for the next school year. Does this pose a risk to investors?
> *Brain:* Well, occasionally—we have Imagine arrangements on a master lease, so there's no loss of rents to the company, although occasionally there are losses of charters in certain areas. . . .[8]

Brain is not concerned about the closures of charters because EPR has a "master lease" with Imagine Schools. As a result, even though schools might close, Brain was confident that EPR would get paid. In fact, he continues by noting that there is "not a lot of risk" because of the bipartisan support for charters. Brain states that both political parties are "solidly behind" charter schools and that "most of the studies have charters at even or better than district public education." He does not name these studies. Strauss closes her article with this comment: "By the way, it isn't true that 'most of the studies have charter schools at even or better than district public education.' But why let the facts get in the way?"[9]

FOR-PROFIT IMAGINE SCHOOLS

As noted in previous chapters, facts most certainly do get in the way of Brian's declaration, with evidence of such facts even on the EPR website. For example, on its 2015 charter school list, EPR includes an Imagine Schools charter named as St. Louis School District. The listing includes no physical address, yet it includes a square-footage notation of 153,000.[10] To further complicate the issue, on its website, Imagine Schools states, "Like all charter schools, Imagine charter schools are publicly funded while privately operated."[11] So then, how is it that the St. Louis School District is named in place of any school name?

At any rate, this reference is outdated, based on an April 18, 2012, *St. Louis Post-Dispatch* article, "Missouri Calls It Quits on Imagine Charter Schools in St. Louis":

JEFFERSON CITY. The Missouri Board of Education put underperforming charter schools statewide on notice Tuesday by voting to close all Imagine charter schools in St. Louis.

The move likely means more than 3,500 students in the city will be looking for new schools before fall. . . . And already, St. Louis Public Schools is determining how to take on the expected influx of children.

The move follows months of increasing scrutiny of the schools' financial, leadership and academic problems. The schools are operated by Virginia-based Imagine Schools Inc., a for-profit charter school management company. Students enrolled at the schools make up about one-third of the city's charter school population.

State test results from 2011 showed that nearly all students at the city's Imagine schools were performing below grade level in reading and math, prompting. . . call for the closure of the schools.

In December [2011], their sponsor, Missouri Baptist University, announced it would close two of them—Imagine Academy of Academic Success and Imagine Academy of Cultural Arts—this spring, and place the other four on probation.

On Monday, [April 16, 2012] Missouri Baptist University relinquished its sponsorship of the six charter schools, handing all regulatory authority over to the state. And one day later, the Board of Education voted to close them.[12]

It seems that the 153,000 square feet of EPR building space in St. Louis is no longer home to any Imagine Schools, though EPR continues to list the building space deceptively as part of what potential EPR investors might read as a listing of active charter schools.

According to the 2012 *St. Louis Post-Dispatch* article, there are no more Imagine Schools in Missouri. Aside from yielding low test scores that certainly do not back Brain's claim of charter schools performing as well or better than public schools, the Imagine Schools in St. Louis were criticized "for spending millions of dollars in state money that came into the schools on rent and administrative costs, rather than on teachers, textbooks and other classroom support."[13]

In 2007, one of Imagine School's Missouri charter schools that closed due to poor performance, Renaissance School for Math and Science, sued Imagine Schools for violations of the Racketeer Influenced Corrupt Organizations (RICO) Act. Imagine Schools controlled the Renaissance School board, which weakened the board's ability to function. Imagine Schools arranged for Renaissance School's board to hand over the school's finances to Imagine Schools via an operating agreement, which Imagine Schools used, in part, to pay for expenses it refused to document. In addition, Imagine Schools was found guilty of self-dealing when it formed its own finance company, SchoolHouse Finance, and then refinanced two Renaissance School buildings without formally disclosing to the Renaissance School board that Imagine Schools was sole owner of SchoolHouse Finance. According to the federal judge's findings, the greater issue in Imagine Schools' operating SchoolHouse Finance rests in undisclosed financial benefits that Imagine Schools incurred from its control of the two Renaissance School buildings:

> There is no evidence that the majority of the Renaissance Board [were told that Imagine Schools and SchoolHouse Finance were related companies.]. . . More importantly, there is no evidence that Imagine Schools ever told any Renaissance board member how Imagine Schools would benefit from the leases. Imagine Schools did not explain that SchoolHouse Finance intended to sell the [two] buildings to a real estate investment trust to recoup the capital expenditures made by SchoolHouse Finance and then lease the real estate back from the real estate trust at a lower rate than SchoolHouse Finance was charging Renaissance. . . . Imagine Schools did not inform the Renaissance Board that the school would incur higher-than-average costs for overhead, including rent, which would result in lower-than-average instructional expenditures, including textbooks, classroom supplies, and teacher salaries, which is exactly what happened.[14]

Imagine Schools' greed turned out to be the undoing of the school it was supposed to manage. Renaissance School's administrative and operating costs for 2007–2008 required 35.09% of its revenue, as compared with the Missouri state average of 19.62%. In contrast, Renaissance School spent 27.9% of its funding on instruction, as compared to the Missouri state average of 64.62%. The court confirmed that such operational-cost-heavy funding was "consistent" for 2007–2011.[15]

Renaissance School closed in 2012. Its worst enemy was its own self-serving charter management organization.

THE CHARTER SCHOOL GRAVY TRAIN

In 2013, *Forbes* magazine carried what was for its time an unusually candid story about the profit potential of the for-profit charter school. Education Opportunity Network writer Jeff Bryant highlights the importance of the *Forbes* article:

> A story that appeared at Forbes in late 2013 foretold a lot of what would emerge [regarding charter school scandals] in 2014. That post "Charter School Gravy Train Runs Express To Fat City" brought to light for the first time in a mainstream source the financial rewards that were being mined from charter schools. As author Addison Wiggin explained, a mixture of tax incentives, government programs, and Wall St. investors eager to make money were coming together to deliver a charter school bonanza—especially if the charter operation could "escape scrutiny" behind the veil of being privately held or if the charter operation could mix its business in "with other ventures that have nothing to do with education."[16]

Indeed, *Forbes'* "Gravy Train" article makes for a pointed and enlightening read. Contributor Addison Wiggin begins the article squarely focused on the profit potential for investors in for-profit education ventures:

> On Thursday, July 25, dozens of bankers, hedge fund types and private equity investors gathered in New York to hear about the latest and greatest opportunities to collect a cut of your property taxes. Of course, the promotional material for the Capital Roundtable's conference on "private equity investing in for-profit education companies" didn't put it in such crass terms, but that's what's going on.[17]

Where hedge funders and equity investors gather, there is money to be made. And the term "for-profit education companies" includes not only for-profit charter schools but also other education-related companies delivering goods and services to schools. Wiggin continues:

> [For these charter schools,] parents don't pay tuition; support comes directly from the school district in which the charter is located. They're also lucrative,

attracting players like the specialty real estate investment trust EPR Properties (EPR). Charter schools are in the firm's $3 billion portfolio along with retail space and movie megaplexes.[18]

An opportunity for the free market to put more reliable, taxpayer money into the market players' pockets. Think about it: This is *Forbes*, a business and investment flagship magazine carrying an article on charter schools. Nevertheless, it isn't necessarily a soft treatment of public education as a money maker. For example, Wiggin also notes that in 2013 in Ohio, for-profit charter schools run by two firms—and comprising 9% of the state's charter school market—collected 38% of Ohio's charter school funds. The article notes that "the operators of both firms both donate generously to elected Republicans." In Arizona, charters purchased goods and services from businesses owned by charter operators and board members. Wiggin writes that most charter schools were exempt from competitive bidding requirements for contracts exceeding $5,000. And in Florida in 2012, the for-profit education industry donated $1.8 million to legislators, mostly Republican.

However, as discussed in this book in Chapter 5 and as Wiggin notes in the *Forbes* article, charters are a bipartisan interest. Both Republicans and Democrats support charter establishment and expansion, with two of the most high-profile Democrats in 2015 being President Obama and former Secretary of Education Arne Duncan. As noted in Chapter 6, the investment incentive for charters includes dazzling tax credits introduced during the Clinton administration. In observing the same, Wiggin hits hard at the financial motives of those behind both for-profit charters and the profit-seeking educational businesses making money from nonprofit charter schools:

> About the only thing charters do well is limit the influence of teachers' unions. And fatten their investors' portfolios.
>
> In part, it's the tax code that makes charter schools so lucrative:. . . firms that invest in charters and other projects located in "underserved" areas can collect a generous tax credit—up to 39%—to offset their costs.[19]

Regarding the tax credit, Wiggin cites a 2010 article by Juan Gonzalez of the *New York Daily News* regarding the tax credit incentive to businesses for creating charter schools. Gonzalez's article is worth examining in its own right, as it provides a great case study in the fiscal exploitation available to businesses that aim to profit from charters by sending money to nonprofit charter management organizations. Hence, the for-profit motive is thinly veiled by nonprofit support—a nonprofit to which charter schools became indebted.

NONPROFIT CHARTERS AND THE CORPORATE TAX BREAK:
BRIGHTER CHOICE

Here is the story Gonzalez tells: In Albany, New York, a city with the highest percentage of charter school enrollment in the state in 2010, a nonprofit charter operator, the Brighter Choice Foundation, received corporate funding to operate several charter schools. As Gonzalez notes, the corporate enticement involved some marvelous corporate tax breaks:

> Under the New Markets program, a bank or private equity firm that lends money to a nonprofit to build a charter school can receive a 39% federal tax credit over seven years.
>
> The credit can even be piggybacked on other tax breaks for historic preservation or job creation.
>
> By combining the various credits with the interest from the loan itself, a lender can almost double his investment over the seven-year period.
>
> No wonder JPMorgan Chase announced this week it was creating a new $325 million pool to invest in charter schools and take advantage of the New Markets Tax Credit.[20]

In short, banks like JPMorgan invest in schools run by nonprofits like Brighter Choice, a scheme that hinges on student enrollments to draw taxpayer money into the charter schools. Despite the student recruiting efforts of Albany schools operated by Brighter Choice, the enrollment was not sufficient to garner enough taxpayer funds for many Brighter Choice schools to pay operating costs, including the rent, which ballooned over the years. One school, for example, paid $170,000 in rent in 2008; by 2009, the rent skyrocketed to $560,000. Thus, the schools ended up in debt to both the bank and to Brighter Choice—which, according to Gonzalez, is itself in debt.

Add to the above the lack of state oversight of charter school spending, as charter schools in New York are not considered public schools when it comes to auditing their books (see Chapter 7). Thus, there is no public watchdog to point out that a number of individuals functioning as board members of individual Albany charter schools were also connected to the "lender," Brighter Choice, which might well constitute a conflict of interest.

One such conflict involves charter school board member Tom Carroll. As Gonzalez details:

> Tom Carroll, the foundation's vice chairman and one of the authors of the state's charter law when he was in the Pataki administration, was a founding board member of Albany Community Charter School and is currently chairman of two other charters, Brighter Choice School for Boys and Brighter Choice School for Girls.

Carroll also sits on the board of directors of NCB Capital Impact, a Virginia organization that used New Market Credits to pull together investors for all the Albany building loans.

A Brighter Choice official confirmed Thursday that the Virginia organization gets "a 3% originating and management fee" for all school construction deals that Brighter Choice arranges.[21]

In sum, Carroll sits on the boards of both the borrowing school, now swimming in debt, and the lending organizer, which benefits financially from arranging the tax-credit-motivated loans. It seems a clear fiscal conflict of interest to sit on both boards when one organization benefits from the other even when the other experiences financial distress. Specifically, Carroll is part of an organization that makes money from arranging school construction even as he sits on a board of a school drowning in debt incurred from construction costs. Carroll notes that he receives no payment for sitting on the Virginia board and that he does not vote on any Brighter Choice "deals." Still, his role as an advocate for the charter school is dulled by his divided interest in, as Gonzalez states, "being part of the landlord, tenant and lending bodies for Albany school construction."[22]

And there is no regulatory agency to step in and sever such fiscal conflicts of interest.

Cut to Albany, New York, in April 2015 and a *Capital New York* article by Scott Waldman, "The Education Model That Fell Apart":

ALBANY—A few blocks from the Capitol, a cluster of vacant buildings testifies to the rapid rise and quick retreat of Albany's charter school sector.

Once heralded as a new beginning for children living in grinding poverty and stuck in a long-troubled school district, Albany's charter system has so far failed to live up to that promise. Five of the 12 charter schools that opened in the last decade have already closed, and others are being skeptically eyed by state officials. . . .

In Albany, all of the charter schools currently operating were supported by the Brighter Choice Foundation. . . .

Once considered a gold standard of charter operations, two Brighter Choice middle schools were closed by the state's Charter Schools Institute after just five years in operation, because 80 percent of the students were not proficient in English and math. Other charter schools in Albany, including an all-girls high school with a graduation rate of 51 percent, could be shuttered in the near future for poor performance.

In total, Albany taxpayers have spent more than $300 million on the city's charter schools in the last decade. . . . Many of those schools have now been closed.[23]

What is important to note is the community disruption caused by the failed Brighter Choice schools. The school construction that yielded corporate lenders a handsome tax break required the leveling of half a city block in a residential area. As Waldman points out, Albany now has "an administrative nightmare" on its hands as it must "establish an entirely new middle school in the next six months to handle the almost 400 charter school students who were enrolled in the failed Brighter Choice schools." The district schools may purchase some of the buildings formerly housing the closed charter schools—buildings funded by "evaporated" taxpayer money squandered "often through leases at above market rates."[24]

As did Gonzalez in 2010, Waldman also highlights Albany charter board member Tom Carroll in his report five years later, noting that former charter lobbyist Carroll was critical of Albany's first charter school, New Covenant Charter School, "which he did not create,"[25] for its rapid growth and underdeveloped curriculum. The New Covenant Charter School closed; Carroll contended that the Brighter Choice schools would be better. However, by 2015, some of Carroll's schools caught the attention of the state charter officials, who decided to close the schools by not renewing the charter. Charter proponents view such closures as evidence of accountability. I disagree. School closure is evidence of an absence of ongoing, systematic accountability that rids a charter school of problematic operators long before it needs closing.

Carroll appears to have done well for himself despite the failure of his schools to offer more to students than the district schools that in 2015 look to buy his vacant buildings draining taxpayer funds. However, Carroll was not available to discuss how handsomely he was paid for failure. As Waldman notes:

> Carroll, who earned more than $400,000 annually from the nonprofits he created to encourage charter growth, raised more than $15 million from the Walton Foundation to help build Albany's charter schools. He also turned to hedge-fund billionaires including Bruce Kovner to bring outside money for help growing Albany's charter sector.
>
> Carroll declined to comment for this story.[26]

In an audit of the closing schools, the New York State comptroller questioned "why $115,779 in payments were made by the school to the Brighter Choice Foundation for 'legal assistance, advocacy, curriculum design and test administration' without any evidence that it received anything of value for those services." Unfortunately, given the ruling protecting New York charter schools from audits (see Chapter 7), this question was raised far too late.

THE PROLIFERATION OF FOR-PROFIT CHARTERS

In 2014, during a discussion on social media regarding the all-charter New Orleans Recovery School District (RSD), I had a commenter from Detroit,

Michigan, write in exasperation that at least RSD had charters run by non-profits, that no one seems to realize how bad it is in Michigan because of the proliferation of for-profit charters.

The commenter's views are supported by a 2011 *Forbes* article that offered a critical examination of the profit motive behind Michigan's charter schools. Contributor Erik Kain draws on both 2011 Michigan State House testimony and the June 2011 U.S. House Education and the Workforce Committee testimony of Gary Miron of Western Michigan State University regarding Michigan's charter schools to offer this caution:

> Four out of five charter schools in Michigan are run by for-profit corporations. Let that sink in a minute. This should be deeply, deeply troubling for anyone thinking about their child's future education, or the future of this country.[27]

Kain's statement taps into issues of allegiance—to children or to dollars. It cannot be both.

Interestingly, Kain's article critical of for-profit charter schools included two ads for a for-profit "online public school," K12. The ad included the statement that K12 schools are "tuition free"—which means that taxpayer money goes to K12 to pay for students to attend.

Miron's testimony on the for-profit takeover of Michigan's charters includes the details behind Kain's surprising assertion. As excerpted from Miron's testimony before the congressional committee in June 2011:

Who Stole My Charter School Reform?

Even as the original goals for charter schools are largely ignored, charter schools fulfill other purposes.

- Promote privatization of public school system. Charter schools have provided an easy route for privatization; many states allow private schools to convert to public charter schools, and increasing the use of private education management organizations is increasingly being seen as the mode for expanding charter schools. Today, one-third of the nation's charter schools are being operated by private education management organizations (EMOs) and this proportion is growing rapidly each year. In states such as Michigan, close to 80% of charter schools are operated by private for-profit EMOs. The recent economic crisis has shown that our economy requires greater public oversight and regulations, a finding that can be reasonably extended to markets in education.
- *Means of accelerating segregation of public schools while placing the "Private Good" ahead of the "Public Good."* State evaluations find that charter schools seem to accelerate the re-segregation of public schools by race, class, and ability, instead of creating homogeneous learning communities based on particular learning styles or pedagogical approaches.

If privatization and accelerated segregation are not outcomes that the federal government wishes to achieve with charter schools, then it would be wise to consider how federal funding can be used to persuade states to revise their charter school reforms. Federal and state policy makers need to revisit the goals and intended purpose of charter schools, clearly articulating values and anticipated outcomes.[28]

A few observations regarding Miron's words. First of all, he supports the idea of charter schools. However, it is important to note that his support is for a charter school model that included autonomy coupled with high accountability. I am not sure how the ideas of autonomy and accountability complement each other since greater autonomy implies lesser oversight. Second, Miron conceived charter schools as working in concert with traditional public schools even as both charter schools and traditional public schools were to compete with one another. A competition implies winners and losers; in the case of school survival, collaboration will lose to competition. Finally, though he supports the idea of charter schools, Miron recognized that "the charter school idea has strayed from its original vision."[29]

In a November 2013 report on "Schoolhouse Commercialism Trends," Miron and University of Memphis Professor Charisse Gulosino, writing for the National Education Policy Center (NEPC), identify Michigan as an anomaly for its high percentage of for-profit charter schools (79%).[30] Nationally, Imagine Schools was the largest for-profit operator, with 89 schools in the 2011–2012 school year; that number dropped to 70 schools by 2015.[31] Other for-profit charter organizations in 2011–2012, as identified in the NEPC report, included Academica (76 schools), National Heritage Academies (68 schools), K12 Inc. (57 schools), and Edison Learning (53 schools). Of these companies, K12 had the highest enrollment by far: 87,091 students to National Heritage Academies' second-place enrollment of 44,338 in that school year.

The remainder of this chapter will consider some of the profit-garnering maneuverings involving three for-profit charter school organizations, Academica, National Heritage Academies, and K12. (Edison Learning was discussed briefly in Chapter 7.) For Academica and National Heritage Academies, a chief payoff is in their brick-and-mortar infrastructure. For the online K12, enrollment is paramount.

FOR-PROFIT ACADEMICA

In April 2014, Academica, based in Miami, Florida, made the news for "potential conflicts of interest in its business practices."[32] Specifically, federal investigators were in the process of examining conflicts of interest between Academica and schools managed by Academica, Mater Academies. Both Academica and Mater Academies share the same board of directors. Thus, the layer of independence between the charter school and the charter management organization—the charter school board—is missing. The absence of a distinct charter school board creates a convenient environment for the charter management organization to exploit the operation of its schools. Consider these details from the *Miami Herald* article:

> Academica President Fernando Zulueta founded the original Mater Academy in 1998 and was a member of its governing board until Sept. 2004.
>
> The auditors found that three of the schools in the Mater network—Mater Academy, Mater High and Mater East—entered into leases with development companies tied to the Zulueta family. Two of the leases were executed while Zulueta sat on the Mater board.
>
> In addition, Mater Academy hired an architectural firm from 2007 through 2012 that employs Fernando Zulueta's brother-in-law. . . .
>
> The report also pointed to a potential conflict of interest between Mater Academy in Hialeah Gardens and its non-profit support organization Mater Academy Foundation.
>
> "Mater Academy shares the same board of directors with the foundation and based on our review of the board of directors meeting minutes at Mater Academy, there is evidence of Mater Academy's board of directors transferring public funds to the foundation," the auditors noted.[33]

Though a federal report on the findings of this investigation, including the Academica conflicts of interest, was expected to be produced in 2014, no such report was made public. However, the conflicts of interest associated with Academica are not new: In November 2006, the Miami-Dade Public Schools Office of Management and Compliance Audits produced an internal audit report, *Investigations of Allegations of Impropriety: Mater Academy Charter School(s) and Academica Charter Corporation: Poor Governance Results in Apparent Self-dealing*. This report echoes the circumstances of Renaissance School and its self-dealing operator, Imagine Schools:

> We did find questionable practices, which suggest that the Board and senior management represented by Academica, did not adequately fulfill their fiduciary duties to the charter schools they represent. . . . Past and present officers and board members placed in major decision making roles. . . had direct ownership in the management company and other undisclosed interests in for profit companies established to provide financing and lease the facility back to the school(s).[34]

The report goes on to detail self-dealing in the form of a company created to buy school property and lease it back to the school for high rates:

> Specifically, a number of senior management and/or their immediate family served simultaneously as officers and directors for companies doing business

with Mater Academy. While serving in these multiple capacities, certain individuals failed to adequately advise the board of the Mater Academy, Inc. regarding the school's right to purchase the property they occupied. Instead, these individuals initiated the purchase of the facility by School Development HG II LLC, a for-profit corporation owned by an offshore corporation they established for that purpose. While denying any direct or indirect benefit, they have refused to disclose the individuals profiting from these questionable transactions. We estimate that the school is paying $1.3 million per year in excessive facility costs, which it otherwise might have had a permanent equity interest in.[35]

Again, this calls to mind the practices of Imagine Schools and Missouri's Renaissance School: Some members of the Academica board form a separate company to cut a business deal on the school real estate, one that ensures the school will have to pay excessive facility costs to an entity that is clearly associated with individuals already having board ties to the charter management organization responsible for overseeing the school.

The audit report is from 2006, 8 years before the 2014 federal investigation into the very same conflicts of interest. This investigation had not published its findings as of early 2016, which further underscores the need for systematic, continued oversight of public dollars flowing to charter schools, whether for-profit or nonprofit, in order to prevent exploitation from happening in the first place. Moreover, the 2006-documented Academica self-dealing that has yet to be resolved highlights the fact that the federal government appears to be either unwilling or unable to efficiently investigate and halt exploitation when it does occur.

FOR-PROFIT NATIONAL HERITAGE ACADEMIES

A major problem with the idea that the free market will produce higher-quality schools is that the free market is highly vulnerable to greed in the form of self-dealing. Indeed, the story of excessive amounts of money being paid for school operations is also true of another for-profit charter organization, National Heritage Academies (NHA), which operates schools in Louisiana. Former Louisiana Department of Education (LDOE) data manager and blogger Jason France wrote an investigative piece on NHA in January 2015, sharing a now-familiar story:

> In the 2012–2013 school year Inspire charter Academy, one of National Heritage Academies schools in Baton Rouge La, took in 6.8 million dollars in revenue from state and federal sources according to their own records. Of that 6.8 million, only about 1.3 million went towards teachers and their salaries. Approximately 2.8 million was classified as instructional expenditures, or about 40%. The remaining 60% went towards management fees, rent and profit. . . .

The rent on the building Inspire is leasing from itself at 5454 Foster Dr. is a little over 1 million dollars a year. The building they acquired is valued at around 5 million according to the assessed value. Inspire has a 5 year charter that is up for renewal for another 5 years at the EBR [East Baton Rouge school district] school board meeting tomorrow. With the rent they have paid to themselves out of the taxpayer funded MFP and Federal Funds an ordinary school district could have purchased the building outright, and owned a 5 million dollar building. NHA will continue to lease this building at 1 million dollars a year (or more) to itself for as long as it stays in business. . . . If/when NHA pulls out or loses its charter the parent corporation will retain ownership of a 5 million dollar building purchased with tax payer funds (that factor in building costs and maintenance) and EBR will have nothing.[36]

France continues by noting that NHA stated publicly that one of its Baton Rouge schools, Willow Charter Academy, will not have bus service because NHA considers the school to be a neighborhood school, "within walking distance." However, the school is located in a shopping center parking lot that is surrounded by four- to six-lane highways on all sides, so parents will need to drive their children to school or enroll them at other schools. But NHA benefits from not providing transportation, as France notes:

This arrangement allows NHA to pocket the money other districts spend on transportation, while also excluding the neediest students, those students without parents with reliable transportation, thus improving their demographics and lowering the higher costs associated with educating the poorest of the poor students.[37]

According to an NHA insider who communicated with France, the company also does not spend a lot of money on technology for its schools because "there is not research that proves [technology] leads to higher test scores, so that's not where they invest their money."[38]

NHA's schools are not known for their stellar school performance. For example, in 2014, the company's Inspire Charter Academy received a school letter grade of D after 5 years in operation. But it is still there and still able to scoop up taxpayer money.

REGAINING PROSPERITY IN THE FOR-PROFIT EDUCATION INDUSTRY(?)

France closes his NHA post with an email advertisement for a one-day "master class" offered by an investment group, Capital Roundtable, on January 14, 2015, in New York. I followed that link and discovered the following information in an ad for a class entitled, "Regaining Prosperity in the

For-Profit Education Industry: Private Equity Investing in For-Profit Education Companies." The conference is targeted at "GPs [general partners], LPs
[limited partners], & managers of buyout, growth equity, mezzanine, and
lending funds, as well as independent sponsors, operating partners, port-
folio company managers, and the bankers, lawyers, accountants, and other
advisors who support them." Here is the heart of the conference ad:

> In today's for-profit education marketplace, investors who truly understand the
> space, and what drives value, are finding that disruption can bring dividends.
>   Investors are encouraging education providers to restructure debt, *sell and
> lease back real estate*, implement efficiency improvements. . . even improve rela-
> tionships with regulators who worry about the cost-benefit gap of the schools'
> curriculums.
>   In addition, investors are increasingly focusing on the service provider
> companies that are targeting for-profit education—from marketing and enroll-
> ment services to course instruction and fundraising.
>   In short, after a rough patch, the future of the for-profit marketplace is
> brightening, and this Capital Roundtable conference will highlight the ways
> many middle-market investors are doing well.[39] [Emphasis added.]

It seems that a major money maker is in "education providers" selling and
leasing back real estate. That way, one can milk taxpayer dollars following the same model as Imagine Schools, Academica, and National Heritage
Academies. The key, though, is to be the owner of the company that holds
the milking lease. Moreover, if most of the taxpayer funds go to the lease,
then there is less money to blow on bothersome issues such as curriculum.
One way to close that curricular "cost-benefit gap" is to spend less money
on the actual education of students. Let's instead put that money in the
pockets of the owners of the school buildings via hamstringing the for-profit
school boards into fat lease payments to those owners.
    The profiteering secret is in the eternal-leasing sauce.
    And who is in charge of offering advice on how to milk public money in
the name of for-profit education? Equity investor Jeff Keith, who is featured
in the Capital Roundtable ad:

> Jeff is an operating partner at Chicago-based Sterling Partners, a $5 billion
> private equity firm focusing on the education marketplace. He has more than
> twenty years of experience leading finance and operations teams, with a wide
> range of senior executive roles under his belt.
>   Currently, Jeff serves as chairman of Sterling portfolio companies—Spartan
> College of Aeronautics, Tribeca Flashpoint Academy, and Educate Online. He
> is also a Director at Ashworth College. Previously, Jeff served as CFO (chief
> financial officer) and EVP (executive vice president) of TCS Education System.

He holds MBA and BS degrees in economics and management from Purdue University, and an MS in finance from the Illinois Institute of Technology.[40]

Jeff is there to help investors make the most of taxpayer-funded public education.

FOR-PROFIT K12

When it comes to profit potential, no brick-and-mortar for-profit charter school compares to the virtual charter. Online charter schools, such as K12, collect money without any building or transportation costs. Virtual schools need only provide online connection to a teacher and some form of online curriculum. That's it. The motivation to complete assignments and log on to submit work and participate in online exchanges with the teacher is up to the student.

Still, when high profit and minimal bottom line are the penultimate goals, one can expect some corner-cutting. In December 2011, *The New York Times* produced an article on virtual charter schools, with particular focus on K12. The article opens with information on one K12 virtual school, Agora Cyber Charter. If one considers educational outcomes, Agora Cyber Charter is a failing school, writer Stephanie Saul contends: Almost 60% of students are behind a grade level in math and almost 50% in reading. In addition, one in three Agora students do not graduate on time, and the student attrition rate is remarkable; "hundreds of children, from kindergartners to seniors, withdraw within months after they enroll."[41]

Yet K12 virtual charter schools are a success for publicly traded K12, for the taxpayer money just keeps rolling in. As Saul notes:

Kids mean money. Agora is expecting income of $72 million this school year, accounting for more than 10 percent of the total anticipated revenues of K12, the biggest player in the online-school business. . . .

A look at the company's operations. . . raises serious questions about whether K12 schools—and full-time online schools in general—benefit children or taxpayers, particularly as state education budgets are being slashed.

Instead, a portrait emerges of a company that tries to squeeze profits from public school dollars by raising enrollment, increasing teacher workload and lowering standards.[42]

According to fiscal information on K12 from marketplace website SeekingAlpha in 2012:

The company [K12] is highly dependent on state funding—Today, K12 receives an average of $5,500 to $6,000 per student from state and local governments. The schools also receive money for federal programs.

The company is also highly dependent on two virtual public schools—Ohio Virtual Academy and the Agora Cyber Charter School of Pennsylvania which produce 12% and 13% of overall revenues (based on FY 2012 Totals).[43]

K12 depends on Agora for profits. Never mind that not all students are intellectually and academically capable enough to thrive in a chiefly isolated, independent-study-styled education format. Nor are all motivated to work on a schedule absent adult supervision, which means that in enrolling their children in a virtual charter school, many parents are agreeing to be that in-home-education, motivating presence for their children. Such could well account for high rates of attrition in the virtual education "classroom."

Then there is the issue of teacher class load. Teaching students at a distance can be challenging and requires intense communication online and by phone. However, that challenge can become "virtually" impossible when profit-driven companies like K12 underpay teachers and then turn around and overload them with hundreds of students—which Saul contends is the case based on correspondence with "current and former staff members of K12."[44]

Add to these issues concerns about teaching ethics and potential enrollment fraud:

> Some teachers at K12 schools said they felt pressured to pass students who did little work. Teachers have also questioned why some students who did no class work were allowed to remain on school rosters, potentially allowing the company to continue receiving public money for them. State auditors found that the K12-run Colorado Virtual Academy counted about 120 students for state reimbursement whose enrollment could not be verified or who did not meet Colorado residency requirements. Some had never logged in.[45]

According to this Colorado state audit, K12 collected money for students it could not confirm as being enrolled. However, even for students who are enrolled, K12 collects more money than is required to educate students virtually. For example, Pennsylvania paid K12 the full amount of over $11,000 per student on average, with actual funding varying by district. Still, in Pennsylvania, K12 walked away with the same amount of student funding as a brick-and-mortar school.[46]

The negative press that K12 garnered from *The New York Times* article was evident in SeekingAlpha's 2012 review of the company—and the SeekingAlpha conclusions did K12 no favors:

> In July 2009, the Pennsylvania Department of Education instituted charter revocation proceedings against the Agora Cyber Charter School based on allegations of charter violations and non-compliance with state charter school and other laws by the independent charter board. However, the charter was renewed

for five years on June 30, 2010, following PDE approval of a new board and management contract with K12.

The Agora School was also the focus of a 2011 investigation courtesy of the *NY Times*, which noted that nearly 60 percent of its students are behind grade level in math, with nearly 50 percent trailing in reading.

The *Times* figures, however, don't seem to really jive with what is advertised on the K12 website, which (as shown below) paints a story that looks a lot rosier. The disparity comes from the fact that K12 utilizes its own 'internal' testing methodology.[47]

The SeekingAlpha review continues by noting that it was able to confirm the high-pressure, profit-driven environment at the expense of "solid education."[48] Moreover, *Financial Investigator* writer Roddy Boyd offered information confirming the high attrition at Agora (in 2009–2010, 2,688, or 35.5%, of students withdrew) and similar attrition at the Colorado Virtual Academy (in 2010–2011, 2,330, or 36.1%, of students withdrew) and even higher attrition at the Ohio Virtual Academy (in 2010–2011, 9,593, or 51.1%, of students withdrew).[49]

In January 2012, K12 investors sued K12 in a class-action lawsuit centered on the company's use of deception to conceal its high rates of student attrition. Saul's article in *The New York Times* apparently served as catalyst for the lawsuit. As Benjamin Herold of *Newsworks* reported in January 2013:

> Former employees allege that K12-managed schools aggressively recruited children who were ill-suited for the company's model of online education. They say the schools then manipulated enrollment, attendance and performance data to maximize tax-subsidized per-pupil funding. . . .
>
> In one example, a former Agora teacher said in court documents that the school continued to bill the home school district of one special education student who was absent for 140 consecutive days.
>
> Pennsylvania requires that cyber charter students who miss 10 straight days be reported as withdrawn.
>
> "What Agora does is keep the kid in inactive limbo and keep billing," said the anonymous former teacher in court documents.[50]

In their lawsuit, investors maintain that K12's efforts to conceal student attrition issues amounts to securities fraud.[51] The lawsuit also concerned teacher-student ratios and academic outcomes.[52]

On July 25, 2013, the U.S. District Court for the Eastern District of Virginia issued a judgment in favor of plaintiffs, K12 investors. The company agreed to pay its stockholders $6.2 million.[53]

In January 2014, K12 founder and CEO Ron Packard resigned.[54] Only months later, in April 2014, investors filed a second class action against

K12 on behalf of investors who purchased K12 stock between March and October 2013.[55] As of this writing, the suit has yet to go to court.

K12 continues to operate. In April 2015, the company offered the following financial information regarding projected fourth quarter 2015 performance, as noted in *Reuters*:

> K12 Inc: Sees Q4 2015 revenue in the range of $225 million to $235 million. Sees Q4 2015 operating income in the range of $4 million to $6 million. Sees FY 2015 revenue in the range of $938 million to $948 million. Sees FY 2015 operating income in the range of $39 million to $42 million.[56]

As I was reading articles in K12 as part of my research for this chapter, most included an ad promoting K12—even articles that revealed the company as a profiteering educational shell.

WHAT ABOUT THE KIDS?

Nothing about the stories in this chapter supports any notion that the bottom line of for-profit education is the student. Though much of the chapter concerns fiscal exploitation associated with for-profit charter schools, it also touches on profiteering that can (and does) occur when nonprofit charter schools are allowed to conduct unchecked business and the potential for exploitation via corporate tax credits.

It's either the profit or the kids. In these cases, the profit wins.

CHAPTER 9

No Excuse Charters, Broken Windows, and Micromanaged Behavior

On the surface, the idea of "no excuses" in the classroom sounds great. If I could do so, I would set up my own list of behaviors for which I would accept No Excuses so that my sophomore English classroom would run as smoothly as a well-oiled machine. For one, I would accept no new students once a semester had begun. So what if your family moved mid-semester, and the move required a change of school? No excuses on my end, because acclimating new students mid-term is a disruption for me and my class. Surely there are no excuses for students not completing their work on time and with sufficient enthusiasm. Thus, only students who complete their assignments would be allowed to attend. All others must go.

How easy teaching would be if only those two rules were part of my classroom. However, I realize that two other issues already confound the instituting and enforcing of those restrictions. For one, American education is compulsory until around age 17 or 18 in most states,[1] and I am a proponent of compulsory education. I believe it to be one of the pillars of a sound democracy. There are those who desire to do away with compulsory education, stating that education should be left up to the parents. However, I know in my own situation that my parents would have been at a loss to assume responsibility for educating my four siblings and me. Plus, there is the assumption that no parents would exploit their children in order to spend education dollars on themselves—leaving their children uneducated—which is neither beneficial to the children or to greater society.

The second reason I could not adhere to my two rules is that I understand child and adolescent development. I know that learning is often messy, especially because students are developing physically, mentally, emotionally, spiritually, and sexually even as I am trying to teach them English. In the course of their development, there will be times of friction, times when students do not complete assignments, when they misbehave—and when I must discipline them with the goal of helping them grow into responsible, healthy, productive adults. Sure, it would be easier for *me* if I could send them away for not completing work or participating productively in class. However, it would not benefit *them*, for human beings learn and grow in relationship with other human beings—and as a teacher of adolescents, I realize the importance of my place in their lives, not only as a provider of information in the core subject of English but also as a mature adult who can help them grow and assume responsibility for their lives. Yes, there are times when I must seek an alternative education arrangement for a student who might be too disruptive for me to teach, or who has excessive emotional difficulty, or who presents a physical danger to my students or me. But these situations are not the norm in my classroom. For most of my students, I am able to teach them English even as I help them grow and mature as human beings.

A set of no excuses rules designed to set my classroom in perfect order would sterilize the "safe place to mess up" atmosphere necessary for healthy human growth.

No excuses might look impressive on the outside, but it doesn't go much farther than that. It offers a shell of appearance at odds with the messy beauty of American public education at work.

REGULATED ENVIRONMENT

The so-called no excuses charter schools are also known as "regulated environment" schools. The idea behind these schools is that the classroom environment should be highly controlled. In March 2013, University of Pennsylvania Professor Joan Goodman published an article in the *Educational Researcher* entitled, "Charter Management Organizations and the Regulated Environment: Is It Worth the Price?"[2] Goodman observes that urban students "are increasingly being educated at public schools run by charter management organizations (CMOs) characterized by a highly rule-ordered and regulated environment." She notes that whereas strictly enforced rules contribute to student safety at school, such rules come with a cost:

> If not counterbalanced with opportunities for genuine choice and personal agency, the rules may quell students' desires and shrink their aspirations. A blanketing emphasis on obedience can create conditions for accepting instruction, but alone, it is dangerous, for students will not have developed their own compass to resist negative models.[3]

In other words, too much emphasis on following rules stifles students' freedom to experiment and dream—and it kills the opportunity for students to sharpen the ability to recognize and resist harmful situations.

The no excuses model of discipline can be oppressive. According to Goodman, these rules involve a pervasive "variety of systematic behavioral engineering techniques":

> A conspicuous feature of the regulated environment is an insistence on continuous compliance to pervasive rules that shadow children throughout the day. The rules [cover] even small details of children's comportment, both in and out of class.[4]

Furthermore, Goodman notes that since the principal focus of charter school success is the standardized test score, "specifically the narrowing of the 'achievement gap' (more aptly described as the 'test gap'),"[5] the means for increasing test scores is largely overlooked. Goodman is critical of such oversight:

> The instructional and behavioral systems used to accomplish this end may be noted but tend not to be critically inspected in evaluations of success, for they are merely instrumental in producing results. However, separating means and ends in this instance may be shortsighted, for the "product" is not merely the test score but the student whose work it represents. One would not consider a competitive runner successful, for example, if he or she won a match but acquired an anxiety disorder from the stress of training or a student worthy of honor if he or she cheated his or her way to success.[6]

In the case of the no excuses charter school, Goodman details what one might expect to witness in the classrooms of such schools based on her research of two no excuses charter operators, KIPP (Knowledge is Power Program) and Young Scholars, including requirements for students to pay full attention to instruction, without deviation; instructor attention to even the most minute of student behaviors; and an intricate system of external rewards and punishments. In the case of elementary-aged students, these may include in-the-moment ratings in which students are assigned colors associated with how well they are behaving. The behavior rating system is reset after lunch at some schools to allow students to begin their behavior ratings afresh. Reports of student progress accompany students home; such reports include daily ratings of student behavior, dress code/uniform compliance, and homework completion.

Goodman notes that for middle grades, the no excuses charter schools have a system of merits and demerits, with students being graded individually and as an entire class. The teacher carries a clipboard for such a purpose; even body language is graded. Positive class behavior grades are eligible for class rewards. At one KIPP school she studied, middle school students are given a tally of their behavior infractions every two weeks. They could be given demerits for infractions as minor as not carrying a behavior tally card.

Many no excuses schools have their own in-school monetary system. For example, at one school, a student whose "account" dips below $30 in school bucks "earns" an after-school detention. If that balance remains below $30 for three weeks, the resulting punishment is either an in- or out-of-school suspension. Six weeks with a low balance incurs both suspension and a "reinstatement meeting."[7] On the other hand, well-behaved students might earn some token entitling them to privileges. At one KIPP school, students who behave well receive a bracelet so that others might know how well-behaved these students are. The bracelets also entitle students to privileges, including being excused from wearing a uniform, preferential seating at lunch, and discounts on purchases that they might make at school with their school money.

Goodman questions the impact of such intense focus on student behavior:

> This laser focus on behavioral compliance through the continuous ministration of sanctions and rewards may or may not be necessary to preserve an educational environment suitable for learning. What students clearly learn is never to lose sight of adult expectations, never to be distracted from what they are expected to do by what they might want to do. Children's initiative is suppressed in favor of conformity, in favor of heteronomy.[8]

Heteronomy is the opposite of autonomy and involves "subordination or subjection to the law of another."[9] In order for my traditional public school classroom to function, as the teacher, I must clarify my expectations of student behavior, I must set consequences for breaches of my expectations, and I must to the best of my ability enforce my system of discipline. However, I must also strike a balance between my authority and student autonomy. As such, I do not micromanage student behavior, just as I do not expect my principal to micromanage mine.

Such an approach certainly confronts the way of the no excuses charter school.

A BIT ABOUT KIPP

Perhaps the most well-known no excuses charter school chain is KIPP, founded in 1994 by two Teach for America (TFA) alumni, Michael Feinberg and Dave Levin. (The TFA-KIPP connection is a tight one: KIPP CEO Richard Barth is married to TFA founder Wendy Kopp.)[10] The KIPP website offers much information (e.g., its history, funding, teachers, number of schools, number of students, and general philosophy); however, there are no details about the behavior management strategies constantly employed for student behavioral micromanagement.[11] Moreover, whereas the KIPP

Parent/Student Handbook offers an extensive listing of student behavior infractions and potential consequences, it might not offer details regarding in-the-moment discipline. For example, the KIPP DC handbook refers to "disruptive behavior" as warranting "in class discipline"; however, it does not detail that students might be given demerits for not following the teacher with their eyes—or even removed from class for sneezing (which happened to a student at KIPP Bronx).[12] All three KIPP handbooks that I accessed (KIPP DC for 2013–2014, KIPP Metro Atlanta for 2013–2014, and KIPP Delta for 2014–2015)[13] offer some detail in the school's "paycheck" system, and one (KIPP DC) states that the school has an "open classroom" policy and invites parents to visit classrooms. None clearly outlines KIPP no excuses behavior management. Therefore, it is possible for parents to enroll their children in a KIPP school without fully understanding the school's behavior management philosophy.

Some KIPP student handbooks apparently offer parents more of a heads-up regarding KIPP's stringent discipline policies than do others. For example, the KIPP Delta student/parent handbook (2014–2015) offers a number of hints as to its no excuses discipline. Regarding bus behavior, students must keep their backpacks on their laps, and they are not allowed to use writing utensils or even talk while riding the bus:

> **Stay silent.** There is no talking on the bus. We value safety and respect. The driver will be able to focus on a safe ride home more if students are quiet. Furthermore, students who want to read or have a peaceful ride home deserve that opportunity.[14]

No unwinding on KIPP Delta's time. No chatting with friends on the bus ride to and from school. Instead, let's inhibit more developmentally appropriate, youthful behavior just because we can.

Regarding the strictures of the KIPP Delta bus ride, there's more. Once the silent ride is over, KIPP Delta's students and bus driver are "expected" to talk on command—but allowed a narrow window for "respectful creativity":

> **Greet your driver and be appreciative.** The expectation is that students and drivers greet each other upon boarding the bus with a friendly good morning, hello, good evening, how are you today, etc. Upon exiting the bus, student should at the very least say thank you, but respectful creativity is applauded such as have a great day/night, much obliged, thanks and see you tomorrow, etc.[15]

Then there are the detailed directives on how to exit the bus:

> **Respectful Dismissal.** When the bus arrives at school, wait until the bus driver has turned to face you and dismisses the bus. Ladies will be dismissed first. If a

student on the window seat needs to get off first, the aisle seat should step out and step back to let the person off the bus.[16]

As for the general behavioral expectations for students attending KIPP Delta, there are hints as to the micromanaged behavioral expectations in the following "non-negotiables":

Non-Negotiable Expectations:

. . .

Be on-task at **all** times during class. While **anyone** is speaking, this means that students will always have their eyes, ears, and brains on that person. Students should be sitting properly during class time (e.g., no heads on their desk; feet on the floor). . . .

Students will be receiving an independent reading book during the first weeks of school. They are expected to have a book on their reading levels in a plastic bag (for protection) at all times. . . .

Respond appropriately to all questions. Tone, reactions, and non-verbal actions matter.[17]

Always sit with both feet on the floor. Whenever anyone is speaking, look at that person. Keep the independent reading book in a plastic bag. Become hyper-aware of voice infection and body language. These are non-negotiable expectations.

I can already think of specific students of mine who would be overwhelmed by the few KIPP Delta bus rules and general rules listed on these pages. I can hear it now:

"All I did was cross my legs."
"All I did was say hello to my friend on the bus ride home."
"All I did was use a pencil while riding the bus."
"All I did was forget to put my independent reading book back in the plastic bag."

And I can visualize the resulting self-esteem erosion and growing dislike for school that such under-researched, no excuses micromanagement must foster in over-inhibited children.

But what of the "open classroom" policy at schools such as KIPP DC? Could a parent gain clear insight into in-the-moment KIPP discipline? Indeed, when parents become more informed regarding the stringent behavior expectations on students, the open classroom policy might not be so "open" to parents wanting to investigate. In 2012, Leonie Haimson of the New York–based advocacy organization Class Size Matters interviewed Celeste, a former KIPP student from the Bronx, and her mother. When

Celeste's mother had concerns about KIPP discipline, she decided to take KIPP up on its open classroom invitation to parents:

> At the very first, I saw the way they were talking to some kids in the line as they're going in. They're like (shouting) "Oh you know you're not supposed to come in here with those!" And I'm saying to myself, it doesn't have to be like that—they were screaming at them. I said to myself, you know, I really have to find out about this school. So I decided that I was going to be very active.
>
> Well, that's where my problems started. Because then it became war. I wasn't welcome there, and I noticed it. Because I used to pop up unexpectedly and I would hear these teachers really being mean! And they would say, "You can't be here, you're interrupting, they're in class, they're in session." And I said, "I have a right to be here."[18]

Perhaps Celeste's mother's presence felt less like a visit and more like investigative research—which KIPP and other no excuse charter schools do not promote. In September 2014, my colleague, fellow education blogger Jennifer Berkshire, interviewed Goodman regarding her 2013 study of no excuses charter schools. Berkshire, whose research expertise is in studying charter schools, called Goodman's research study "the single best overview of 'no excuses' charter schools that I've seen."[19]

NO EXCUSES ACADEMIC RESEARCH SHYNESS

In July 2015, Berkshire and I discussed the interview, and she noted that it has received more public attention than she anticipated. (I first read it in the September 19, 2014, *Washington Post*.[20]) Berkshire believes the public interest was largely due to the fact that there is a notable lack of academic research on the no excuses charter school model. Berkshire and Goodman discussed this lack of research in their interview, which Berkshire titled "The High Cost of No Excuses":

Berkshire: With the exception of KIPP, which has allowed *Mathematica* to study its admission policies and test results, these schools haven't been receptive to academic studies. How did you manage to study them?
Goodman: I'm the academic director of our Teach for America program at UPenn and our TFA students are teachers in these schools. So I can go in to look at what our students and their teachers are doing, and then students tell me a lot about what's going on. I have also done a good bit of visiting. The charters are hospitable to that. A lot of this (Goodman's research) is

anecdotal, and much is based on what the schools have written, which is public. My work is investigative, I think, more than formal research. But you're right—it takes a huge effort to try to get into these schools for any systematic research. They don't welcome outsiders to study them. And they have a point. What academics do when they go in is criticize, and you can see why they might not like that. I think they'll let just about anybody in for a visit. But to go in and have the schools really cooperate with an investigator, that's a whole lot harder. What are the day-to-day processes that are happening in the classroom? How do teachers feel about these processes? How much range of behavior is there? It would be great to be able to investigate these sorts of questions, but the schools wouldn't welcome that.[21]

Even though there is a lack of formal research on no excuses charter schools like KIPP, these schools are known for their micromanagement of student behavior—and the expectation that students can and will control their behavior when required to do so under clearly expressed adult expectations. The next exchange between Berkshire and Goodman reveals the bending of the student will necessary in no excuses classrooms—classrooms that tend to be popular in cities populated with children of color:

> *Berkshire:* Minority children in urban areas are increasingly being educated at schools run by the types of charter management organizations you study, yet I find that people know little if anything about the way these schools view the world.
>
> *Goodman:* These schools start with the belief that there's no reason for the large academic gaps that exist between poor minority students and more privileged children. They argue that if we just used better methods, demanded more, had higher expectations, enforced these higher expectations through very rigorous and uniform teaching methods and a very uniform and scripted curriculum geared to being successful on high-stakes tests, we can minimize or even eradicate these large gaps, high rates of drop outs and the academic failures of these children. *To reach these objectives, these schools have developed very elaborate behavioral regimes that they insist all children follow, starting in kindergarten. Submission, obedience, and self-control are very large values. They want kids to submit. You can't really do this kind of instruction if you don't have very submissive children who are capable of high levels of inhibition and do whatever they're told.* [Emphasis added.][22]

In her 2012 interview with Celeste, a former KIPP Bronx fifth-grade student, Haimson captures the pressure placed on students to submit even minor body movement to the no excuses system:

> I had to sit like this. [demonstrates] It's called S.L.A.N.T.: Sit straight. Listen. Ask a question. Nod your head. Track. Track is, if the teacher is going that way you have to. . . [demonstrates] follow. . . If you didn't do that, they'll yell at you: "You're supposed to be looking at me!" [points to demerit sheet] "No SLANTing." They'll put that on there (the demerit sheet).
>
> If I got into an argument with a teacher, I would have to stand outside the classroom on the black line, holding my notebook out. [Stands up and demonstrates, holding arms out] I would have to stand there until they decided to come out. For 20 minutes, 30 minutes, sometimes they'll forget you're out there and you'll be there the whole period—an hour and forty minutes standing. if you have necklaces you have to tuck them away so they can't see them—or else they'll have you write four pages of a sentence about KIPP—"I must follow the rules of the KIPP Academy" or "I must not talk" for four pages.
>
> They would have us stand on the black line for as many minutes as they felt was right for what I did. I would never get my homework during that hour when I was outside on the line. And I'd ask for the homework, they'd be like "I'll give it to you later." And the next day I would come in without homework and it goes directly on my paycheck [the demerit system]. . . .
>
> At KIPP, I would wake up sick, every single day. Except on Sunday, 'cause that day I didn't have to go to school. *All the students called KIPP the "Kids in Prison Program."*[23]

Perhaps KIPP should put its schools on its own demerit system based on the negative psychosomatic reactions of students to the overbearing discipline.

ESCAPING FROM NO EXCUSES

Psychosomatic reactions are not the only means that KIPP students have for dealing with the stress associated with no excuses micromanaged behavior. As Celeste observes, attrition is a way to escape no excuse pressure—for students and teachers alike:

> I noticed that a lot of kids left. In 5th grade, there were about 50 students. 6th grade, I came back and there were 30. 7th grade: 20. About 10 of them were held back and a lot of them left.
>
> A lot of the teachers left too. When I got to 6th grade, the 5th grade teachers had all changed. By the time I got to 8th grade, there were only about four teachers left that I knew. And now it's all new teachers. None of them are there that I went to school with.[24]

I wrote about KIPP in my first book, *A Chronicle of Echoes*. Regarding student attrition at KIPP, here is an excerpt concerning what I discovered:

As reported by Gary Miron (of Western Michigan) and others in [a] 2011 [analysis of KIPP via a national education database using 2007–2008 data], KIPP had an attrition rate of 30% between sixth and eighth grade. This means that almost one in three KIPP students who make it to sixth grade will not make it to ninth grade. Furthermore, 40% of African American males leave KIPP between sixth and eighth grades. To consider this latter stat another way: Of every five African American boys who enroll at a KIPP school, only three will stay to reach ninth grade. . . .

Whenever one reads of an amazing KIPP statistic, one should factor in KIPP student attrition. . . . [The Miron et al.] study shows that KIPP loses approximately 15% of its students from each grade cohort each year. Results of a three-year study of KIPP conducted by *Mathematica* found KIPP attrition to be 37% over three years, comparable to the public schools it used for comparison. The Western Michigan study notes that those leaving KIPP are likely to be low-performing students who likely return to the local community school.[25]

Note that the 2013 *Mathematica* follow-up to its 2010 study of KIPP middle school students found that KIPP "substantially" retained students in 5th and 6th grades as compared to local districts (2010–2011 data). Moreover, students in 5th and 6th grades were more likely to repeat a grade than they were in district schools. Finally, KIPP was more likely to accept new students in 7th and 8th grades, and the new students choosing to transfer to KIPP tended to be higher-achieving.[26]

The *Mathematica* study of KIPP is focused on middle grades (5th through 8th). For the students who remain at KIPP for at least 3 years, *Mathematica* notes that their reading and math score gains are likely to be both positive and statistically significant. As Goodman and Berkshire note previously in this chapter, the *Mathematica* study does not include examination of the impact of the No Excuses behavioral emphasis on student development, including the ability to exercise one's individuality.

No standardized test measures student developmental health.

Student mental and emotional development and well-being aside, one additional issue is worthy of discussion regarding KIPP academics. The 2014–2015 KIPP Delta student handbook specifies as a requirement for graduation "acceptance to at least one (1) 4-year colleges or universities."[27] The implication is that KIPP Delta students who are not accepted into at least one four-year college/university prior to graduation—or who believe that they will not be even before they reach their senior year—must either face retention or graduate from some other school. Since no non-magnet, traditional, board-run public school holds such a requirement over the heads of its students, one might assume that KIPP high school students who do not meet its college-acceptance requirement might choose to return to traditional public school.

So, when one reads the following stellar December 2013 KATV announcement of KIPP Delta success, one must remember that the school requires college admission for receipt of a diploma:

> KIPP Delta is a K–12 charter school located in Helena-West Helena. Its enrollment, over 900 students, almost all African-American. Eighty-eight percent of them qualify for free or reduced lunch, 100 percent of this year's graduating class was accepted into college.[28]

The KATV article did not include information about how many students enrolled as freshmen at KIPP Delta versus how many graduated four years later from the school.

I also found that KIPP Austin advertises the following on its website:

> KIPP Austin is a network of 9 schools serving more than 3,900 students in Austin. With 100% of the Class of 2014 accepted to college, KIPP Austin continues to prove that demographics do not define destiny.[29]

However, I could find no publicly available copy of the KIPP Austin Student/Parent handbook to examine to see if this school had the same college-acceptance requirement as does KIPP Delta. I did find the 2014–2015 KIPP San Antonio student handbook, which includes no college acceptance requirement as a condition for high school graduation.[30]

And now, a bit about KIPP teacher attrition.

The 2013 *Mathematica* study cited previously also captured the high teacher attrition rates at KIPP middle schools on average: 21% for teachers in general, as compared to 15% nationally for public school teachers. However, the KIPP lottery schools in the study had unusually low teacher turnover: 12%.[31]

In 2014, KIPP reported that 76% of its teachers returned from one year to the next;[32] in 2012, 74% returned. In their 2011 study, Miron, Urschel, and Saxton found that 11 out of 12 KIPP districts spend less per student on teacher salaries and benefits than did their host districts.[33] Moreover, the 2013 *Mathematica* study noted that 86% of KIPP principals found it difficult to fill teacher vacancies; 61% noted as the reason that "applicants are not a good fit for the school culture or goals" (*Mathematica's* words).[34]

I can only imagine that being a good no excuses teacher requires one to accept and rigidly adhere to the micromanagement of the most seemingly insignificant of student movements. Every movement, every moment.

I would make a terrible no excuses teacher.

BROKEN WINDOWS THEORY

Journalist Sarah Carr of the *Hechinger Report* also captures the effects of no excuses submission on students in a November 2014 article including the experiences of a student at a no excuses school in New Orleans, entitled, "The Painful Backlash Against 'No Excuses' School Discipline":

> From the moment Summer Duskin arrived at Carver Collegiate Academy in New Orleans (Louisiana) last fall, she struggled to keep track of all the rules. There were rules governing how she talked. She had to say thank you constantly, including when she was given the "opportunity"—as the school handbook put it—to answer questions in class. And she had to communicate using "scholar talk," which the school defined as complete, grammatical sentences with conventional vocabulary. When students lapsed, they were corrected by a teacher and asked to repeat the amended statement.
>
> There were rules governing how Summer moved. Teachers issued demerits when students leaned against a wall, or placed their heads on their desks. (The penalty for falling asleep was 10 demerits, which triggered a detention; skipping detention could warrant a suspension.) Teachers praised students for shaking hands firmly, sitting up straight, and "tracking" the designated speaker with their eyes. The 51-page handbook encouraged students to twist in their chairs or whip their necks around to follow whichever classmate or teacher held the floor. Closed eyes carried a penalty of two demerits. The rules did not ease up between classes: students had to walk single file between the wall and a line marked with orange tape.[35]

Regarding schools adhering to this stringent approach to discipline, Carr observes, "The schools, most of them urban charters, share an aversion to even minor signs of disorder." But why attention to such minute behaviors? Such attention is based on what is known as "broken windows theory." As *Encyclopedia Britannica* notes:

> Broken windows theory, academic theory proposed by James Q. Wilson and George Kellingin 1982 that used broken windows as a metaphor for disorder within neighbourhoods. Their theory links disorder and incivility within a community to subsequent occurrences of serious crime. . . .
>
> Prior to the development and implementation of various incivility theories such as broken windows, law enforcement scholars and police tended to focus on serious crime; that is, the major concern was with crimes that were perceived to be the most serious and consequential for the victim, such as rape, robbery, and murder. Wilson and Kelling took a different view. They saw serious crime as the final result of a lengthier chain of events, theorizing that crime emanated from disorder and that if disorder were eliminated, then serious crimes would not occur.[36]

In her interview with Goodman, Berkshire asks about broken windows theory as it might apply to K–12 classrooms. Goodman notes that adherence to this idea in no excuses schools is to prevent "bedlam" resulting from seemingly inconsequential events:

> *Berkshire:* The "broken windows" theory is well known when it comes to policing, but as you write, these charter management organizations apply that theory to schools. Explain.
>
> *Goodman:* These schools believe that behaviors that you might not think are directly related to academic learning can have a domino effect if left unaddressed. Getting up from your chair to go to the bathroom without explicit permission, for example, or not having your hands folded on your desk, or not looking at the teacher every minute, or not having your feet firmly planted on each side of the center of the desk are problematic behaviors. *Because if you don't conform to these rules then you are going to precipitate the next domino and the next domino. It's going to have a cascading effect on your behavior and pretty soon you're going to be very disruptive.* If you get up to sharpen your pencil, maybe you're going to throw your pencil at someone. Or if you get up and get something out of your backpack that you forgot, maybe you're going to elbow another student on your way back to your seat, or make eye contact with them and divert them from looking at the teacher. Any one of these little behaviors they see as leading to the next behavior. Before you know it there will be bedlam.[37] [Emphasis added.]

It is true that order in the classroom is important, and structure is an indispensable component for achieving a healthy and productive classroom atmosphere. However, my concern about applying broken windows theory in the classroom is the degree of control, which could oppressive on its face.

I remember watching a movie in which the main character was narrating a sequence of seemingly insignificant events that he believed culminated in a tragic car accident. His view was that altering one of the minor events leading up to the accident would have prevented it—if only the timing of the car striking the pedestrian had been changed so that the car and pedestrian had not been in the same place in the same street at the same moment. If only the pedestrian had not waited for her friend who had to change shoes because of a broken shoelace. If only the driver of the car had not had to wait those extra moments for his late passenger. If only. If only. Watching the film made me think about how difficult it would be for human beings to live life freely if we had to choreograph all moments precisely to achieve some desired result—and what we might miss as a matter of unanticipated outcomes from our own intense choreography.

I think students at no excuses schools are missing a school-day *joie de vivre* that can only thrive in an atmosphere in which independence and submission are balanced.

So does Joan Goodman.

THE UP-SIDE OF NO EXCUSES

In the *Hechinger Report*, Carr notes that the motivation behind the strict behavior regimen appears to be both a concern that student scores well on standardized tests to keep the school open and a genuine desire for students to succeed by attending college in the future.[38] Thus, the concern that students must behave in order to score well on tests because such is good for the combined futures of school and students appears to be, at least to some degree, a decent motivation.

Berkshire asks Goodman about the positive side of no excuses:

> *Berkshire:* I think it's important to point out that you also have some
>   very positive things to say about these schools—you're not just a
>   straight-up hater.
> *Goodman:* Not at all. I'm certainly not a hater. I think the basic idea
>   of order, of developing habits—you walk into class, you put
>   your things away, you sit down, you take out your book, teacher
>   says good morning, shakes hands, you look at her—some of the
>   habits they're cultivating will be helpful to kids. And certainly the
>   prohibition on violence makes for a safe community. The problem
>   is that the approach is unbalanced. I think a certain amount of
>   routine, habit forming, strictness, limiting certain behavior is
>   good—but I would always be working towards reducing that.
>   Once you've established a safe environment, for example, why
>   not loosen up on the behavior regulations? If I were running one
>   of these schools I would feel that "OK—I have to do this" but
>   I would always be working towards turning over more authority
>   to the kids. That would be my goal all of the time. Let the kids
>   be responsible for their behavior. Have more group work, more
>   student councils, more kids in charge of their own lives.[39]

Putting more kids in charge of their own lives is the direction that discipline should take. Discipline should lead to self-discipline, to an individual maturing and becoming increasingly in charge of oneself. However, the transition to greater student autonomy is messy—and no excuses abides no mess.

IF YOU CAN'T BEND 'EM, SUSPEND 'EM

The question remains whether the no excuses price is worth paying—or even if it can be maintained. For example, the student suspension rates at no excuses schools are extremely high, which makes sense if student behavior is being micromanaged. A 2010 report by the National Economic and Social Rights Initiative (NESRI) and Families and Friends of Louisiana's Incarcerated Children (FFLIC) notes the following regarding student out-of-school suspensions:

> In Louisiana, already higher-than-average suspension rates have been on the rise over the past decade as state and local zero-tolerance policies have imposed harsh punishments for minor misbehavior. The total number of students suspended out of school at least once per year increased from 75,601 (9.7% of students) in 2000–2001, to 86,120 (12.1% of students) in 2007–2008. This is almost twice the national rate of 6.9%.[40]

As Carr of the *Hechinger Report* observes, "As New Orleans students who entered kindergarten after Katrina make their way into the city's new high schools, Summer Duskin isn't the only one questioning the doctrinaire approach to discipline. Some educators themselves are wondering whether it has become an obstacle to progress."[41] The school that Duskin attends, Carver Collegiate, had a suspension rate of 69% in 2012–2013. Another no excuses school in New Orleans, Carver Prep, had a 2012–2013 suspension rate of 61%. In comparison, Carr cites the national rate of student out-of-school suspensions as 11%. Comparing Carr's statistic to the 2010 national suspension rate of 6.9%, the question arises of whether the presence of no excuses discipline practices is slowly increasing the national suspension rate. A 2015 UCLA study on suspension rates concluded the opposite—that overall, suspension rates have leveled off, at least through the 2011–2012 school year:

> The national summary of suspension rate trends for grades K–12 indicates that these rates increased sharply from the early 1970s to the early 2000s, and then more gradually, until they leveled off in the most recent three-year period (2009–12). We conclude that in this recent period, no real progress was made in reducing suspension rates for grades K–12.[42]

Still, the UCLA researchers conclude that there is a "discipline gap," with both African American and Latino students much more likely to be suspended than White students.[43] The UCLA study does not focus specifically on suspension rates for no excuses charter schools; however, given that these schools tend to be located in urban areas, which have high populations of children of color, then the rigid disciplinary practices of the no excuses schools arguably exacerbate the already present problem of uncharacteristically high suspension rates for students of color.

It is difficult to justify the no excuses approach to so-called public education. Whereas a thorough study of the effects of no excuses school discipline on students is long overdue, it seems that anyone with a cursory knowledge of human development would realize that constant, scripted attention to the slightest physical movement must surely negatively affect the human psyche even into adulthood.

In closing this chapter, I leave readers with this reflection from my colleague Jennifer Berkshire based on her experience in studying the no excuses charter school model:

> No excuses charter schools are quickly becoming the predominant style of education for poor and minority students in cities across the country, yet there is virtually no academic research on the long-term impact that this approach has on students. While "broken windows" policing has inspired entire fields of study, its education equivalent, "broken windows" schooling hasn't, so we're left to guess the effects of, say, routinely punishing students for small acts of non-compliance such that compliance itself becomes the goal. The anecdotal evidence is troubling. I've heard about college students who are the product of no excuses schools, and who say that challenging authority is difficult for them. Students, by the way, understand exactly what is at stake in this kind of education. When a high school student described the trouble that her young cousin had run into at a Boston charter middle school, including ever mounting demerits, leading to constant suspensions, she said of the school: "they're trying to change his character."

The kids get it. It's time for the adults to catch up.

CHAPTER 10

Gulen Charters

A Powerful Turkish Cleric's Followers Find a Cozy Home in the American Taxpayer Pocket

On May 13, 2012, *60 Minutes* journalist Leslie Stahl reported on American charter schools run by "mysterious Turkish cleric Fetullah Gulen,"[1] an acknowledged cult leader in Turkey who lives in the Poconos in Pennsylvania in a gated community.

THE STAHL TREATMENT OF GULEN

Here is how Stahl opens her 13-minute segment:

> Over the last decade, scores of charter schools have popped up all over the U.S., all sharing some common features. Most of them are high achieving academically; they stress math and science. And one more thing: They're founded and largely run by immigrants from Turkey who are carrying out the teachings of a Turkish Islamic cleric, Fetullah Gulen. He is the spiritual leader of a growing and increasingly influential force in the Muslim world, known as the Gulen Movement, with millions upon millions of disciples, who compare him to Gandhi and Martin Luther King. Gulen promotes tolerance, interfaith dialogue, and, above all, he promotes education. And yet, he's a mystery man. He's never seen or heard in public, and the more power he gains, the more questions are raised about his motives and the schools.[2]

Is America so enamored with high academic achievement that the nation is willing to surrender its children to questionable individuals for the sake of good grades and high test scores?

Do we no longer care to know exactly who is molding the minds of our children?

These things ought not to be. And yet, in the case of Fethullah Gulen, they are.

Note that from the outset, Stahl is receiving her information not from direct interactions with "mystery man" Gulen, but through what his followers say about him—followers allowed to establish schools on American soil, teach American children, *and* draw American tax dollars for doing so— "nearly $150 million a year," according to Stahl.[3]

Here is a question: Why is the U.S. educational system allowing its largest chain of charter schools (130 schools in 26 states in 2012,[4] up to 139 schools in 26 states in 2014[5]) to be run by a man who is a mysterious, established power in a foreign country and lives in posh seclusion in the United States?

Stahl does not delve into that question. She does address the issue of Gulen's mysterious persona later in her piece, and she uncovers additional reasons that U.S. citizens should be concerned about Gulen. However, for the seriousness of what she uncovers, Stahl's feature lacks power. She begins and ends soft on Gulen and his schools, despite touching on some critical information in the middle. Still, in her 13-minute 2012 broadcast, Stahl did bring national attention to Gulen charter schools. For that reason, I will detail her 2012 Gulen report in this chapter.

In the opening of Stahl's 2012 *60 Minutes* news segment, she is obviously impressed by the Gulen school that she features, Harmony Public School in Houston, one of "an expanding chain of 36 [Gulen] charter schools in Texas."[6] And what she shows of the school is nominally impressive: The broadcast features a handful of happy students speaking much better English than their Gulen teachers and demonstrating their science projects, along with a discussion with an American administrator of Gulen's Harmony Schools, Julie Norton, about the waiting list of 30,000 students hoping for a chance to become one of Gulen's students, who numbered 20,000 at that time.[7] The segment shows students sitting at computers doing school work with an American teacher teaching a lesson in front of a class.

Then comes Stahl's interview with one of the numerous Turkish teachers, "some just recently arrived and hard to understand." The brief segment in which she interviews one Turkish teacher is notably unintelligible.

Stahl is able to access Gulen on the web (just as you or I might do) and features him in part of a video as stating that teaching science is worshiping God. Apparently, Gulen tells his followers not to build mosques, but schools to teach science.[8]

And so, because America opens her doors to allow questionable individuals from other countries to just come on in and establish their own schools in the name of offering Americans "choice," it seems that Gulen's followers have decided to establish their presence in America. Plus, there are those under regulated tax dollars sweetening the deal—and that can be sent back to the likes of Fetullah Gulen and his followers. Note, however, that the Gulen school presence is global, with the number of Gulen schools totaling roughly 1,000 worldwide.

In the *60 Minutes* segment, Stahl calls the apparent success of Gulen schools in America "counterintuitive."[9] One Gulen follower tells Stahl that the opportunity for these schools arose because the performance of American schools in math and science "is not good, and many parents complain about that."[10] The logic here is that Gulen saw a major business opportunity and seized it: Harmony schools were worth $346 million in end-of-year total assets in 2013,[11] up from $308 million in 2011[12] and $327 million in 2012.[13]

Harmony Schools were also featured in a June 2011 *New York Times* article by reporter Stephanie Saul:

> TDM Contracting was only a month old when it won its first job, an $8.2 million contract to build the Harmony School of Innovation, a publicly financed charter school that opened last fall in San Antonio.
>
> It was one of six big charter school contracts TDM and another upstart company have shared since January 2009, a total of $50 million in construction business. Other companies scrambling for work in a poor economy wondered: How had they qualified for such big jobs so fast?. . .
>
> For her report, Stahl traveled to Turkey, which is populated with Gulen schools. While there, Stahl found that the schools are "multi-million-dollar, high-tech facilities" in which English is taught beginning in early grades and both girls and boys are educated equally.
>
> While educating schoolchildren across Texas, the group has also nurtured a close-knit network of businesses and organizations run by Turkish immigrants. The businesses include not just big contractors like TDM but also a growing assemblage of smaller vendors selling school lunches, uniforms, after-school programs, Web design, teacher training and even special education assessments.[14]

Gulen charter schools provide remarkable opportunities for their founder's followers to maximize profits. And maximizing profits appears to be a central focus of Gulen's teachings. In Turkey, Stahl learned that for years, Gulen has taught his followers to emulate Western culture, including the drive for financial success. In fact, Stahl cites another Internet video in which Gulen tells followers, who reportedly number in the millions,[15] that not seeking to be wealthy is sinful.[16] Heeding Gulen's advice to become Western wealthy, his followers have established the Gulen empire worth multiple billions and including schools, a television station, a Turkish bank, and its principal trade association and newspaper.

Gulen is a very powerful man.

He declined an interview with Stahl, but she was allowed to see his prayer chair. She noticed the medicine bottles by that chair, adding that Gulen first came to the United States in 1999 for medical treatment. She also referenced a video apparently released once Gulen came to America in which he advises his followers to move into positions of power in Turkish government. Gulen's suggestion at what amounted to a coup was illegal in

Turkey. Even though he was formally cleared of committing treason in 2008, he chose to remain in Pennsylvania. But his followers did take over those key government positions, as they were advised to do by their absent leader.

Gulen is a powerful man.

Gulen is not the only individual Stahl tries to interview to no avail. She tells her audience that critics of the Gulen movement also refuse to be interviewed. If Gulen preaches tolerance, as Stahl said in her introduction, why would critics of the movement avoid discussing Gulen? Freelance reporter Andrew Finkel, who has reported from Turkey for more than two decades, tells Stahl a few individuals who have written books critical of the Gulen movement ended up in jail.

This report does not delve into Gulen's control and motives in any depth, though Stahl does raise some questions about the U.S. government's tolerance for both his American residency and schools. It appears that the U.S. State Department's concerns about Gulen's agenda arose a full decade after he came to this country. Stahl refers to State Department communications dated December 2010. Yet Gulen is allowed to operate 100 schools on American soil—and funded with American taxpayer money—as of Stahl's 2012 report.

That American charter schools lack sufficient oversight is glaringly obvious in the case of cult leader Fetullah Gulen.

Stahl notes that Gulen's lack of transparency invites conspiracy theories, not the least of which involves the ability of Turkish nationals to immigrate to the United States by way of visas issued to them as teachers at the Gulen schools. David Dunn of the Texas Charter Schools Association tells Stahl these Turkish teachers are needed because the United States has a shortage of math and science teachers. Stahl counters that numerous Turkish nationals are being granted visas to teach English, not math and science, which seems to surprise Dunn. He stumbles through a response that ends with, "I don't look at the visas that they bring in."[17]

Then there is the story of former Gulen school teacher, Mary Addi.

MARY ADDI ALERTS THE FBI

Mary Addi taught at Horizon Science Academy, a Gulen chain in Cleveland, Ohio, for two years. She married a Turkish national who was also a Gulen school teacher; according to Addi, she learned from him that Turkish teachers are required to pay a percentage of their salaries back to the Gulen movement. Addi's husband handed over 40% of his paycheck. Addi shared this information with the FBI, and Stahl reports that her actions helped launch a bureau investigation into potential visa fraud and misappropriation of taxpayer money in a number of states.[18]

I first heard of Addi and her role in uncovering the Gulen salary skimming scheme by way of her February 2013 interview by Frank Gaffney of the Center for Security Policy.[19] Addi had just spoken before the Loudon County (Virginia) Public School Board regarding its consideration of an application for a Gulen school in the district. In her interview with Gaffney, Addi mentioned her interest in applying for an administrative position at her school. To her surprise, her husband told her not to bother because the open administrative positions were already "hand selected" to be filled by Turkish men. According to Addi, all administrators are Turkish men in order to conceal the salary-skimming operation:

> Slowly but surely, [my husband] told me what was going on. After we were married, he told me that he was required to give back forty percent of his salary back in cash. So, every pay period, after he was paid, he would have to go to the bank, withdraw a certain amount of cash, take it back to the office manager [who] was Turkish. . . . Anybody in a higher administrative position is Turkish because . . . they keep that little secret among themselves.
>
> So, they keep a second set of books for the [cash kickback] money. . . . [My husband] did not volunteer to give that money back. It's a kind of form of extortion. He, they held his H-1B (work permit) visa, and he knew that if he didn't give the money back, they would be shipping him back to Turkey.[20]

Stahl's report only briefly presents Addi's story—without the details that Gaffney captures in his interview with Addi regarding the visa blackmail component. In fact, coverage of Addi's extortion charge gets about one minute of airtime in the segment, which devotes a full three minutes to Harmony Public Schools and reports that students are thriving academically in those schools. What seems to be missing are critical questions about how a Turkish cult leader came to open a network of publicly-funded American schools. Texas Charter School representative Dunn even denies that the schools are connected to the Gulen movement, though they obviously are the product of the cult leader's teachings.

In her closing, Stahl notes that Gulen's representative in the Poconos "says the man behind the door has no hidden agenda."[21]

Not everyone buys this tidy ending to Stahl's report. The day after this story aired on May 14, 2012, education historian Diane Ravitch devoted part of her blog to Stahl's reporting:

> I was curious to see how Lesley Stahl and *60 Minutes* would deal with the Gulen Charter schools in their program last night.
>
> The Gulen charters are the largest charter chain in the United States, with something like 135–140 charters. Few people realize that the Gulen charter chain is far larger than the KIPP chain.

They focus mainly on math and science. Some of the Gulen charters get high test scores.

That seems to seal the deal for *60 Minutes*. Stahl was very impressed with the schools' test scores and with the students' interest in math and science.

The show points out that the Gulen schools are tied, in some non-specific way, to a Turkish imam named Fetullah Gulen, who lives in seclusion in the Poconos in Pennsylvania. It notes that the Gulenists run a vast media, financial, and political empire inside Turkey, and that critics of the Gulen movement in Turkey are reluctant to appear on camera. Stahl made no reference to the page one story in the *New York Times* about the critics of Gulen in Turkey who are fearful and intimidated.[22]

THE GULEN FORCE IN TURKEY

The New York Times story to which Ravitch refers was published April 24, 2012, only weeks before Stahl's Gulen feature aired. Written by Dan Bilefsky and Sebnem Arsu, the article "Turkey Feels Sway of Reclusive Cleric in the U.S." demonstrates the power of the Gulen movement, which is only hinted at in Stahl's report. The infiltration of Gulen's followers into positions of governmental influence in Turkey enables persecution of any who would publicly criticize Gulen. As Bilefsky and Arsu report:

ISTANBUL—When Ahmet Sik was jailed last year on charges of plotting to overthrow the government, he had little doubt that a secretive movement linked to a reclusive imam living in the United States was behind his arrest.

"If you touch them you get burned," a gaunt and defiant Mr. Sik said in an interview in March at his apartment here, just days after being released from more than a year in jail. "Whether you are a journalist, an intellectual or a human rights activist, if you dare to criticize them you are accused of being a drug dealer or a terrorist."

Mr. Sik's transgression, he said, was to write a book, "The Army of the Imam." It chronicles how the followers of the imam, Fethullah Gulen, have proliferated within the police and the judiciary, working behind the scenes to become one of Turkey's most powerful political forces—and, he contends, one of its most ruthless, smearing opponents and silencing dissenters.

The case quickly became among the most prominent of dozens of prosecutions that critics say are being driven by the followers of Mr. Gulen, 70, a charismatic preacher who leads one of the most influential Islamic movements in the world, with millions of followers and schools in 140 countries. . . .

Critics say the agenda is threatening the government's democratic credentials just as Turkey steps forward as a regional power.

"We are troubled by the secretive nature of the Gulen movement, all the smoke and mirrors," said a senior American official, who requested anonymity to avoid breaching diplomatic protocol. "It is clear they want influence and power. We are concerned there is a hidden agenda to challenge secular Turkey and guide the country in a more Islamic direction."[23]

Bilefsky and Arsu cite a "culture of fear" associated with speaking against Gulen in Turkey to the degree that individuals refused even to discuss the matter over the phone because they are afraid that the conversation is being recorded. (Stahl noted as much in a statement but did not pursue it.) If dozens of individuals who have openly criticized Gulen end up imprisoned, then the culture of fear is substantiated. Apparently people have a reason to fear.

The implications of these reports are exacerbated by Gulen's decision to distance himself for the most part from public discourse. His reticence feeds the mystery, and the mystery surrounding Fethullah Gulen has afforded him a a devoted following—many of whom now hold positions of power and are therefore able to silence via fear much of the criticism surrounding the Gulen movement in Turkey.

Meanwhile, in the United States, Turkish nationals are allegedly being blackmailed into relinquishing substantial percentages of their teaching salaries to the Gulen movement, which has led to an FBI investigation spanning several American states. More to come on that investigation.

In Turkey, the Gulen movement is difficult to pin down and hold responsible, as Bilefsky and Arsu report:

> Ayse Bohurler, a founding member of the Justice and Development Party, said that the lack of transparency and clear organizational structure made it impossible to hold the group accountable. "There is no reference point; they are kicking in the shadows," Ms. Bohurler said. "They are everywhere and nowhere."[24]

MORE ON ADDI, THE FBI, AND GULEN ENTANGLEMENTS

Even though citizens in Turkey are afraid to discuss the Gulen movement, Mary Addi has spoken out in the United States. She offered additional details in her 2013 interview at a Virginia school board meeting:

> The majority of them are all Turkish board members. . . . We have copies of emails, and they're always, their administrative emails are always sent in Turkish to each other and to board members. . . . But they refer to Americans that show up at the board meetings as "foreigners," and that they will have to have a second meeting if the "foreigners" show up.
>
> We have uncovered evidence of vast immigration fraud with the H-1B visas and the green card applications. We have uncovered money laundering. . . . My husband and I have been actively involved in federal investigations for the past five years, and it is my hope that within the near future that this will come to

fruition and we're going to start seeing some people arrested and deported, as they well should be.[25]

As of June 2014, as part on its ongoing investigation into Gulen school operations, the FBI had raided 20 charter schools in Ohio, Illinois, Indiana, and Louisiana.[26] In July 2014, Doug Livingston of the Ohio *Beacon Journal* reported briefly about the FBI investigation into Gulen operations as part of a greater article on the influence of the Gulen presence in schools in Ohio and Illinois:

> Three of the Ohio schools have been visited by the FBI as part of a multistate probe. The agency said it is part of a white-collar criminal investigation.
>
> Federal agents have not disclosed details, only that the investigation originated in Cleveland, has spread to Indiana and Illinois, and may or may not be connected to previous investigations at related schools in Baton Rouge, La., and Philadelphia.
>
> Last school year, these Ohio charter schools, called Horizon and Noble Academies, received nearly $50 million in public funding transferred from local school districts where students otherwise would have attended.[27]

By way of public records and state audits, Livingston discovered more entanglement in the Gulen influenced web: The charter school chains in Ohio, Horizon and Noble Academies, are part of a larger network of schools operated by Chicago-based Concept Schools. According to its 2013 990 tax form, Concept Schools listed 31 schools it operates, 19 of which are in Ohio. An additional eight are located in Illinois, Michigan, Indiana, Missouri, Wisconsin, and Minnesota, and four have no physical address listed.[28] Livingston notes that Concept Schools has strong fiscal and member ties to the nonprofit Niagara Foundation, which is known for providing lawmakers at all levels—local, state, and federal—with free trips to Turkey. The nature of those trips raises concerns about conflicts of interest and attempts to influence oversight and funding of the Gulen charter schools in Ohio and Illinois:

> Among those touring Turkey has been State Rep. Cliff Rosenberger, a Clarksville Republican on the powerful finance and appropriations committee and considered to be a leading candidate for House speaker next year. He was joined on the trip by at least four other state legislators and local government leaders from his area in southwest Ohio.
>
> There have been other trips from Ohio, and in Illinois, there are allegations that state officials who took trips showed favoritism in disbursing public dollars to Concept schools.
>
> Public records show that since late 2009, the U.S. Department of Labor has allowed 19 of these schools in Ohio to hire 325 educators almost exclusively from Turkey.[29]

Then comes the evidence from Ohio state audits extending back to at least 2002 showing that thousands of taxpayer dollars were misspent to assist Turkish nationals and their families with expenses associated with immigrating to the United States. Livingston notes that these Turkish nationals tend to be recent college graduates with no classroom teaching background. The Ohio audit also revealed that some taxpayer money might have even been used to repay personal loans in Turkey for these Turkish nationals. Moreover, Livingston adds, "State audits also show reimbursement to high-level employees for their pursuit of MBA degrees, along with credit card purchases for alcohol, shampoo, Red Bull and other non-school-related goods."[30]

According to its 2013 990 tax form, Concept Schools is making money. The organization reported end-of-year total assets of $7.5 million; it had received $6.5 million in "management fees," $6.8 million in "per capita tuition," and $826,000 in "government grants."[31]

As to additional opportunities for Gulen's followers to make money through American charter schools, there is always real estate. Former leaders of Chicago-based Concept Schools (the operator of Ohio's Horizon and Nobel networks) also operate a real estate company, Breeze, Inc., which owns many of the Concept Schools buildings. Livingston reports that the buildings are leased back to the schools, making Breeze, Inc., a landlord collecting of taxpayer money. Both Concept Schools and Breeze, Inc., share the same physical address in Des Plaines, Illinois.[32]

GULEN SCHOOLS IN LOS ANGELES

Ohio is not the only state producing questionable results from auditing Gulen charter school spending. A June 2014 audit of eight Gulen charter schools in Los Angeles produced some eyebrow-raising findings, as Southern California Public Radio blogger Annie Gilbertson reports:

> The Los Angeles Unified school district is investigating a network of eight charter schools for misuse of public school funds.
>
> An audit showed Magnolia Public Schools used classroom cash to help six non-employees with immigration costs. The schools had trouble justifying another $3 million expense. . . .
>
> A June audit, which the district is calling a "forensic review," revealed $2.8 million flowed from schools sites to the network's management organization in the form of sloppy loans—much of which were never paid back. The management organization was then found to be operating on a $1.7 million deficit, meeting the IRS's definition of insolvent. . . .
>
> For years, the Magnolia's books and bank account didn't match.

An audit in 2012 based on a sampling of transactions found $43,600 miss-
ing from accounts: school records showed double payments made to vendors
with duplicate invoices attached.[33]

Gilbertson writes that the Los Angeles school board was prepared to allow
two high-performing Magnolia schools to remain open when it appeared that
the charter operator had indeed set Magnolia's financial books in order by
March 2014. However, an audit three months later showed that Magnolia's
finances were not so tidy after all: The company had spent $3 million over
four years for services it had already declared that it had taken care of
in-house, such as curriculum development and teacher training.[34]

Despite years of audits uncovering fiscal irregularities, the two schools
in question were allowed to remain open and a third was approved after
Magnolia sued the Los Angeles school board and settled in March 2015; a
follow-up audit exonerated Magnolia in part.[35] As Teresa Watanabe reports
in a May 2015 Los Angeles Times article:

> California state audit has found that a charter school organization accused of
> financial mismanagement by the Los Angeles Unified School District has im-
> proved its bottom line but still needs stronger controls over spending.
>   The audit, released Thursday by State Auditor Elaine M. Howle, also found
> that the expenditure of $127,000 by the Magnolia Educational and Research
> Foundation to process immigration papers for foreign staff was lawful and
> reasonable. . . .
>   The audit found that some of L.A. Unified's concerns had merit. It con-
> firmed that some of the academies were insolvent at points in the last three
> fiscal years, in part because of delays in state funding, but that all were back
> in the black. It also questioned 52 of 225 transactions reviewed, the financial
> relationship with one vendor and controls over fundraisers. [Magnolia CEO
> Caprice] Young, who was hired in January, said her new leadership team has
> moved swiftly to address the concerns. Magnolia's improvements, she said, in-
> clude a new chief financial officer and controller, stronger controls over spend-
> ing and staff training. Under the legal settlement with L.A. Unified, the charter
> chain also agreed to submit to fiscal oversight by a state financial management
> organization.[36]

Here are some of the details regarding Magnolia's questionable spending from its May 2015 follow-up audit by California State Auditor Elaine
Howle:

> In fiscal year 2012–13, the Foundation (Magnolia) spent $1,609 at a restau-
> rant and supported the expense with a receipt and handwritten note that the
> lunch was for professional development, along with an agenda of a profes-
> sional activity. However, the Foundation did not document who attended the

activity, where the activity was located, or why the Foundation paid for lunch at a training program run by another entity, leading us to question if the expense was necessary to support the Foundation's mission or whether it was a private benefit for the attendees. Similarly, the Foundation spent $2,120 in fiscal year 2012–13 for a summer retreat program for Foundation staff that it supported by providing us with an invoice for a cabin rental and an agenda for a training program that occurred on the same dates as the rental. However, the Foundation could not provide documentation demonstrating that the location of the training was at or near the cabin rental, nor was it able to give us a sign-in sheet of employees who attended the event. Without documentation that expenses were incurred for a public benefit or were necessary to provide services to the academies, we question their appropriateness.[37]

It seems that "fiscal oversight by a state financial management organization," as called for in Watanabe's article, is long overdue for Magnolia Schools. And what of the years of questionable financial transactions preceding this single, improved audit? Is Magnolia allowed a free pass? Since the chain is allowed to keep its schools open as part of a negotiated legal settlement, it appears so. Clean slate for Magnolia.

These things ought not to be. Magnolia should have been under direct fiscal supervision from the state in 2013, the year following its first shaky audit. Magnolia is raking in American taxpayer money. According to its 990 tax form for 2012, it received over $28 million in "government grants." The charter chain is a taxpayer-dependent operation—and a wealthy one, with 2012 end-of-year total assets at $11.8 million.[38]

Magnolia has a vested interest in keeping its taxpayer-supported charter school business venture afloat; as with other for-profit and nonprofit charter school ventures supporting profit-seeking partners, this interest is not primarily the education of the children in their classrooms. However, Magnolia's financing differs from some other private charter school operations in notable ways. For example, New York charter operator Eva Moskowitz (see Chapter 6) draws notable cash from private sources (over $22 million in 2013)[39] as compared to taxpayer money ($2.5 million in 2013).[40] Moskowitz has both reason and leverage to fight a public audit of the public money she receives: She wants to keep her operation out of the public eye, and she has the backing to do so in New York given the political connections that accompany her vast private financing. In contrast, the Gulen schools appear to be primarily dependent on taxpayer money and therefore do not have the political positioning that allows them to dodge state audits.

States need to use Gulen dependence on public funding—and the resulting inability to avoid these audits—to their advantage in holding Gulen charter schools fiscally accountable.

Back in Los Angeles, Gulen-operated Magnolia schools are allowed to remain open—and allowed to fund immigration fees for Turkish nationals associated with the schools. In the 2015 follow-up audit, Howle noted that $40,000 paid to Homeland Security and $59,000 paid to immigration attorneys and consultants "appeared reasonable" for helping Turkish nationals with the expense of immigrating to the United States to teach in American schools.[41] However, Magnolia is a Gulen charter chain, and Gulen schools are known for employing disproportionate numbers of Turkish teachers. Though beyond the scope of a state financial audit, it should not be beyond the scope of charter school oversight to require Gulen schools to advertise their teaching positions to American teachers before importing scores of Turkish nationals to assume these teaching positions. Has any agency in any state asked Gulen schools to provide evidence that they have in good faith sought to fill teaching slots with qualified American teachers before such positions were filled with Turkish nationals, who often graduate from college with degrees outside of education? It seems not, given the example of the surprised reaction from Texas Charter Schools Association Executive Director David Dunn in the *60 Minutes* segment when he was asked about Turkish teachers immigrating to the United States to teach English.[42]

GULEN IN GEORGIA (NO LONGER)

In June 2012, *New York Times* writer Stephanie Saul again reported on Gulen schools, this time in Georgia. Again, Saul's report included the Gulen interest in profiting from charter schools. However, the group of three Gulen charter schools (one elementary, one middle school, and one high school) defaulted on bonds, which led to an audit by the entity overseeing the three charters: The Fulton County Board of Education.[43] The audit primarily focused on the middle school, the Fulton Science Academy Middle School, which had been denied renewal of its charter. As Saul reports:

> A group of three publicly financed charter schools in Georgia run by followers of Fethullah Gulen, a prominent Turkish imam, have come under scrutiny after they defaulted on bonds and an audit found that the schools improperly granted hundreds of thousands of dollars in contracts to businesses and groups, many of them with ties to the Gulen movement.
> The audit, released Tuesday [June 05, 2012] by the Fulton County Schools near Atlanta, found the schools made purchases like T-shirts, teacher training and video production services from organizations with connections to school officials or Gulen followers. Those included more than $500,000 in contracts since January 2010 with the Grace Institute, a foundation whose board has included school leaders. In some cases the awards skirted bidding requirements, the audit said.
> "I would just question how those vendors were selected when price in many instances wasn't part of the decision making," said the Fulton County

superintendent, Robert Avossa, who criticized the schools for conflicts of interest. "And those are public dollars."[44]

The three schools were in default of their $19 million bond with Wells Fargo Bank because the charter operators did not inform bank officials that the middle school was in danger of losing its charter. The elementary and high schools, Fulton Sunshine Academy and Fulton Science Academy High School, remained open for three more years. In November 2014, the Fulton County School Board voted to close both schools at the end of the 2014–2015 school year. According to its press release (as noted in the Roswell *Patch*), the board decided to close the two remaining Gulen charters because of "serious and recurring concerns regarding governance and transparency that have been documented through various audits and reviews."[45] *Patch* writer Kristal Dixon adds:

> The published report cited poor governance in both schools that has resulted in the default on a $19 million bond, a self-perpetuating board membership structure that has been dominated by individuals who did not represent the community, a general lack of transparency and associations with individuals and organizations now under Federal investigation.[46]

The Fulton County School Board decision followed an August 2014 decision by the State Charter Schools Commission of Georgia to deny both Fulton Sunshine and Fulton Science the right to operate as their own "local education agency" (LEA), separate from school board oversight.[47] Had the Georgia state charter board authorized the Gulen charter schools' request to function as their own LEA, the schools could have potentially escaped closure at the hands of the Fulton County School Board that had audited them and found their financial management wanting.

The level of oversight by state and county officials of these schools in Georgia might provide a worthy model for officials in other states in ensuring that charter schools serve the educational needs of their students first or foremost rather than financial interests of the companies behind them. Unfortunately, the end result even in Georgia was the loss of taxpayer money and the disruption to children and community by what has become known as "charter churn."

GULEN: GOOD FOR AMERICAN PUBLIC EDUCATION?

State audits and the ongoing FBI investigation of Gulen charter schools have provided evidence that warrants continued examination into the operations of these schools. In sum, these investigations and published reports cited in this chapter indicate that a powerful, secretive Turkish leader, Fethullah

Gulen, living in an exclusive Pennsylvania community has followers around the world estimated to number in the millions, including some who have assumed influential government positions in Turkey. Turkish citizens who publicly criticize this powerful leader and his movement have reportedly ended up in jail, and some Turkish citizens say they are afraid to openly criticize this individual for fear of reprisal.

In the United States, Gulen followers serve as the principal faculty at scores of American charter schools; these Turkish immigrants come to America via necessity visas without education degrees or experience in teaching. These schools apparently do not seek to hire qualified American teachers. The Gulen school administrators have access to millions of dollars in American taxpayer money; at least one former employee turned FBI informant has shared details of a purported kickback scheme. At the very least, these findings underscore the need for both continued scrutiny of an organization to which the education of American children is entrusted through the largest charter school network in the nation and stronger controls over a chartering system that would allow a cult leader to operate schools in the first place.

CHAPTER 11

Some Final Thoughts on School Choice

Generally speaking, the term *school choice* involves either the use of vouchers to allow taxpayer money to follow students to private schools or the establishment and promotion of charter schools, an alternative to traditional neighborhood public schools overseen by locally elected boards. Charter schools are publicly funded (at least in part) and operate under a charter agreement; they typically have greater autonomy in their use of taxpayer money and less oversight on how that money is spent. Even though vouchers were the first system in the history of school choice, charters are far more prevalent, as of 2015. Still, vouchers remain in use and continue to drain funding away from public schools.

CHALLENGES TO VOUCHERS

In several states, including Florida, Colorado, Louisiana, Alabama, and Oklahoma,[1] vouchers have been declared unconstitutional based on the language of various state constitutions. These decisions are often based on either the finding that public money should go to public schools or that public money should not be spent on religious schools. However, in some states, such as Louisiana and Florida, a change in the source of voucher funding has allowed these programs to continue. The Louisiana voucher program is not popular with the public, serving only approximately 2% of eligible public school students and with seats and line-item funding left over in 2014.[2] In Florida, former Governor Jeb Bush's voucher program, declared unconstitutional by the Florida Supreme Court in 2006, morphed into a corporate-tax-credit-funded program. The so-called "opportunity scholarships" served thousands more students in 2014, but the program once again finds itself in Florida courts under charges of being unconstitutional because of tax credits amounting to having a voucher program that is taxpayer funded through a back door.[3] According to the Florida Department of Education, the "opportunity scholarships" began in 1999 as a "program [that] offered students who attended or who were assigned to attend failing public schools the option to choose a higher performing public school or a participating private school."[4] In 2015, these Florida corporate-tax-credit-funded vouchers are intended for students to leave Florida public schools that receive a school letter grade of F or three consecutive years of Ds.

Failing public schools? Still? Florida has been subject to well over a decade of Jeb Bush–styled corporate education reform heavily reliant on high-stakes testing as its centerpiece, including grading of schools using an A–F system, attempts to curb social promotion from grade 3 to grade 4, basing teacher pay on student testing outcomes, using nontraditional avenues for teacher certification, and promoting school choice in the form of charters, online schools, and of course, vouchers.[5] So, here is the looming question: What results have all these "reforms" produced? If school improvement as measured by test scores is supposed to revive Florida's public education system, and if Florida has been subject to such reforms since Jeb Bush's A-Plus Plan in 1999,[6] then why do the state's public school students need vouchers to enable them to exit "failing schools" in 2015?

Even as Florida's revised voucher program heads back to court, an August 2014 North Carolina Superior Court ruling[7] that the state's voucher program was unconstitutional for allowing taxpayer money to go to schools unaccountable to taxpayers was reversed by the North Carolina Supreme Court in July 2015 in a 4–3 decision.[8] As a result, North Carolina taxpayer money will be taken from its public schools and sent with lower-income students to private schools supposedly of their parents' choosing. However, as Supreme Court Judge Cheri Beasley states in her dissenting opinion, use of vouchers in North Carolina has its roots in avoiding federally mandated desegregation. Moreover, Beasley maintains that providing public money for tuition alone is "cruel," given that the families of lower-income children could well be hooked into paying for additional costs not currently incurred by students attending public schools.

Beasley recalls the history of vouchers in North Carolina as tied to efforts to keep the state's schools racially segregated, a history detailed in Chapter 3:

> Free public education historically has been, and today remains, vital to American life. Its diminishment in quality or its concentration among a few invites despots to power and risks oppressing the rest. With continued necessity for preserving and promoting free public education clearly in view, I turn to the Opportunity Scholarship Program. . . .
>
> When public funds are used for nonpublic initiatives to fulfill the constitutional public education mandate, the appropriation may violate the public purpose clause, especially if the grant recipients are chosen because the public school system fails to meet their educational needs. . . .
>
> Given North Carolina's history of public education and the State's continued efforts to address shortcomings to deliver on its constitutional mandate

[to fulfill the mandate to offer North Carolina children a public education], the General Assembly's decision to pursue vouchers at this time and in this way is vexing. The majority notes that the purpose of the grants is to address grade level deficiencies of a "large percentage of economically disadvantaged students," but as shown below, it is unclear whether or how this program truly addresses those children's needs. . . .

In endeavoring to provide its citizens with a sound basic education, North Carolina has long embraced a complex variety of educational initiatives. . . .

Our legislature has met the standard with varying degrees of success. It is worth observing that our General Assembly previously embraced vouchers for approximately a decade as a means to avoid the State's obligation under the U.S. Constitution to desegregate public schools as required by the Supreme Court of the United States in its seminal *Brown v. Board* decisions. . . . Indeed, some of our schools are only now achieving unitary status under long-standing federal orders to desegregate. . . . Even those victories, however, are tempered by a different reality:

> The rapid rate of de facto resegregation in our public school system in recent decades is well-documented. As one scholar put it, "Schools are more segregated today than they have been for decades, and segregation is rapidly increasing." Erwin Chemerinsky, Separate and Unequal: American Public Education Today, 52 Am. U. L. Rev. 1461, 1461 (2003). . . .

For now, as noted by the majority, the program is available only to lower income families. This availability assumes that private schools are available within a feasible distance, that these families win the grant lottery, and that their children gain admission to the nonpublic school of their choice. With additional costs for transportation, tuition, books, and, at times, school uniforms, for the poorest of these families, the "opportunity" advertised in the Opportunity Scholarship Program is merely a "cruel illusion." Tenn. Small Sch. Sys. v. McWherter, 851 S.W.2d 139, 154-55 (Tenn. 1993) ("[E]ducational opportunity of the children in this state should not be controlled by the fortuitous circumstance of residence. . . . Such a system only promotes greater opportunities for the advantaged while diminishing the opportunities for the disadvantaged. . . . 'The notion of local control was a "cruel illusion" for the poor districts due to limitations placed upon them by the system itself. . . .'") . . . (quoting Dupree v. Alma Sch. Dist. No. 30, 279 Ark. 340, 346, 651 S.W.2d 90, 93 (1983).

Without systemic and cultural adjustments to address social inequalities, the further cruel illusion of the Opportunity Scholarship Program is that it stands to exacerbate, rather than alleviate, educational, class, and racial divides.[9]

Beasley maintains that vouchers are not a cure for issues plaguing public schools. If the public schools are not of a suitable quality, then address the issue. Don't remove students (and funding) via a voucher program that funds private schools and exacerbates the divide between the most economically disadvantaged—those who are clearly unable to shoulder the added costs above the amount of a state stipend associated with private schooling—and their more economically advantaged peers.

Too often, those willing to point fingers at so-called failing public schools stop short of examining the public school within the larger economic system of a district, state, or even region. If, for example, a state has poor economic policy—if the legislature offers amazing tax breaks to business and industry without requiring job growth and local economic development—then the residents of that state suffer the loss of the revenue forfeited to those corporations. The fiscal loss to a state is aggravated when outside companies employ few locals or chiefly employ locals in underpaid positions that create scores of "working poor." In addition, due to the corporate tax breaks afforded such companies, fewer taxes are collected to support the state infrastructure, which includes local schools.

As to the supposed marvel of school vouchers: What is the point of removing money from a public system tasked with carrying out the compulsory education mandates of a state and sending it to schools outside of the control of the state? It is naïve to believe that schools outside of state jurisdiction will do right by students and in a manner consistent with the very state education laws from which they escape accountability.

Those who advocate for school choice do not necessarily believe that equity of educational opportunity will result from it. This realization was a real eye-opening moment for me. In June 2015, I attended a session at the Education Research Alliance of New Orleans (ERA) conference, which focused on determining the success of what is now a 100% state-run charter school district in New Orleans, the Recovery School District (RSD), and its local-board-run remnant district, the Orleans Parish School Board (OPSB). In discussing the issue of educational opportunity inequities present in New Orleans' "choice" system, Margaret Raymond, director of the Center for Research on Education Outcomes (CREDO) based at Stanford University, remarked, "In designing a system . . . [there is] a trade-off between equity and designing a system to educate all students. . . . I think we could tolerate that."[10]

I was amazed to hear that. Raymond is a proponent of charter schools and of charter school systems like New Orleans' RSD. But until that moment, I had assumed she believed that educational equity should be a nonnegotiable in American public education. Apparently not. If embracing a choice system means having less desirable students (such as those with additional needs or those who are not stellar test takers) fall through the cracks, it seems to be a "tolerable trade-off."

Raymond and I did not discuss the issue of just how tolerable the growing list of cases of charter school operator fiscal exploitation might be.

Before proceeding to the topic of charters, let us return briefly to the issue of choice in the name of the school vouchers and then to charter school promotion, both at the federal level.

THE FEDS AND SCHOOL CHOICE

Though school vouchers appear to have a shaky foothold in few states, the chiefly Republican push for school vouchers is not dead on either the state or federal level. In the July 2015 Senate work on its version of the proposed reauthorization of the Elementary and Secondary Education Act of 1965 (ESEA), known as the Every Child Achieves Act of 2015 (ECAA),[11] Senate education committee chair Lamar Alexander sponsored an amendment to include vouchers as part of ECAA, Senate Amendment 2139.[12] On July 8, 2015, Alexander's voucher amendment was rejected in the Senate in a 45–52 vote.[13]

Meanwhile, the House version of the ESEA reauthorization, known as the Student Success Act (SSA),[14] which passed the House on July 8, 2015 in a 218–213 vote,[15] alters the way in which states disburse Title I funding to districts. According to this House bill, Title I funding is supposed to follow the student, a characteristic of vouchers. In the case of SSA, this individualized, per-child measure of Title I funding could be used to fund either public or private school education.

The Democratic Obama administration did not support Title I funding portability,[16] and Obama had the power to veto a resulting, ECAA-SSA conference draft.

Thus, at least on the federal level, the voucher concept is less likely, at least until around the next potential ESEA reauthorization in 2020. However, support for America's underregulated, endlessly-in-scandal charter schools is a different story. As was the case 25 years ago, in the early 1990s (see Chapter 6), charter schools continue to garner bipartisan support. In the ESEA reauthorization under the Clinton administration, the Improving America's Schools Act of 1994, Title X, "Programs of National Significance," included a part allowing for the "enhancement of parent and student choices" by way of charter schools, which "should . . . be restricted from restrictive rules and regulations if the leadership of such school commits to attaining specific and ambitious results."[17] By the next ESEA reauthorization, the George W. Bush administration's No Child Left Behind Act of 2001 (NCLB), federal funding for charter schools was moved into Title V, "Promoting Informed Parental Choice and Innovative Programs." The purpose of Title V was supposed to be "to implement promising educational reform programs and school improvement programs based on scientifically based research."[18] However, there is no conclusive body of research substantiating that students who attend charter schools consistently outperform those attending traditional public schools on state or national tests. Research is mixed. What is clear is that charter schools are allowed to operate with less oversight than traditional public schools, which has resulted in an ever-increasing number of news stories and research reports about charter school operators financing their own self-interest using taxpayer money that has been taken from local-board-run, neighborhood public schools. And as for federal funding for charter schools, even the "accountability-buzzword" NCLB does not carefully account for Title V funds spent on charter schools. In a paragraph titled "Accountability for Charter Schools," NCLB simply states, "The accountability provisions under this Act shall be overseen for charter schools in accordance with State charter school law."[19] And in the absence of either conclusive research regarding the superiority of the charter school model or investigation into the potential or actual exploitation of under-regulated public money send to charter schools, NCLB declared its intent to "increase national understanding of the charter schools model by . . . expanding the number of high quality charter schools across the Nation."[20]

NCLB chiefly defines "high quality charter" as a school that keeps the chartering agreement made with the state, where the agreement involves "meeting clear and measurable objectives for the educational progress of the students attending the schools."[21] In NCLB, "high quality" did not include any in-depth federal study of charter school fiscal management and educational equity. NCLB did encourage states to financially support charter schools "for facilities financing in an amount more nearly commensurate to the amount the States have typically provided for traditional public schools."[22]

Thus the NCLB language surrounding "high quality charter schools" was narrowly focused on test score outcomes, and states were called to increase the number of these testing-outcome-driven schools.

Even as the news of charter school financial scandals continued, the idea of the federal government confronting such reality was trumped by school choice ideology. Consider this language of the 2015 House version of the ESEA reauthorization, SSA, regarding the marvel of charter schools as part of Title III, "Parental Engagement and Local Flexibility." In SSA, Congress appears to have researched charter schools. However, the research is superficial and reads more like a charter school promotional brochure than a piece of legislation founded on solid documentation:

Subpart 1—Charter School Program
SEC. 3101.SENSE OF CONGRESS; PURPOSE.
(a) SENSE OF CONGRESS.—
(1) FINDINGS.—The Congress finds the following:
    (A) The number of public charter schools has dramatically
        increased in recent years. Between the 2008–2009 school
        year and the 2013–2014 school year, there was a 77 percent

increase in the number of students attending public charter
schools and a 39 percent increase in the number of schools.

(B) Charter schools serve a very diverse population of students.
Nationally, 57 percent of students enrolled in charter schools
are minority students, while only 39 percent of students in
non-charter public schools are minority students.

(C) For the 2014–2015 school year, there are more than 6700
public charter schools serving about 2.9 million students.
This represents a 4 percent growth in the number of open
charter schools, and a 14 percent increase in student
enrollment from the 2013–2014 school year.

(D) There are more than one million student names on charter
school waiting lists.

(E) Charter schools are open in areas where students need better
education options, including areas that serve economically
disadvantaged kids. Almost 50 percent of the students
attending charter schools qualify for free or reduced priced
lunch, a slightly larger percentage than non-charter public
schools.

(F) Charter schools serve students in all areas, from urban cities
to rural towns through traditional brick and mortar schools,
blended learning models, and online programs, giving
parents across the Nation options to find the best learning
environment for their children.

(G) Charter schools give parents the opportunity to find the
right place for their child to learn. Whether they are looking
for digital learning, Montessori, or a more structured
environment, charter schools provide a variety of education
options for families.

(H) Charter schools have strong accountability to parents
and the community because they have to meet the same
State academic accountability requirements as all other
public schools, satisfy the terms of their charter with their
authorizing authority, and satisfy parents who have selected
the school for their children.

(2) SENSE OF CONGRESS.—It is the sense of the Congress that
charter schools are a critical part of our education system in this
Nation and the Congress believes we must support opening more
quality charter schools to help students succeed in their future.[23]

The statistics that the House offers in support of charter school growth
and expansion via its SSA involve numbers of charter schools, the increase
in those numbers, the numbers of students reported on charter waiting lists,
and large proportion of children of color that charter schools serve. The SSA

offers no empirical evidence that charter schools serve children of color *well*. Also, the SSA draft does not question whether charter schools are serving children equitably and offers no solid evidence of any investigation into whether specific subpopulations are being slighted by charter admission and retention practices.

As to those charter waiting lists, the SSA "sense of Congress" on charters does not offer any information regarding auditing such lists to determine if they are updated or simply involve cumulatively collecting names of students who might be on multiple lists and accepted into a school, or who have even been accepted into the very school that continues to have the student's name on the waiting list.

Another limitation of the SSA is that it offers no accounting of the numbers of students who leave the charter schools, much less an accounting of the reasons why students leave and where they go when they leave—which may well be right back to that traditional public school that is not eligible for Title V money.

Through the unreserved charter school support evidenced at the outset of SSA Title III, the House appears willing to assume charter school quality based on the shaky notion that charters must adhere to the same academic standards as traditional public schools and that this requirement ensures "strong accountability." In this ESEA draft, the House does not address what might be lost to children and to our nation by enabling the likes of no excuses KIPP schools or Gulen schools, which are the subject of an FBI investigation.

The SSA document continues with some gentle language about the need for accountability. However, the language again evidences a clear disconnect between the proliferation of charter school operator fiscal exploitations and the faith of Congress that states just need encouragement to suitably oversee charters:

> (b) PURPOSE.—It is the purpose of this subpart2 to—
>   (7) support efforts to strengthen the charter school authorizing process to improve performance management, including transparency, oversight, monitoring, and evaluation of such schools; and
>   (8) support quality accountability and transparency in the operational performance of all authorized public chartering agencies, which include State educational agencies, local educational agencies, and other authorizing entities.[24]

In its Title III requirements, SSA reflects a belief that states will take care of charter accountability for what are obviously schools superior to traditional public schools if only the federal government politely asks. Now, as one continues in the Title III requirements of state oversight of charters, one reads about an oversight that is not preventing charter school fraud from occurring. Moreover, this oversight depends on school closure as the final solution, and that closure disrupts the lives of children and communities.

> [The State entity] will provide oversight of authorizing activity, including how the State will help ensure better authorizing, such as by establishing authorizing standards that may include approving, actively monitoring, and re-approving or revoking the authority of an authorized public chartering agency based on the performance of the charter schools authorized by such agency in the areas of student achievement, student safety, financial and operational management, and compliance with all applicable statutes and regulations.[25]

Yet even as SSA addresses oversight, it calls for charter school autonomy under the heading of "assurances": "Each charter school receiving funds under the State entity's program will have a high degree of autonomy over budget and operations."[26]

If the states were adequately monitoring charter schools, there would not be the vast and growing charter school operator exploitation as reported by the media. Yet to monitor charters too closely is to infringe upon an autonomy that they are supposed to have and that makes them somehow inherently superior to local-board-run neighborhood schools.

Such federal leaning toward charters appears to be ideologically motivated, at least in part. Another motivator that speaks to public officials who endorse a free-market presence in K–12 education is money, and the money is there in the form of pro-charter lobbying. Between 2007 and mid-2015, the National Alliance for Public Charter Schools (NAPCS) spent $2.36 million on lobbying.[27]

There is one more component worth noting regarding the SSA criteria for the Title III grant money for charters, and that concerns facilities financing. SSA seeks to offer Title III grant money to entities that "demonstrate innovative methods of assisting charter schools to address the cost of acquiring, constructing, and renovating facilities by enhancing the availability of loans or bond financing."[28] SSA assumes that charter schools will have private-sector financing and requires an explanation of how the charter operator will maximally leverage such private funding relative to the amount of public funding, "including how the eligible entity will offer a combination of rates and terms more favorable than the rates and terms that a charter school could receive without assistance from the eligible entity."[29] This entity is also supposed to be able to demonstrate that it is somehow able to gauge charter school success in order to determine that the facilities investment is worth making.

The potential for profiteering through school facilities is significant, as discussed in Chapters 8 and 10. Let's say that I want to make money from charter schools via property that I have supposedly located but that

I actually have a fiscal connection to by a couple degrees of separation. My plan is to promote myself as CEO of a real estate company specializing in education property sales and management. I could argue that I see potential in this group of charter schools but that I want to be cautious—I don't want to rush the schools to purchase because it is not in the best interest of the schools or of the federal government, whose money I am hoping to secure. Being a careful real estate CEO who always puts the interests of children first, I want to see if the school is able to produce those expected, marvelous test grades before I arrange for the school to purchase the property. I suggest that the best course of action is for the schools to *lease* for a number of years and then to possibly purchase. I argue that it is best to not be burdened with an empty building should the schools fail. I convince the state and the state convinces the federal government to support my leasing idea with Title III funding.

I benefit financially from my arrangement, and I use up the Title III funding before enough time passes to call me on finally selling property to the charter school. The school might even fail in part due to an inability to afford the likely-ballooning terms of my lease using other funding sources, including state funding.

Now, here is my question:

Why does the federal government not see through the potential real estate exploitation to the degree that it directly confronts such leasing scam potential in the language of SSA?

It truly baffles me that this potential for corruption is not obvious to all.

Yet another issue introduced by the federal government's expectation that charter schools secure private funding concerns the promoting of the public–private hybrid akin to Eva Moskowitz's heavily private-funded Success Academies in New York. As noted in Chapter 7 a New York judge ruled that Moskowitz's schools could avoid public audit because Success Academies are not considered "units of the state." The public–private hybrid model of many charter schools allows for such ducking of public accountability for public funding for these schools' ability to selectively hide behind the unaccountable cloak of private entity.

The 2015 Senate draft of the ESEA reauthorization, ECAA, is equally as generous to a charter school expansion that outweighs true fiscal and operational accountability. In ECAA's Title V, "Empowering Parents and Expanding Opportunity Through Innovation,"[30] ECAA also encourages states to expand the number of "high quality" charter schools, especially for low-income families, and to "maximize charter school participation in Federal and State programs for charter schools." Even though charter schools are supposed to be about parental choice, in order to receive ECAA's Title V funding, states must explain how they will "work with charter schools on recruitment practices, including efforts to engage groups that may otherwise have limited opportunities to attend charter schools."[31]

There is no language in ECAA requiring states to demonstrate that they will assist traditional public schools with student retention and recruitment *from* charter schools. The ECAA bias is in favor of charters over traditional public schools. And even though ECAA follows SSA in encouraging states to "strengthen the charter school authorizing process,"[32] the Senate through its ECAA notes no serious concerns with well-publicized cases of charter school fiscal fraud. Like SSA, ECAA calls for states to demonstrate how they will hold charter schools accountable, but there is no requirement that states specifically address their past charter school scandals and to present specific measures for preventing such scandals before they become scandals.

There is also no requirement in either SSA or ECAA for states to report losses in terms of state and local taxpayer money for issues related to charter school mismanagement and closure.

Like SSA, ECAA also calls for states to "leverage the maximum amount of private-sector financing capital relative to the amount of government funding used and otherwise enhance credit available to charter schools."[33]

Yet another similarity between the House and Senate bills is a call for states applying for charter school grant money to include "a description of how the autonomy and flexibility granted to a charter school is consistent with the definition of a charter school in section 5110 [including 'no significant issues . . . in financial management']."[34] In other words, the ECAA does not broach accounting for past problems with school fiscal issues, for the impact of previous charter school closures on students and community, and for whether the state's charter accountability really works in practice—which should include the degree to which the charter school presence contributes to a stable learning environment for students.

Adequate monitoring of charter schools is not happening, by and large, and those individuals using taxpayer money to serve their own interests by operating charter schools only contribute to damaging American public education. Furthermore, if in general, charter schools are not "out-testing" traditional public schools—which is currently the ultimate marker of educational worth according to the corporate reform promotion of charter school choice—then the point in a proliferation of underregulated charter schools must be to provide a less stable, Plan B system to aggravate the stability of the American cornerstone of the neighborhood public school.

On December 10, 2015, President Obama signed into law the SSA-ECAA compromise bill known as the Every Student Succeeds Act (ESSA).[35] As expected, based on SSA and ECAA's language regarding charter schools, the ESSA language is just as generous in its goal to expand charter schools and just as negligent in addressing the rampant charter school fraud perpetrated in the name of autonomy.

THE CONFRONTATION

How might America address the issue of the systematic defunding of the local-board-run public school in favor of underregulated charter schools? It will not be by any quick fix because ideology defies reason and evidence—it just knows it's right—and because the profit motive serves self and does not really care if children and communities are cheated. That noted, quitting because a right and noble effort requires much time and energy is not the way to live a productive life.

First, the public must become aware of the situation, which is my chief aim in writing this book and my other books on education reform issues. Through my writings, I consider myself to chiefly deal in munitions—to provide ammunition for the public to use in confronting the destructiveness of education reform driven by profit and measured by test scores.

Second, the public must develop enough discomfort over corporate reform destructiveness to act on our collective discontent. It is not enough to throw up one's hands and say, "Well, what can you do?" One can do something—writing letters to the editor, protesting, joining with others as part of a community group to organize and put pressure on local and state officials to hold charters accountable—and the more publicity that something receives the better. But it will take time and effort. "Choice at all costs" ideology and profit motive die hard.

Third, the public must have some alternative course of action to offer in order to confront this crippling of American public education in the name of underregulated choice competition. To simply declare that "school choice needs to end" is not realistic. I do believe the current push for vouchers and charters does need to end if compulsory public education is to survive. But one must begin with realistic efforts, and that beginning is in pushing for greater accountability of choice that will counteract the likes of money-follows-the-child-styled public school defunding and charter churn.

Even though the defunding of local public education via vouchers is problematic in some states, the greater threat is the destabilization of the community school via parasitic squandering of taxpayer money in the name of charter choice. Thus, for those public activists wishing to rescue the traditional public school from hemorrhaging money to self-serving charter operators or boards, let me suggest as a first course of action to pursue the passage of statutes requiring a halt to endless charter school churn. Simply put, if a traditional public school becomes a charter and that charter's operator or board becomes embroiled in fiscal scandal, that charter is not allowed to become yet another charter. Instead, it must be returned to a local school board and converted back to a traditional, local school. Furthermore, a charter that fails for other reasons—including not being able to achieve the test score gains it promises, being unable to retain a given enrollment, or being found to creatively select and deselect its student population—should be limited to only one "redo" opportunity to open as a charter school. If the second try does not succeed for any reason, then that school is to return to local board control as a traditional school.

And if there is no longer a local school board to which such a school might return, then the school might be operated by a local school board in a contiguous city or county until such a local school board is (re)established.

These suggestions are not a quick fix. However, such accountability crucially confronts endless charter churn. These solutions promote the stabilization of public education and hold charter authorizers accountable for their decisions, the risk being that a state's/locale's charter authorization could be significantly slowed or even halted if authorizers are sloppy with such decisions.

Not a quick fix, but a focus for action for all who are wondering what they might do next.

It is important to comprehend the unmistakable reality that efforts to defend and protect American public education will be confronting unflappable, choice-is-superior-period ideology or opportunistic, self-serving greed, and neither will easily succumb.

Even so, if we are to halt the capricious, crippling effects of so-called school choice on the democratic institution of the community school, fight we must.

Notes

Chapter 1

1. Schneider, Mercedes. (2015, May 14). Yong Zhao's NPE speech, transcribed—part V [Web log post]. Retrieved from deutsch29.wordpress.com/2015/05/14/yong-zhaos-npe-speech-transcribed-part-v-all-done/

2. China Education Center, Ltd. (2015). Overview of education in China. Retrieved from www.chinaeducenter.com/en/cedu.php

3. Tan, Kenneth. (2008, December 27). Chinese nationalism indoctrination 101 [Web log post]. Retrieved from shanghaiist.com/2008/12/27/chinese_nationalism_indoctrination.php

4. Fei Chang Dao. (2015, February 25). A chronicle of China's campaign to rectify political ideology at universities: 2014–2015 [Web log post]. Retrieved from blog.feichangdao.com/2015/02/a-chronicle-of-chinas-campaign-to.html

5. Ravitch, Diane. (2013). *Reign of Error: The Hoax of the Privatization Movement and the Danger to America's Public Schools*. New York: Alfred A. Knopf.

6. See note 5.

7. Clark, Nick. (2013, June 1). Education in South Korea. *World Education News and Reviews*. Retrieved from wenr.wes.org/2013/06/wenr-june-2013-an-overview-of-education-in-south-korea/

8. See note 7.

9. Ursulinesenior. (2014, December 10). Academic success in South Korea and happiness: Can they co-exist? [Web log post]. Retrieved from bearmarketreview.wordpress.com/2014/12/10/academic-success-in-south-korea-and-happiness-can-they-co-exist/

10. Sharma, Yojana. (2014, February 14). Rising unemployment—Are there too many graduates? *University World News*. Retrieved from www.universityworldnews.com/article.php?story=20140213153927383

11. Shim, Elizabeth. (2015, April 28). Suicide is leading cause of death among South Korean teens, says report. *United Press International*. Retrieved from www.upi.com/Top_News/World-News/2015/04/28/Suicide-is-leading-cause-of-death-among-South-Korean-teens-says-report/3871430235561/

12. Costa-Roberts, Daniel. (2015, March 15). South Korea announces app to combat student suicide [Web log post]. *PBS Newshour*. Retrieved from www.pbs.org/newshour/rundown/south-korea-announces-app-prevent-student-suicides/

13. Laine, Jarmo. (2015, April). Parliamentarism in Finland. *This Is Finland*. Retrieved from finland.fi/public/default.aspx?contentid=160051

14. Tung, Stephen. (2012, January 20). How the Finnish school system outshines U.S. education. *Stanford News*. Retrieved from news.stanford.edu/news/2012/january/finnish-schools-reform-012012.html

15. Ministry of Education and Culture; Finnish National Board of Education; CIMO. (2013). Finnish education in a nutshell [Report]. Retrieved from web.archive.org/web/20130718111301/www.minedu.fi/export/sites/default/OPM/Julkaisut/2013/liitteet/Finnish_education_in_a_nuttshell.pdf

16. See note 5, p. 69.

17. See note 14.

18. Darling-Hammond, Linda, & Rothman, Richard. (2015). *Teaching in the Flat World: Learning from High-Performing Systems*. New York: Teachers College Press, pp. 30–31.

19. See note 18, p. 32.

20. See note 18.

21. See note 18, p. 43.

Chapter 2

1. U.S. Supreme Court. (1973, March 21). *San Antonio Independent School District v. Rodriguez*. Retrieved from www.law.cornell.edu/supremecourt/text/411/1

2. See note 1.

3. Massachusetts Foundation for the Humanities. (n.d.). Massachusetts passes first education law, April 14, 1642. *Mass Moments* [Online education project]. Retrieved from www.massmoments.org/moment.cfm?mid=113

4. See note 3.

5. Massachusetts Legislature. (n.d.). *Constitution of the Commonwealth of Massachusetts*. Retrieved from www.malegislature.gov/laws/constitution

6. United States Bureau of Education. (1913). Expressions on education [Bulletin no. 28, p. 13]. Retrieved from books.google.com

7. Altenbaugh, Richard J. (Ed.). (1999). *Historical Dictionary of American Education*, p. 224. Westport, CT: Greenwood Press. Retrieved from books.google.com

8. Opal, J. M. (2008). *Beyond the Farm: National Ambitions in Rural New England*, pp. 97–98. Philadelphia: University of Pennsylvania Press. Retrieved from books.google.com

9. Kindig, Thomas. (n.d.). Signers of the Declaration of Independence: Benjamin Rush. Independence Hall Association. Retrieved from www .ushistory.org/declaration/signers/rush.htm

10. Runes, Dagobert D. (Ed.). (2015). *The Selected Writings of Benjamin Rush*. New York: Philosophical Media, pp. 99–100. Retrieved from https:// archive.org/stream/selectedwritings030242mbp/selectedwritings030242 mbp_djvu.txt

11. Foley, John P. (Ed.). (1900). *The Jeffersonian Cyclopedia: A Comprehensive Collection of the Views of Thomas Jefferson*, p. 275. New York: Funk and Wagnalls. Retrieved from books.google.com

12. Holowchak, M. Andrew. (2014). Jefferson and democratic education. *Democracy and Education* 22(1). Retrieved from democracyeducationjournal .org/cgi/viewcontent.cgi?article=1159&context=home

13. Wagoner, Jennings L., & Haarlow, William N. (2002). Common school movement. *Encyclopedia of Education*. Retrieved from www .encyclopedia.com/topic/Common_School_Movement.aspx

14. See note 13.

15. Microsoft Encarta Reference Library. (2002). Who was Horace Mann? Retrieved from mann.spps.org/who_was_horace_mann

16. See note 15.

17. Alexander, Kern, & Alexander, M. David. (2012). *American Public Schools Law* 8th ed., p. 35. Belmont, CA: Wadsworth. Retrieved from books.google.com

18. Mann, Horace. (1852). *The Common School Journal*. Retrieved from archive.org/details/commonschooljou00manngoog

19. The Library Company of Philadelphia. (2005). Portraits of American women writers that appeared in print before 1861: Catharine E. Beecher. Retrieved from www.librarycompany.org/women/portraits/ beecher.htm

20. Harvard University. (2015). Harvard University open collections program: Women working, 1800–1930: Catharine Beecher. Retrieved from ocp.hul.harvard.edu/ww/beecher.html; Newman Library Collections. (n.d). An American family: The Beecher tradition. Catharine Beecher. Retrieved from www.baruch.cuny.edu/library/alumni/online_exhibits/digital/2001/beecher/catherine.htm

21. See note 13.

22. U.S. Department of Education. (n.d.). The federal role in education. Retrieved from www2.ed.gov/about/overview/fed/role.html

23. Reform Movements. (n.d.). Education reform. Retrieved from reformmovements1800s.weebly.com/education.html

24. Massachusetts Foundation for the Humanities. (2015). Mass moments: Teachers' features. Massachusetts chapter 256, desegregating public schools, 1855 [Legislation]. Retrieved from massmoments.org/teachers/primedoc.cfm?pid=47

25. U.S. Supreme Court. (1954, May 17). Brown v. Board of Education of Topeka. Retrieved from supreme.justia.com/cases/federal/us/347/483/case.html

26. Marcus, Frances F. (1988, September 20). Chalmette journal; after 20 years, the girls are where the boys are. *The New York Times*. Retrieved from www.nytimes.com/1988/09/20/us/chalmette-journal-after-22-years-the-girls-are-where-the-boys-are.html

27. Legal Information Institute. (n.d.). Civil rights: An overview. Retrieved from www.law.cornell.edu/wex/civil_rights

28. See note 22.

Chapter 3

1. Rothstein, Richard. (2013, May). Why our schools are segregated. *Educational Leadership, 70*(8). Retrieved from www.ascd.org/publications/educational-leadership/may13/vol70/num08/Why-Our-Schools-Are-Segregated.aspx

2. Meyer, Ali. (2015, January 28). GOP leaders: School choice is a "civil rights issue." CNS News. Retrieved from cnsnews.com/news/article/ali-meyer/gop-leaders-school-choice-civil-rights-issue

3. *Biographical Directory of the United States Congress*. (n.d.). Byrd, Harry Flood, Jr. Retrieved April 08, 2016, from http://bioguide.congress.gov/scripts/biodisplay.pl?index=b001209

4. Tarter, Brent. (n.d.). Byrd Organization. *Encyclopedia Virginia*. Virginia Foundation for the Humanities. Retrieved April 08, 2016, from http://www.encyclopediavirginia.org/byrd_organization

5. Reed, Douglas S. (2014). *Building the Federal Schoolhouse: Localism and the American Education State*. New York: Oxford University Press. Retrieved from books.google.com

6. Old Dominion University Libraries. (n.d.). Digital collections: School desegregation in Norfolk, Virginia. Retrieved from dc.lib.odu.edu/cdm/timeline/collection/sdinv/

7. See note 6, p. 34.

8. U.S. Supreme Court. (1955, May 31). Brown v. Board of Education. Retrieved from caselaw.lp.findlaw.com/scripts/getcase.pl?court=US&vol=349&invol=294

9. Day, John K. (2014). *The Southern Manifesto: Massive Resistance and the Fight to Preserve Segregation*. Jackson: University of Mississippi Press. Retrieved from books.google.com

10. See note 9.

11. See note 9, p. 35.

12. See note 9.

13. Thomas, William G., III, and Rector and Board of Visitors, University of Virginia. (2005). Television news of the civil rights era, 1950–1970: Tuition grants. Retrieved from www2.vcdh.virginia.edu/civilrightstv/glossary/topic-024.html

14. Virginia Historical Society. (n.d.). Massive resistance. Retrieved from www.vahistorical.org/collections-and-resources/virginia-history-explorer/civil-rights-movement-virginia/massive; Herschman, James H. (2011, June 29). Massive resistance. *Encyclopedia Virginia*. Retrieved from www.encyclopediavirginia.org/Massive_Resistance#its3

15. Brown vs. Board of Education: Virginia responds. Exhibit of the Library of Virginia. Originally displayed December 2003–June 2004 [Online document archive]. Retrieved from www.lva.virginia.gov/exhibits/brown/browndocs.htm

16. Court of Appeals of Virginia. (1959, January 19). Harrison v. Day. Retrieved from www.courtlistener.com/opinion/1328174/harrison-v-day/

17. United States District Court E.D. of Virginia. (1959, January 19). James v. Almond. Retrieved from www.leagle.com/decision/1959501170FSupp331_1432.xml/JAMES%20v.%20ALMOND

18. See note 16.

19. Herschman, see note 14.

20. Bonastia, Christopher. (2012). *Southern Stalemate: Five Years Without Public Education in Prince Edward County, Virginia*, p. 95. Chicago: University of Chicago Press. Retrieved from books.google.com

21. See note 25, p. 96.

22. Herschman, see note 14.

23. See note 20.

24. Herschman, see note 14.

25. Dunn, Adrienne. (2009). Pearsall plan. North Carolina History Project (John Locke Foundation). Retrieved from www.northcarolinahistory.org/commentary/318/entry

26. Hale, Jon. N. (2009). *A History of the Mississippi Freedom Schools, 1954–1965* [Doctoral dissertation]. University of Illinois, Urbana-Champaign. Retrieved from books.google.com

27. Davies, David R. (Ed.). (2001). *The Press and Race: Mississippi Journalists Confront the Movement*. Jackson: University Press of Mississippi. Retrieved from books.google.com

28. See note 27.

29. Dittmer, John. (1994). *Local People: The Struggle for Civil Rights in Mississippi*, p. 29. Champaign: University of Illinois Press. Retrieved from books.google.com

30. Virginia Historical Society. (n.d.). The closing of Prince Edward County's schools. Retrieved from www.vahistorical.org/collections-and-resources/virginia-history-explorer/civil-rights-movement-virginia/closing-prince

31. See note 26, p. 53.

32. U.S. District Court for the Eastern District of Louisiana. (1961, August 30). Hall v. St. Helena Parish School Board. Retrieved from law.justia.com/cases/federal/district-courts/FSupp/197/649/1419413/

33. See note 32.

34. U.S. District Court for the Eastern District of Louisiana. (1966, August 3). Poindexter v. Louisiana Financial Assistance Commission. Retrieved from law.justia.com/cases/federal/district-courts/FSupp/258/158/1510964/

35. U.S. District Court for the Eastern District of Louisiana. (1968, January 15). Poindexter v. Louisiana Financial Assistance Commission. Retrieved from law.justia.com/cases/federal/district-courts/FSupp/275/833/1458865/

36. United States District Court M.D. Alabama E.D. (1964, July 13). Lee v. Macon County Board of Education. Retrieved from www.leagle.com/decision/1964974231FSupp743_1831.xml/LEE%20v.%20MACON%20COUNTY%20BOARD%20OF%20EDUCATION

37. United States District Court, D. South Carolina. (1968, May 31). Brown v. South Carolina State Board of Education. Retrieved from www.courtlistener.com/opinion/1982763/brown-v-south-carolina-state-board-of-education/

38. The Southern Manifesto (text and signatories). (1956, March). Retrieved from kdentify.wordpress.com/texas-am-university-commerce-academics/rhetoric-race-and-the-digital-humanities-2/the-southern-manifesto-text-and-signatories/

39. Federal Judicial Center. (n.d.). Bush v. Orleans Parish School Board and the desegregation of New Orleans Schools: Historical documents. History of the Federal Judiciary. Retrieved from www.fjc.gov/history/home.nsf/page/tu_bush_doc_6.html

40. See note 39.

41. See note 39.

42. See note 39.

43. Waller, Mark. (2012, February 01). Leander Perez: The Times-Picayune covers 175 years of New Orleans history. *Times Picayune.* Retrieved from http://www.nola.com/175years/index.ssf/2012/02/leander_perez_the_times-picayu.html

44. Carl, Jim. (2011). *Freedom of Choice: Vouchers in American Education.* Santa Barbara, CA: Praeger. Retrieved from books.google.com

45. United States Court of Appeals Fifth Circuit. (1962, August 28). Bush v. Orleans Parish School Board. Retrieved from openjurist.org/308/f2d/491/bush-v-orleans-parish-school-board

46. See note 45.

47. Smith, Ralph L. (1960, October 1). The South's pupil placement laws: Newest weapon against integration. *Commentary Magazine.* Retrieved from www.commentarymagazine.com/article/the-souths-pupil-place-ment-lawsnewest-weapon-against-integration/

48. See note 45.

49. See note 45.

50. See note 44.

51. See note 44.

52. U.S. District Court for the Eastern District of Louisiana, New Orleans Division. (1968, January 15). Poindexter v. Louisiana Financial Assistance

Commission. Retrieved from www.courtlistener.com/opinion/1458865/poindexter-v-louisiana-financial-assistance-commis/

53. See note 44.

Chapter 4

1. Friedman, Milton. (1955). The role of government in education [book chapter]. In Solo, Robert (Ed.), *Economics and the Public Interest: Practical Applications of Economics to Problems of Public Welfare.* New Brunswick, NJ: Rutgers University Press. Copyright © 1955, 1983 by Robert A. Solo. Reprinted by permission of Rutgers University Press. Retrieved from www.edchoice.org/The-Friedmans/The-Friedmans-on-School-Choice/The-Role-of-Government-in-Education-%281995%29.aspx

2. Doherty, Brian. (1995, June). Best of both worlds: An interview with Milton Friedman. *Reason.com.* Retrieved from reason.com/archives/1995/06/01/best-of-both-worlds/1

3. *Investopedia.* (n.d.). Keynesian economics. Retrieved June 12, 2015, from www.investopedia.com/terms/k/keynesianeconomics.asp

4. Pongracic, Ivan. (2007, September 1). The Great Depression according to Milton Friedman. *Foundation for Economic Education.* Retrieved from fee.org/freeman/detail/the-great-depression-according-to-milton-friedman; Norton, Justin M. (2006, November 16). Economist Milton Friedman dies at 94. *Boston.com News.* Retrieved from www.boston.com/news/education/higher/articles/2006/11/16/economist_milton_friedman_dies_at_94_1163724554/?page=full; Library of Economics and Liberty. (2008). The concise encyclopedia of economics: Milton Friedman. Retrieved from www.econlib.org/library/Enc/bios/Friedman.html

5. Jahan, Sarwat, Mahmud, Ahmed S., & Papageorgiou, Chris. (2014, September). What is Keynesian economics? *Finance and Development.* Retrieved from www.imf.org/external/pubs/ft/fandd/2014/09/basics.htm

6. See note 2.

7. *International Encyclopedia of the Social Sciences.* (2008). Milton Friedman. Retrieved from www.encyclopedia.com/topic/Milton_Friedman.aspx

8. See note 6.

9. See note 6.

10. Friedman Foundation. (n.d.). About us. Retrieved from www.edchoice.org/About-Us

11. See note 1.

12. See note 1.

13. Bryant, Jeff. (2014, December 19). Education newsmaker of the year: Charter school scandals. Education Opportunity Network [Newsletter]. Retrieved from educationopportunitynetwork.org/educations-newsmaker-of-the-year-charter-school-scandals/; Dyer, Stephen. (2015, June 4). Ohio charter schools' terrible, horrible, no good, very bad week (and it's not even over yet) [Web log post]. Retrieved from www.10thperiod.com/2015/06/ohio-charter-schools-terrible-horrible.html?m=1; Cotto, Robert, Jr. (2015, May 20). Show me the (charter management fee) money! *Connecticut News Junkie.* Retrieved from www.ctnewsjunkie.com/archives/entry/op-ed_show_me_the_charter_management_fee_money/#.VWuOGQzWlh8.twitter; Boccella, Kathy. (2015, May 24). School board group seeks charters' data. *Philly.com.* Retrieved from www.philly.com/philly/education/20150523_School_board_group_seeks_charters__data.html#WT6XPfUmfspjz7KZ.99; Koew, Morgan. (2015, May 06). While many public schools struggle, some charter chains profit. *CBS5AZ.com.* Retrieved from www.kpho.com/story/28999644/while-many-public-schools-struggle-some-charter-chains-profit; Klonsky, Mike. (2015, May 10). I'm not 'anti-charter," but I'm anti-this . . . [Web log post]. Retrieved from michaelklonsky.blogspot.nl/2015/05/im-not-anti-charter-but-i-am-anti-this.html?m=1

14. Schneider, Mercedes K. (2013, July 5). New Orleans "parental choice" and the Walton-funded OneApp [Web log post]. Retrieved from deutsch29.wordpress.com/2013/07/05/new-orleans-parental-choice-and-the-walton-funded-oneapp/

15. Schneider, Mercedes K. (2015, January 18). My thoughts on Doug Harris' January 15, 2015, New Orleans community meeting [Web log post]. Retrieved from deutsch29.wordpress.com/2015/01/18/my-thoughts-on-doug-harris-january-15-2015-new-orleans-community-meeting/

16. See note 15.

17. Jabbar, Huriya. (2015, March 26). How do school leaders respond to competition? Education Research Alliance [Policy brief]. Retrieved from deutsch29.files.wordpress.com/2015/03/era-policy-brief-how-do-school-leaders-respond-to-competition.pdf

18. See note 15.

19. Schneider, Mercedes K. (2013, May 22). Louisiana charter school audit reveals faux accountability [Web log post]. Retrieved from deutsch29.wordpress.com/2013/05/22/louisiana-charter-school-audit-reveals-faux-accountability/; Schneider, Mercedes K. (2014, August 10). RSD school construction overspending and substandard concrete: Time for Jindal admin

to expand its audit [Web log post]. Retrieved from deutsch29.wordpress
.com/2014/08/10/rsd-school-construction-overspending-and-substandard-
concrete-time-for-jindal-admin-to-expand-its-audit/; Dreilinger, D. (2013,
December 16). Louisiana school voucher program needs better oversight,
auditor says. *The Times-Picayune.* Retrieved from deutsch29.wordpress
.com/2013/12/16/the-2013-legislative-audit-of-louisiana-voucher-schools/

20. See note 1.

21. See note 1.

22. Friedman, Milton. (1970, September 13). The social responsibility of
business is to increase its profits. *New York Times Magazine.* Retrieved from
www.colorado.edu/studentgroups/libertarians/issues/friedman-soc-resp-
business.html

23. Denning, Steve. (2013, June 26). The origin of "the world's dumb-
est idea": Milton Friedman. *Forbes.* Retrieved from www.forbes.com/sites/
stevedenning/2013/06/26/the-origin-of-the-worlds-dumbest-idea-milton-
friedman/

24. See note 23.

25. Center for Popular Democracy & Integrity in Education. (2014,
May). *Charter School Vulnerabilities to Waste, Fraud, and Abuse.* Retrieved
from integrityineducation.org/charter-fraud/

26. See note 25.

27. Sanandaji, Tino. (2014, July 21). Sweden has an education crisis, but
it wasn't caused by school choice [Web log post]. *National Review.* Retrieved
from www.nationalreview.com/agenda/383304/sweden-has-education-crisis-
it-wasnt-caused-school-choice-tino-sanandaji

28. See note 27.

29. Sommers, Roseanna. (2009). School vouchers in Sweden.
Writing@Swathmore. Retrieved from www.swarthmore.edu/writing/school-
vouchers-sweden

30. Böhlmark, Anders, Holmlund, Helena, & Lindahl, Mikael. (2015).
School choice and segregation: Evidence from Sweden [Working paper]. Retrieved from www.ifau.se/Upload/pdf/se/2015/wp2015-08-School-choice-
and-segregation.pdf

31. Doherty, Brian. (2006, December 15). The economist and the dictator. *Reason.com.* Retrieved from reason.com/archives/2006/12/15/the-
economist-and-the-dictator

32. See note 31.

33. Encyclopaedia Britannica. (2015, April 20). Augusto Pinochet: President of Chile. Retrieved from www.britannica.com/biography/Augusto-Pinochet

34. Lopez, Veronica, Madrid, Romina, & Sisto, Vincente. (2012, August 17). "Red light" in Chile: Parents participating as consumers of education under global neoliberal policies [Book chapter]. In Cuadra-Monteil, Hector (Ed.), *Globalization—Education and Management Agendas.* New York: InTech. Retrieved from www.intechopen.com/books/globalization-education-and-management-agendas/-red-light-in-chile-parents-participating-as-consumers-of-education-under-global-neoliberal-policies

35. Arveseth, Lucinda G. (n.d.). Friedman's school choice theory: The Chilean education system [Digital commons paper]. Retrieved from digitalcommons.usu.edu/cgi/viewcontent.cgi?article=1378&context=gradreports

36. See note 34.

37. Organisation for Economic Cooperation and Development. (2000). *Investing in Education: Analysis of the 1999 World Education Indicators*, p. 111. Paris: Author. Retrieved from books.google.com

38. See note 34.

39. Council on Hemispheric Affairs. (2010, September 08). Rescue, relief, reconciliation: Sebastián Piñera's full plate [Web log post]. Retrieved from www.coha.org/rescue-relief-reconciliation-sebastian-pinera%E2%80%99s-full-plate/

40. See note 34.

41. Wisconsin Legislative Reference Bureau. (2001, January). Milwaukee school choice voucher program. *Wisconsin Briefs.* Retrieved from legis.wisconsin.gov/lrb/pubs/wb/01wb4.pdf

42. Schmidt, George N. (2011, June 02). Wal-Mart 'scholars' at the University of Arkansas prove, once again (again!), that the Walton family's voucher and pro-'choice' ideologies are beautiful good and true . . . *Substance News.* Retrieved from www.substancenews.net/articles.php?page=2305

43. Cowen, Joshua M., Fleming, David J., Witte, John J., Wolf, Patrick J., & Kisida, Brian. (2012, February). *Student Attainment and the Milwaukee Parental Choice Program: Final Follow-up Analysis.* Retrieved from web.archive.org/web/20120625034431/www.uark.edu/ua/der/SCDP/Milwaukee_Eval/Report_30.pdf

44. Schneider, Mercedes K. (2013, April 02). In Ravitch's defense: Milwaukee voucher study found wanting [Web log post]. Retrieved from deutsch29.wordpress.com/2013/04/02/in-ravitchs-defense-milwaukee-voucher-study-found-wanting/

45. 2013–14 Wisconsin Student Assessment Results by Grade [Assessment results table]. Retrieved from watchdog.wpengine.netdna-cdn.com/wp-content/blogs.dir/1/files/2014/04/test-scores.png

46. Borsuk, Alan J. (2012, December 1). Scores show voucher schools need accountability. *Milwaukee Journal Sentinel*. Retrieved from www.jsonline.com/news/education/scores-show-voucher-schools-need-accountability-t87s06b-181693671.html

47. Schilling, Jennifer. (2015, April 28). GOP giving up on voucher school accountability. *Urban Milwaukee*. Retrieved from urbanmilwaukee.com/pressrelease/gop-giving-up-on-voucher-school-accountability/

48. Miner, Barbara. (2015, April 17). School vouchers in Milwaukee, religious freedom and discrimination. *Milwaukee Journal Sentinel*. Retrieved from www.jsonline.com/news/opinion/school-vouchers-in-milwaukee-religious-freedom-and-discrimination-b99480751z1-300392801.html

49. United States General Accounting Office. (2001, August). School vouchers: Publicly funded programs in Milwaukee and Cleveland [Report to the Honorable Judd Gregg, U.S. Senate]. Retrieved from www.gao.gov/new.items/d01914.pdf

50. Supreme Court of the United States. (2002, June 27). Zellman v. Simmons-Harris. Retrieved from www.law.cornell.edu/supct/html/00-1751.ZS.html; Walsh, Mark. (2002, June 27). Supreme Court upholds Cleveland voucher program. *Education Week*. Retrieved from www.edweek.org/ew/articles/2002/06/27/42voucher_web.h21.html

51. Ohio Department of Education. (n.d.). Cleveland scholarship program. Retrieved from education.ohio.gov/Topics/Other-Resources/Scholarships/Cleveland-Scholarship-Tutoring-Program

52. National Conference of State Legislatures. (2015). School voucher laws: State-by-state comparison. Retrieved from www.ncsl.org/research/education/voucher-law-comparison.aspx

53. Ohio Department of Education. (n.d.). EdChoice and Cleveland Scholarships: Assessment data. Retrieved from education.ohio.gov/Topics/Other-Resources/Scholarships/EdChoice-Scholarship-Program/EdChoice-Cleveland-Assessment-Data

54. Ohio Department of Education. (2015, February). Cleveland summary [Voucher data spread sheet]. Retrieved from education.ohio.gov/getattachment/Topics/Other-Resources/Scholarships/EdChoice-Scholarship-Program/EdChoice-Cleveland-Assessment-Data/Cleveland_Summaries_Notes_2015.pdf.aspx; Ohio Department of Education. (2014, January). Cleveland summary [Voucher data spread sheet]. Retrieved from education.

ohio.gov/getattachment/Topics/Other-Resources/Scholarships/EdChoice-Scholarship-Program/EdChoice-Cleveland-Assessment-Data/ClevelandSummaryandAll_Scholarship_Summaries_2013-Final.xlsx.aspx

55. U.S. Department of Education. (2014, December 12). Legislation, regulations, and guidance: DC School Choice Incentive Act of 2003. Retrieved from www2.ed.gov/programs/dcchoice/legislation.html

56. See note 55.

57. Strauss, Valerie, & Turque, Bill. (2008, June 09). Fate of D.C. voucher program darkens [Web log post]. *Washington Post*. Retrieved from www.washingtonpost.com/wp-dyn/content/article/2008/06/08/AR20080 60802041_2.html?hpid=topnews

58. Turque, Bill, & Murray, Shailiagh. (2009, May 07). Obama offers compromise on D.C. tuition vouchers [Web log post]. *Washington Post*. Retrieved from www.washingtonpost.com/wp-dyn/content/article/2009/05/06/ AR2009050603852.html

59. Executive Office of the President, Office of Management and Budget. (2011, March 29). Statement of administration policy: H.R 471—Scholarships for Opportunity and Results Act. Retrieved from www.whitehouse .gov/sites/default/files/omb/legislative/sap/112/saphr471r_20110329.pdf

60. United States Government Accountability Office. (2013, September). District of Columbia opportunity scholarship program: Actions needed to address weaknesses in administration and oversight [Report to the Chairman, Subcommittee on Financial Services and General Government, Committee on Appropriations, U.S. Senate]. Retrieved from www.gao.gov/ assets/660/658416.pdf

61. See note 60.

62. See note 60.

Chapter 5

1. University of Massachusetts Amherst. (2005, June 20). Obituary: Ray Budde, taught in school of education. Retrieved from webcache.googleusercontent.com/search?q=cache:OWkVRZL2YggJ:www.umass.edu/newsoffice/article/obituary-ray-budde-taught-school-education+&cd=2&hl=en &ct=clnk&gl=us

2. See note 1.

3. Budde, Ray. (1988). *Education by Charter: Restructuring School Districts*. Regional Laboratory for Educational Improvement of the Northeast and Island, pp. 39–40. Retrieved from www.edreform.com/wp-content/

uploads/2014/12/Education-by-Charter-Restructuring-School-Districts-Ray-Budde.pdf

4. See note 3.

5. See note 3, p. 43.

6. See note 3.

7. Berger, Joseph. (1997, February 24). Albert Shanker, 68, combative leader who transformed teachers union, dies. *New York Times*. Retrieved from www.nytimes.com/1997/02/24/nyregion/albert-shanker-68-combative-leader-who-transformed-teachers-union-dies.html

8. Shanker, Albert. (1988, March 31). National Press Club speech, p. 5. Retrieved from reuther.wayne.edu/files/64.43.pdf

9. See note 8, pp. 5–6.

10. See note 8, p. 7.

11. See note 8, p. 11.

12. See note 8, p. 12.

13. See note 8, pp. 13–15.

14. See note 8, p. 17.

15. *New York Times* staff. (1988, April 1). Shanker asks greater autonomy for teachers and schools: Special to *The New York Times*. Retrieved from www.nytimes.com/1988/04/01/us/shanker-asks-greater-autonomy-for-teachers-school-special-new-york-times.html

16. Budde, Ray. (1996, September 1). The evolution of the charter school concept: Special section on charter schools. *Phi Delta Kappan, 78*(1), 72–73. This excerpt is reprinted with permission of Phi Delta Kappa International, www.pdkintl.org. All rights reserved.

17. Shanker, Albert. (1988, July 10). Convention plots new course: A charter for change. *New York Times*. Retrieved from source.nysut.org/weblink7/DocView.aspx?id=1886

18. See note 17.

19. See note 17.

20. See note 16.

21. See note 16.

22. Hartocollis, Anemona. (1999, January 3). The nation; test tube babies; private public schools. *New York Times*. Retrieved from www.nytimes.com/1999/01/03/weekinreview/the-nation-test-tube-babies-private-public-schools.html; Kolderie, Ted. (2008, June). How the idea of "chartering" schools came about: What role did the Citizens League

play? *Minnesota Journal*. Retrieved from www.educationevolving.org/pdf/ Origins-of-Chartering-Citizens-League-Role.pdf

23. School Structure Committee. (1988, November 17). *Chartered Schools = Choices for Educators + Quality for All Students*. Retrieved from web.archive.org/web/20110725173043/www.citizensleague.org/ publications/reports/424.Report.Chartered%20Schools%20Choices%20 for%20Education%20Quality%20for%20All%20Students.PDF

24. See note 23.

25. Minnesota Office of the Revisor of Statutes. (2014). 124D.10 Charter school [Statute]. Retrieved from www.revisor.mn.gov/statutes/?id=124D.10

26. See note 22.

27. Shanker, Albert. (1994, July 3). Noah Webster Academy. *New York Times*. Retrieved from source.nysut.org/weblink7/DocView.aspx?id=1010

28. See note 27.

29. See note 7.

30. Shanker, Albert. (1994, December 18). Questions about charters. *New York Times*. Retrieved from source.nysut.org/weblink7/DocView. aspx?id=967

31. Shanker, Albert. (1996, December 22). Dangerous minds. *New York Times*. Retrieved from source.nysut.org/weblink7/DocView.aspx?id=1006

32. See note 31.

33. See note 32.

34. See note 16.

Chapter 6

1. Education Commission of the States. (2015). Charter schools [Online database]. Retrieved from www.ecs.org/html/educationIssues/ CharterSchools/CHDB_intro.asp

2. Minnesota Legislative Reference Library. (n.d.). ReichgottJunge, Ember D. [Legislative record]. Retrieved from www.leg.state.mn.us/legdb/ fulldetail.aspx?id=10301

3. Minnesota Legislative Reference Library. (n.d.). Carlson, Sr., Arne Helge. [Legislative record]. Retrieved from www.leg.state.mn.us/legdb/ fulldetail.aspx?ID=10084

4. Gillam, Jerry. (1992, August 27). Wilson signs law on safer roofing shingles. *Los Angeles Times*. Retrieved from articles.latimes.com/1992-08-27/local/me-6602_1_san-francisco-giants

5. National Governors Association. (2011). California Governor Pete Wilson [Biographical sketch]. Retrieved from www.nga.org/cms/home/governors/past-governors-bios/page_california/col2-content/main-content-list/title_wilson_pete.html

6. DeGrow, Ben. (2013, June 18). Voices: As state charter law turns 20, one of its champions seeks new role. *Chalkbeat Colorado*. Retrieved from co.chalkbeat.org/2013/06/18/voices-as-state-charter-law-turns-20-one-of-its-champions-seeks-new-role/#.VYjDghtVikp

7. New York City Charter School Center. (2014, April). New York State Charter Schools Act of 1998 (as amended). Excerpt from New York State Consolidated Laws: Education. Retrieved from www.nyccharterschools .org/sites/default/files/resources/NYSCharterSchoolsActof1998_with-2014amendments.pdf

8. McLaughlin, Seth. (2015, May 28). George Pataki, former New York governor, announces White House bid. *Washington Times*. Retrieved from www.washingtontimes.com/news/2015/may/28/george-pataki-former-new-york-governor-announces-w/?page=all

9. Levy, Clifford J. (1998, December 18). Senate passes charter plan for schools. *The New York Times*. Retrieved from www.nytimes .com/1998/12/18/nyregion/senate-passes-charter-plan-for-schools.html

10. See note 9.

11. Clinton, William J. (1998, October 2). Statement on signing the Charter School Expansion Act of 1998 [Speech]. Retrieved from www .presidency.ucsb.edu/ws/?pid=55127

12. See note 11.

13. Goenner, James N. (2011). The origination of Michigan's charter school policy: An historical analysis [Doctoral dissertation]. University of Michigan. Retrieved from etd.lib.msu.edu/islandora/object/etd%3A872/datastream/OBJ/view

14. National Governors Association. (2011). Michigan governor John Engler [Biographical sketch]. Retrieved from www.nga.org/cms/home/governors/past-governors-bios/page_michigan/col2-content/main-content-list/title_engler_john.html

15. See note 13.

16. Miron, Gary, Nelson, Christopher D., & Lubienski, Christopher. (2002). Charter schools and the public-private synthesis [Book chapter draft]. In Miron & Nelson, *What's Public about Charter Schools?* Thousand Oaks, CA: Corwin Press. Retrieved from www.sagepub.com/upm-data/7218_miron_ch_1.pdf

17. Supreme Court of Michigan. (1997, July 30). Council of Organizations v. Governor. Retrieved from www.leagle.com/decision/1997774566NW2d208_1753.xml/COUNCIL%20OF%20ORGANIZATIONS%20v.%20GOVERNOR

18. Sabedra, David C. (1994, May 26). [Letter to Eric Gilbertson]. Retrieved from web.archive.org/web/19970728093250/www.mackinac.org/mea/letter.htm

19. Public law 107-11. (2002, January 08). [Legislation]. Retrieved from www2.ed.gov/policy/elsec/leg/esea02/107-110.pdf

20. Ravitch, Diane. (2010). *Death and Life of the Great American School System*. New York: Basic Books.

21. Bush, George W. (2002, January 08). President signs landmark No Child Left Behind education bill [Speech]. Retrieved from georgewbush-whitehouse.archives.gov/news/releases/2002/01/20020108-1.html

22. Dillon, Sam. (2007, November 6). For a key education law, reauthorization stalls. *The New York Times*. Retrieved from www.nytimes.com/2007/11/06/washington/06child.html

23. See note 19, p. 364.

24. See note 19, p. 365.

25. See note 19, p. 366.

26. See note 19, p. 366.

27. U.S. Department of Education. (2009, December). Race to the Top [Fact sheet]. Retrieved from www2.ed.gov/programs/racetothetop/factsheet.html

28. Duncan, Arne. (2009, June 22). Turning around the bottom five percent [Speech]. Retrieved from www2.ed.gov/news/speeches/2009/06/06222009.html

29. See note 28.

30. See note 28.

31. Rebarber, T., & Zgainer, Alison C. (Eds.). (2014). *Survey of America's Charter Schools*. Retrieved from www.edreform.com/wp-content/uploads/2014/02/2014CharterSchoolSurveyFINAL.pdf

32. Berkshire, Jennifer. (2015, June 24). Disrupt this! [Web log post]. Retrieved from edushyster.com/disrupt-this/

33. U.S. National Labor Relations Board Region 8. (2014, October 31). Northeast Ohio College Preparatory School et al. and Cleveland Alliance of Charter Teachers and Staff et al. [Labor relations board consolidated complaint and notice of hearing]. Retrieved from media.cleveland.com/

plain_dealer_metro/other/I%20CAN%20Unionizing%20attempt%20
CPT.08-CA-132977.issued%2010-31-14.pdf

34. Berkshire, Jennifer. (2015, June 24). The Marshall note [Flier]. Retrieved from edushyster.com/wp-content/uploads/2015/06/dollar-bill_FINAL.pdf

35. O'Donnell, Patrick. (2015, January 21). Groundbreaking fight to unionize two Cleveland charter schools is delayed while the schools and union negotiate. *The Plain Dealer.* Retrieved from www.cleveland.com/metro/index.ssf/2015/01/groundbreaking_fight_to_unionize_two_cleveland_charter_schools_is_delayed_while_the_schools_union_negotiate.html

36. See note 35.

37. Schneider, Mercedes K. (2014). The big three foundations: Gates, Walton, and Broad [Book chapter]. In *A chronicle of echoes: Who's who in the implosion of American public education.* Charlotte, NC: Information Age.

38. The Walton Family Foundation. (2013). [Grant Report]. Retrieved from dbd7853403f6a0e4167e-9fe3b5899f298e1c7d591332d27bb114.r52.cf1.rackcdn.com/documents/46315af7-4637-4c25-b288-0c141ee94cbb.pdf

39. Inside Philanthropy. (2014). Walton Family Foundation: Grants for charter schools. Retrieved from www.insidephilanthropy.com/charter-school-grants/walton-family-foundation-grants-for-charter-schools.html

40. See note 37.

41. See note 39.

42. See note 38.

43. See note 38.

44. Schmidt, George N. (2011, June 2). Wal-Mart 'scholars' at the University of Arkansas prove, once again (again!), that the Walton family's voucher and pro-'choice' ideologies are beautiful good and true . . . *Substance News.* Retrieved from www.substancenews.net/articles.php?page=2305

45. Brantley, Max. (2015, March 15). Following the money on the Walton-Hutchinson takeover of Little Rock Schools [Web log post]. *Arkansas Times.* Retrieved from www.arktimes.com/ArkansasBlog/archives/2015/03/15/following-the-money-on-the-walton-hutchinson-takeover-of-little-rock-schools

46. Brantley, Max. (2015, March 17). Breaking: School privatization bill pulled for this session [Web log post]. *Arkansas Times.* Retrieved from www.arktimes.com/ArkansasBlog/archives/2015/03/17/breaking-school-privatization-bill-pulled-for-this-session

47. See note 47.

48. Brantley, Max. (2015, February 20). Suit filed over Little Rock School District takeover [Web log post]. *Arkansas Times*. Retrieved from www.arktimes.com/ArkansasBlog/archives/2015/02/20/suit-filed-over-little-rock-school-district-takeover

49. Brantley, Max. (2015, March 19). Supreme Court grants halt of Little Rock school lawsuit [Web log post]. Retrieved from www.arktimes.com/ArkansasBlog/archives/2015/03/19/supreme-court-grants-halt-of-little-rock-school-lawsuit

50. Cashing in on Kids. (2015). Tell the Walmart heirs to hold charter schools accountable [Petition]. Retrieved from org2.salsalabs.com/dia/track.jsp?v=2&c=lxTAQnEWAUN1RTK34Kenn4rZ55H%2FYFlY

51. In the Public Interest & the American Federation of Teachers. (n.d.). *Cashing in on Kids: Brought to You by Wal-mart? How the Walton Family Foundation's ideological pursuit is damaging charter schooling.* Retrieved from cashinginonkids.com/brought-to-you-by-wal-mart-how-the-walton-family-foundations-ideological-pursuit-is-damaging-charter-schooling/

52. See note 51.

53. See note 51.

54. See note 51.

55. See note 51.

56. American Legislative Exchange Council. (2015). Mission. Retrieved from www.alec.org/news/mission/

57. Schneider, Mercedes K. (2014). The American Legislative Exchange Council (ALEC): Manipulating the nation state by state [Book chapter]. In *A chronicle of echoes: Who's who in the implosion of American public education.* Charlotte, NC: Information Age.

58. Center for Media and Democracy. (n.d.). ALEC Exposed. Retrieved from www.alecexposed.org/wiki/ALEC_Exposed

59. Common Cause. (2015). ALEC whistleblower complaint. Retrieved from www.commoncause.org/issues/more-democracy-reforms/alec/whistleblower-complaint/?referrer=www.google.com/

60. See note 40.

61. Wilce, Rebekah. (2014, August 21). Microsoft and more leave ALEC, 80 corporations out. *Center for Media and Democracy's PR Watch*. Retrieved from www.prwatch.org/news/2014/08/12573/microsoft-and-more-leave-alec-80-corporations-out; Center for Media and Democracy. (n.d.). Corporations that have cut ties with ALEC. Retrieved from www.sourcewatch.org/index.php/Corporations_that_Have_Cut_Ties_to_ALEC

62. American Legislative Exchange Council. (n.d.). History. Retrieved from www.alec.org/about-alec/history/

63. Schneider, Mercedes K. (2014). *A chronicle of echoes: Who's who in the implosion of American public education,* p. 391. Charlotte, NC: Information Age.

64. American Legislative Exchange Council. (2011, September 16). Charter school growth and quality act [Model legislation]. Retrieved from www.alec.org/model-legislation/charter-school-growth-with-quality-act/

65. American Legislative Exchange Council. (2007, September). Next generation charter schools act [Model legislation]. Retrieved from www.alec.org/model-legislation/the-next-generation-charter-schools-act/

66. American Legislative Exchange Council. (2011, August 5). Indiana education reform package [Model legislation]. Retrieved from www.alec.org/model-legislation/indiana-education-reform-package/

67. See note 65.

68. See note 66.

69. Surgey, Nick. (2012, January 31). ALEC exposed, for 24 hours [Web log post]. Retrieved from www.commonblog.com/2012/01/31/alec-exposed-for-24-hours/

70. Center for Education Reform. (2015). Board of directors. Retrieved from www.edreform.com/about/people/board-of-directors/

71. Singer, Alan. (2014, May 20). Why hedge funds love charter schools [Web log post]. *Huffington Post.* Retrieved from www.huffingtonpost.com/alan-singer/why-hedge-funds-love-char_b_5357486.html

72. Jackson, Abby. (2015, March 17). The Walmart family is teaching hedge funds how to profit from publicly funded schools. *Business Insider.* Retrieved from www.businessinsider.com/walmart-is-helping-hedge-funds-make-money-off-of-charter-schools-2015-3

73. See note 72.

74. Strauss, Valerie. (2014, October 29). Cuomo calls public school system a "monopoly" he wants to bust [Web log post]. *Washington Post.* Retrieved from www.washingtonpost.com/blogs/answer-sheet/wp/2014/10/29/cuomo-calls-public-school-system-a-monopoly-he-wants-to-bust/

75. Joseph, George. (2015, March 19). 9 billionaires are about to re-make New York's public schools—here's their story. *The Nation.* Retrieved from www.thenation.com/article/201881/9-billionaires-are-about-remake-new-yorks-public-schools-heres-their-story

76. Wilson, Jenny. (2015, May 29). Hedge fund managers back charter schools, democrats' campaigns. *Hartford Courant.* Retrieved from www.courant.com/politics/hc-charter-school-campaign-money-20150529-story.html#page=1

77. See note 76.

Chapter 7

1. Graham, Kristen. (2008, June 19). City takes 6 schools back from managers. *Philadelphia Inquirer.* Retrieved from articles.philly.com/2008-06-19/news/25250078_1_school-reform-commission-charter-schools-edison-schools

2. Saltman, Kenneth. (2005). *The Edison Schools: Corporate Schooling and the Assault on Public Education,* p. 36. New York: Routledge. Retrieved from books.google.com

3. Vaughn, Jason M. (2012, November 21). UUMKC: No new charter for Derrick Thomas Academy. *Fox4KC.com.* Retrieved from fox4kc.com/2012/11/21/umkc-no-new-charter-for-derrick-thomas-academy/

4. Williams, Mara Rose. (2013, July 3). Broke KC charter leaves teachers without final paycheck. *Kansas City Star.* Retrieved from www.kansascity.com/news/local/article322449/Broke-KC-charter-school-leaves-teachers-without-final-paycheck.html; Koepp, Paul. (2013, July 23). Closing of Derrick Thomas Academy leaves legal mess. *Kansas City Business Journal.* Retrieved from www.bizjournals.com/kansascity/news/2013/07/24/closure-of-derrick-thomas-academy.html

5. St. Tammany Parish School Board. (2015). 2014–15 Quick Facts. Retrieved from www.stpsb.org/PDFFiles/quickfacts.pdf

6. Sentell, Will. (2011, October 6). Almost half of Louisiana schools get failing grades. *Baton Rouge Advocate.* Retrieved from theadvocate.com/home/1011993-79/story.html

7. Louisiana Division of Administration. (2015, April). Louisiana administrative code: Title 28, education: Part LXXXIII. Bulletin 111—The Louisiana school, district, and state accountability system.

8. Silvernail, David L., Sloan, James E., Paul, Chelsea R., Johnson, Amy F., & Stump, Erika K. (2014, January). *The Relationship Between School Poverty and Student Achievement in Maine.* Retrieved from usm.maine.edu/sites/default/files/cepare/poverty_achievement_Web.pdf; Resseger, Jan. (2015, February 25). Helen Ladd: A–F letter grades for schools hide what we must do to support school children [Web log post]. Retrieved from janresseger.wordpress.com/2015/02/25/helen-ladd-a-f-letter-grades-for-

schools-hide-what-we-must-do-to-support-school-children/; Center for Student Achievement. (2014, September 3). If not now, when will we improve the data used in our school letter grades? [Web log post]. Retrieved from www.centerforstudentachievement.org/blog/if-not-now-when-will-we-improve-the-data-used-in-our-schools-letter-grades; Stranahan, Harriet A., Borg, J. Rody, & Borg, Mary O. (n.d.). School grades based on standardized test scores: Are they fair? *Journal of Academic and Business Ethics.* Retrieved from www.aabri.com/manuscripts/08006.pdf; Scott S. Cowen Institute for Public Education Initiatives. (2012, March). 2012 regular session of the Louisiana legislature: PK-12 public education in Louisiana. Retrieved from www.coweninstitute.com/wp-content/uploads/2012/03/SPELA-2012-web-final-3-6-12.pdf

9. Ellis, Ralph, and Lopez, Elwyn. (2015, April 30). Judge reduces sentences for three educators in Atlanta cheating scandal. *CNN.* Retrieved from http://www.cnn.com/2015/04/30/us/atlanta-schools-cheating-scandal/

10. Silvernail et al., see note 8.

11. Fiske, Edward B., & Ladd, Helen F. (2015, February 11). Addressing the impact of poverty on student achievement. *EducationNC.* Retrieved from www.ednc.org/2015/02/11/addressing-impact-poverty-student-achievement/

12. Center for Student Achievement, see note 8.

13. Stranahan et al., see note 8.

14. Myslinski, David. (2010, October 28). American Legislative Exchange Council 35-day mailing, education task force meeting [Memorandum, conference application, and task force materials], p. 46. Retrieved from www.commoncause.org/issues/more-democracy-reforms/alec/whistleblower-complaint/original-complaint/National_ALEC_Exhibit_4_Education_SNPS_2010.pdf

15. Myslinski, David. (2010, October 28). American Legislative Exchange Council 35-day mailing, education task force meeting [Memorandum, conference application, and task force materials]. Retrieved from www.commoncause.org/issues/more-democracy-reforms/alec/whistleblower-complaint/original-complaint/National_ALEC_Exhibit_4_Education_SNPS_2010.pdf

16. Myslinski, David. (2011, July 1). American Legislative Exchange Council 35-day mailing, 38th annual meeting [Memorandum, conference application, and task force materials]. Retrieved from www.commoncause.org/issues/more-democracy-reforms/alec/whistleblower-complaint/original-complaint/National_ALEC_Exhibit_4_Education_2011_Annual_Meeting.pdf; American Legislative Exchange Council. (2011, August 3). Hundreds

of state legislators gather to discuss policy solutions promoting economic growth and limited government. Retrieved from www.alec.org/hundreds-of-state-legislators/

17. Scott S. Cowen Institute, see note 8.

18. Smith, Greg B. (2014, March 14). Judge rules that state controller Thomas DiNapoli cannot audit charter schools. *New York Daily News.* Retrieved from www.nydailynews.com/new-york/education/state-comptroller-audit-charter-schools-judge-article-1.1721265

19. PR Watch. (2014). Appendix 1: Federal tax dollars spent to create and expand charter schools [Chart]. Retrieved from www.prwatch.org/files/ed_charter_school_funding.png

20. Persson, Jonas. (2015, May 7). Special report: Feds spent $3.3 billion fueling charter schools but no one knows what it's really bought [Report]. Retrieved from www.prwatch.org/news/2015/04/12799/new-documents-show-how-federal-taxpayer-money-wasted-charter-schools

21. See note 20.

22. Miron, Gary, Mathis, William, & Welner, Kevin. (2015, February). Review of *Separating Fact & Fiction* [Report review]. National Education Policy Center, p. 3. Retrieved from nepc.colorado.edu/files/ttr-charterclaims-mmw.pdf

23. See note 22, p. 3.

24. See note 22, pp. 9–10.

25. Louisiana's minimum foundation program for 2013–14: Overview and fact sheet. (2013, November). Retrieved from deutsch29.files.wordpress.com/2013/11/2013-14-mfp-overview.pdf

26. Louisiana Developmental Disabilities Council. (2015, May 23). [Report on Louisiana Senate Bill 267]. Retrieved from myemail.constantcontact.com/LaTEACH-Alert--Charter-schools-bank-funding-intended-for-students-with-disabilities-in-traditional-schools--House-.html?soid=1102605778958&aid=cNUXrs97xWI; see also note 23.

27. Campanile, Carl. (2013, October 3). Charter schools cheaper than public schools: Study. *New York Post.* Retrieved from nypost.com/2013/10/03/study-charter-schools-actually-cheaper-than-public-schools/

28. Center on Reinventing Public Education. (2010, Summer). *Teacher Attrition in Charters vs. District Schools.* Retrieved from www.crpe.org/sites/default/files/brief_ics_Attrition_Aug10_0.pdf

29. See note 22.

30. Ozimek, Adam. (2015, January 11). The unappreciated success of charter schools. *Forbes*. Retrieved from www.forbes.com/sites/modeledbehavior/2015/01/11/charter-success/

31 Center for Research on Education Outcomes. (2013). *National Charter School Study*. Retrieved from credo.stanford.edu/documents/NCSS%20 2013%20Final%20Draft.pdf

32. Gabor, Andrea A. (2015, April 28). New CREDO study, new credibility problems: from New Orleans to Boston [Web log post]. Retrieved from andreagabor.com/2015/04/28/new-credo-study-new-credibility-problems-from-new-orleans-to-boston/

33. See note 32.

34. Kamenetz, Anya. (2015, April 18). Falling through the cracks: Young lives adrift in New Orleans. *NPR*. Retrieved from www.npr.org/sections/ed/2015/04/18/393849058/in-new-orleans-young-lives-adrift

35. Louisiana Department of Education. Orleans-RSD enrollment counts 2004–05 2006–07 to 2013–14 [Excel file]. Retrieved from deutsch29.files.wordpress.com/2015/06/orleans-rsd-enrollment-counts-2004-05-2006-07-to-2013-14.xlsx

36. See note 34.

37. See note 34.

38. Sturgis, Chris. (2014, May 28). Reports from New Orleans: Opportunity youth and high school reform. *Youth Transition Funders Group*. Retrieved from ytfg.org/2014/05/reports-from-new-orleans-opportunity-youth-and-high-school-reform/

39. See note 34.

40. Welner, Kevin G., & Miron, Gary. (2014, May). Wait, wait. Don't mislead me! Nine reasons to be skeptical about charter waitlist numbers [Policy brief]. National Education Policy Center. Retrieved from nepc.colorado.edu/files/nepc-policymemo_waitlists.pdf

41. National Alliance for Public Charter Schools. (2013, June 27). National charter school waitlist numbers approach one million [Survey results brief]. Retrieved from www.publiccharters.org/press/national-charter-school-waitlist-numbers-approach-million/

42. See note 40.

43. See note 40.

44. Gleason, Phillip, Clark, Melissa, Tuttle, Christina C., Dwoyer, Emily, & Silverberg, Marsha. (2010, June). The evaluation of charter

school impacts: Final report. Retrieved from www.mathematica-mpr.com/ publications/PDFs/education/charter_school_impacts.pdf

45. Sackler, Madeline (Dir). (2010). *The Lottery* [DVD]. Great Curve Films.

46. Gonzalez, Juan. (2014, June 18). Gonzalez: Students of much-touted Success Academy charter school score too low on entrance exam for top city high schools. *New York Daily News*. Retrieved from www.nydailynews .com/new-york/education/gonzalez-success-charter-students-fail-top-city-schools-article-1.1833960

47. See note 40.

48. Decker, Geoff. (2015, March 24). In interview, Eva Moskowitz addresses backfill and test prep critiques. *Chalkbeat New York*. Retrieved from ny.chalkbeat.org/2015/03/24/in-interview-eva-moskowitz-addresses-backfill-and-test-prep-critiques/#.VZn15htViko

49. Democracy Builders. (n.d.). *Our team*. Retrieved from democracy-builders.org/team/

50. Democracy Builders. (n.d.). *No Seat Left Behind: The Unfilled Potential, Opportunity and Seats in Charter Schools*. Retrieved from democracybuilders.org/no-seat-left-behind-report-view-now/

51. See note 50.

52. Petrilli, Michael J. (2015, February 3). Backfilling charter seats: A backhanded way to kill charter autonomy [Web log post]. Retrieved from edexcellence.net/articles/backfilling-charter-seats-a-backhanded-way-to-kill-school-autonomy

53. See note 52.

54. See note 40.

55. See note 46.

Chapter 8

1. Wiggin, Addison. (2013, September 10). Charter school gravy train runs express to fat city. *Forbes*. Retrieved from www.forbes.com/sites/greatspeculations/2013/09/10/charter-school-gravy-train-runs-express-to-fat-city/

2. Bryant, Jeff. (2014, December 19). Education's newsmaker of the year: Charter school scandals. *Education Opportunity Network*. Retrieved from educationopportunitynetwork.org/educations-newsmaker-of-the-year-charter-school-scandals/

3. Center for Popular Democracy & Alliance to Reclaim Our Schools. (2015, April). *Tip of the Iceberg: Charter School Vulnerabilities to Waste,*

Fraud, and Abuse. Retrieved from www.scribd.com/doc/263415503/ New-Report-Finds-Over-200-Million-in-Fraud-and-Abuse-at-Charter-Schools#scribd

4. Strauss, Valerie. (2012, August 16). The big business of charter schools [Web log post]. *Washington Post*. Retrieved from www.washingtonpost .com/blogs/answer-sheet/post/the-big-business-of-charter-schools/2012/08/ 16/bdadfeca-e7ff-11e1-8487-64e4b2a79ba8_blog.html

5. EPR Properties. (2015). Public charter schools [Facilities investment overview]. Retrieved from www.eprkc.com/portfolio-overview/public-charter-schools/

6. See note 4.

7. See note 4.

8. Rosen, Steve. (2015, February 24). David Brain is retiring as chief executive of EPR properties. *Kansas City Star*. Retrieved from www.kansas-city.com/news/business/article11089067.html

9. EPR Properties. (2015). [Fact sheet]. Retrieved from www.eprkc.com/ pdf/eprfactsheet.pdf

10. EPR Properties. (2015). Public charter schools list. Retrieved from www.eprkc.com/portfolio-overview/public-charter-schools-list/

11. Imagine Schools. (n.d.). About us. Retrieved from www.imagine-schools.com/about-us/

12. Crouch, Elisa. (2012, April 18). Missouri calls it quits on Imagine charter schools in St. Louis. *St. Louis Post-Dispatch*. Retrieved from www.stltoday.com/news/local/education/missouri-calls-it-quits-on-imagine-charter-schools-in-st/article_e721e842-1a93-5e15-a673-f9766d19ee37.html

13. See note 10.

14. United States District Court for the Western District of Missouri, Central Division. (2014, December 18). Renaissance Academy for Math and Science of Missouri, Inc., v. Imagine Schools, Inc. Retrieved from docs.justia.com/cases/federal/district-courts/missouri/mowdce/4:2013 cv00645/110158/136

15. See note 14.

16. See note 2.

17. See note 1.

18. See note 1.

19. See note 1.

20. Gonzalez, Juan. (2010, May 6). Albany charter cash cow: Big banks making a bundle on new construction as schools bear the cost. *New York*

Daily News. Retrieved from www.nydailynews.com/new-york/education/
albany-charter-cash-big-banks-making-bundle-new-construction-schools-
bear-cost-article-1.448008

21. See note 20.

22. See note 20.

23. Waldman, Scott. (2015, April 3). The education model that fell
apart. *Politico New York.* Retrieved from www.capitalnewyork.com/article/
albany/2015/04/8564874/education-model-fell-apart

24. See note 23.

25. See note 23.

26. See note 23.

27. Kain, Erik. (2011, September 29). 80% of Michigan charter
schools are for-profits. *Forbes.* Retrieved from www.forbes.com/sites/
erikkain/2011/09/29/80-of-michigan-charter-schools-are-for-profits/

28. Miron, Gary. (2011, June 1). Testimony prepared for June 1, 2011,
hearing of the House Committee on Education and the Workforce [Written
testimony]. Retrieved from edworkforce.house.gov/uploadedfiles/06.01.11_
miron.pdf

29. See note 28.

30. Miron, Gary, & Gulosino, Charisse. (2013, November). *Profiles of
For-Profit and Nonprofit Education Management Organizations*, 14th ed.
2011–12. Retrieved from nepc.colorado.edu/files/emo-profiles-11-12.pdf

31. See note 11.

32. McGrory, Kathleen. (2014, April 20). South Miami-based charter
school management company under federal scrutiny. *Miami Herald.* Retrieved from www.miamiherald.com/news/local/community/miami-dade/
article1963142.html

33. See note 32.

34. Miami Dade-County Public Schools Office of Management and
Compliance Audits. (2006, November). Investigation of allegations of im-
propriety, Mater Academy Charter School(s) and Academica Corporation.
Poor governance results in apparent self-dealing. Retrieved from mca.dade-
schools.net/AC_Reports_0607/AC_1-30-07/MATER%20ACADEMY%20
REPORT_REVISED11-2-06.pdf

35. See note 34.

36. France, Jason. (2015, January 15). National Heritage Academies
makes money for themselves but no sense for taxpayers [Web log post].

Retrieved from crazycrawfish.wordpress.com/2015/01/15/national-heritage-academies-makes-money-for-themselves-but-no-sense-for-taxpayers/

37. See note 36.

38. See note 36.

39. Capital Roundtable. (2014). Regaining prosperity in the for-profit education industry: Private equity investing in for-profit education companies [Advertisement]. Retrieved from www.capitalroundtable.com/masterclass/CapitalRoundtableEducationA2015.html

40. See sote 39.

41. Saul, Stephanie. (2011, December 12). Profits and questions at on-line charter schools. *The New York Times*. Retrieved from www.nytimes.com/2011/12/13/education/online-schools-score-better-on-wall-street-than-in-classrooms.html?_r=0

42. See note 41.

43. Shortzilla. (2012, September 14). K12 Inc.: School might be out of session, this is why we're short [Company financial history]. Retrieved from seekingalpha.com/article/868191-k12-inc-school-might-be-out-of-session-this-is-why-were-short

44. See note 41.

45. See note 41.

46. Herold, Benjamin. (2013, January 21). Ex-workers claim operator of cyber-charters played games with enrollment figures. *Newsworks*. Retrieved from www.newsworks.org/index.php/homepage-feature/item/49878-k12cyber21?Itemid=1&

47. See note 43.

48. See note 44.

49. Boyd, Roddy. (2012, February 27). K12: A corporate destiny manifested. *Financial Investigator*. Retrieved from www.thefinancialinvestigator.com/?p=649

50. See note 46.

51. See note 46.

52. K12 settles one lawsuit, and another is filed, and then another [Web log post]. (2014, May 9). Retrieved from cyberschools.wordpress.com/2014/05/09/k-12-settles-one-lawsuit-and-another-is-filed/

53. Labaton Sucharow. (2013, July 25). In re K12 Inc. securities litigation [Lead council statement on litigation outcomes]. Retrieved from www.labaton.com/en/cases/In-re-K12-Inc-Securities-Litigation.cfm

54. Ho, Catherine. (2014, January 8). K12 founder Ron Packard steps down to start new online education venture. *Washington Post*. Retrieved from www.washingtonpost.com/business/capitalbusiness/k12-founder-ron-packard-steps-down-to-start-new-online-education-venture/2014/01/08/7a 2d4656-77f0-11e3-8963-b4b654bcc9b2_story.html

55. *Reuters*. (2014, February 13). Law offices of Howard G. Smith files class action lawsuit against K12 Inc. Retrieved from www.reuters.com/finance/stocks/LRN/key-developments/article/2921866

56. See note 55.

Chapter 9

1. National Center for Education Statistics. (n.d.). Table 174: Age range for compulsory school attendance and special education services, and policies on year-round schools and kindergarten programs, by state: Selected years, 2000 through 2010 [Spread sheet]. Retrieved from nces.ed.gov/programs/digest/d10/tables/dt10_174.asp

2. Goodman, Joan F. (2013, March). Charter management organizations and the regulated environment: Is it worth the price? *Educational Researcher, 42*(2), 89–96. Reprinted by permission of Sage Publications, Inc. Retrieved from edr.sagepub.com/content/42/2/89.full.pdf

3. See note 2.

4. See note 2.

5. See note 2.

6. See note 2.

7. See note 2.

8. See note 2.

9. Free Dictionary by Farlex. (n.d.). Heteronomy [Dictionary entry]. Retrieved from www.thefreedictionary.com/heteronomy

10. Schneider, Mercedes K. (2014). Knowledge Is Power Program (KIPP): What money cannot seem to do [Book chapter]. In *A Chronicle of Echoes: Who's Who in the Implosion of American Public Education*, pp. 337–352. Charlotte, NC: Information Age.

11. KIPP. (2015). KIPP public charter schools. Retrieved from www.kipp.org/

12. Haimson, Leonie. (2012, March 22). "At KIPP, I would wake up sick, every single day" [Interview]. Retrieved from webcache.googleusercontent.com/search?q=cache:jjrL1-vWknEJ:nycpublicschoolparents.blogspot

.com/2012/03/at-kipp-i-would-wake-up-sick-every.html&hl=en&gl=us&s
trip=1&vwsrc=0

13. KIPP: DC. (2013). KIPP DC parent/student handbook 2013–14. Retrieved from www.kippdc.org/wp-content/uploads/2013/10/KIPP-DC-Handbook-PDF.pdf; KIPP: Metro Atlanta. (2013). KIPP: Metro Atlanta parent and student handbook 2013–14. Retrieved from www.kippmetroatlanta .org/sites/default/files/u22/parent_and_student_handbook_13-14_final.pdf; KIPP: Delta College Preparatory School. (2014). Student and family handbook 2014–15. Page 48. Retrieved from www.kippdelta.org/sites/default/ files/resources/Final%20Revised%20KIPP%20DCPS%20Handbook%20 (2014-2015)_1.pdf

14. KIPP: Delta, see note 13, p. 48.

15. KIPP: Delta, see note 13, p. 48.

16. KIPP: Delta, see note 13, p. 48.

17. KIPP: Delta, see note 13, p. 47.

18. See note 12.

19. Berkshire, Jennifer. (2014, September 10). The high cost of no excuses [Web log post]. Retrieved from edushyster.com/the-high-cost-of-no-excuses/

20. Strauss, Valerie. (2014, September 19). Why "no excuses" charter schools mold "very submissive" students—starting in kindergarten [Web log post]. *Washington Post*. Retrieved from www.washingtonpost.com/blogs/ answer-sheet/wp/2014/09/19/why-no-excuses-charter-schools-mold-very-submissive-students-starting-in-kindergarten/

21. See note 19.

22. See note 19.

23. See note 12.

24. See note 12.

25. See note 10, pp. 342, 344.

26. Tuttle, Christina C., Gill, Brian, Gleason, Phillip, Knechtel, Virginia, Nichols-Barrer, Ira, & Resch, Alexandra. (2013, February 27). KIPP middle schools: Impacts on achievement and other outcomes. *Mathematica Policy Research*. Retrieved from www.kipp.org/files/dmfile/KIPP_Middle_Schools_ Impact_on_Achievement_and_Other_Outcomes1.pdf

27. KIPP Delta, see note 13, p. 32.

28. KATV.com. (2013, December 11). Beating the odds: 100 percent of Delta charter school accepted into college. Retrieved from www.katv.com/ story/24199809/charter-school-in-impoverished-delta

29. KIPP: Austin Public Schools. (2012.). About us. Retrieved from www.kippaustin.org/about-us

30. KIPP: San Antonio College Preparatory Schools. (2014). 2014–15 student handbook. Retrieved from webcache.googleusercontent .com/search?q=cache:7vYBBjhn7O0J:kippsa.org/wp-content/ uploads/2014/11/FINAL-2014-2015-KIPP-UPREP-Student-Handbook .docx+&cd=3&hl=en&ct=clnk&gl=us

31. See note 26.

32. KIPP. (2015, January 26). 2014 report card. Retrieved from www .kipp.org/view-report-card

33. Miron, Gary, Urschel, Jessica L., & Saxton, Nicholas. (2011, March). What makes KIPP work? A study of student characteristics, attrition, and school finance [Report]. Retrieved from www.edweek.org/media/ kippstudy.pdf

34. See note 26.

35. Carr, Sarah. (2014, November 17). The painful backlash against "no excuses" school discipline. *Hechinger Report*. Retrieved from hechingerreport.org/painful-backlash-excuses-school-discipline/

36. McKee, Adam J. (2015). Broken windows theory. *Encyclopaedia Britannica*. Retrieved from www.britannica.com/topic/broken-windows-theory

37. See note 19.

38. See note 35.

39. See note 19.

40. Sullivan, Elizabeth, & Morgan, Damekia. (2010, Spring). Pushed out: Harsh discipline in Louisiana schools denies the right to education: A focus on the Recovery School District in New Orleans. Retrieved from fflic. org/wp-content/uploads/2010/06/Pushed_Out_Report.pdf

41. See note 35.

42. Losen, Daniel, Hodson, Cheri, Keith, Michael A., Morrison, Katrina, & Belway, Shakti. (2015, February 23). Are we closing the school discipline gap? Center for Civil Rights Remedies, University of California at Los Angeles (UCLA) Civil Rights Project. Retrieved from civilrightsproject.ucla.edu/ resources/projects/center-for-civil-rights-remedies/school-to-prison-folder/ federal-reports/are-we-closing-the-school-discipline-gap

43. Losen, Daniel, Hodson, Cheri, Keith, Michael A., Morrison, Katrina, & Belway, Shakti. (2015, February). Are we closing the school discipline gap? Center for Civil Rights Remedies, University of California

at Los Angeles (UCLA) Civil Rights Project. Retrieved from civilrightsproject.ucla.edu/resources/projects/center-for-civil-rights-remedies/school-to-prison-folder/federal-reports/are-we-closing-the-school-discipline-gap/losen-are-we-closing-discipline-gap-2015-summary.pdf

Chapter 10

1. Stahl, Lesley. (2012, May 13). US charter schools tied to powerful Turkish imam [Video]. Retrieved from www.cbsnews.com/videos/us-charter-schools-tied-to-powerful-turkish-imam/

2. See note 1.

3. See note 1.

4. See note 1.

5. Citizens Against Special Interest Lobbying in Public Schools. (n.d.). Gulen charter schools: Introduction to Gulen charter schools. Retrieved from gulencharterschools.weebly.com/

6. See note 5.

7. See note 5.

8. See note 5.

9. See note 5.

10. See note 5.11. Harmony Public Schools. (2013). IRS Form 990. Retrieved from pdfs.citizenaudit.org/2015_03_EO/76-0615245_990_201406.pdf

12. Harmony Public Schools. (2011). IRS Form 990. Retrieved from pdfs.citizenaudit.org/2013_04_EO/76-0615245_990_201208.pdf

13. Harmony Public Schools. (2012). IRS Form 990. Retrieved from pdfs.citizenaudit.org/2014_03_EO/76-0615245_990_201306.pdf

14. Saul, Stephanie. (2011, June 6). Charter schools tied to Turkey grow in Texas. *The New York Times*. Retrieved from web.archive.org/web/20120607214425/www.nytimes.com/2011/06/07/education/07charter.htm

15. Bilefsky, Dan, & Arsu, Sebnem. (2012, April 24). Turkey feels sway of reclusive cleric in the U.S. *The New York Times*. Retrieved from www.nytimes.com/2012/04/25/world/middleeast/turkey-feels-sway-of-fethullah-gulen-a-reclusive-cleric.html?pagewanted=all&_r=0

16. See note 1.

17. See note 1.

18. See note 1.

19. Act for America Houston. (2013, February 20). Must watch: Remarks by Mary Addi, a former Gulen charter school teacher [Video web log post]. Retrieved from actforamericahouston.wordpress.com/2013/02/20/must-watch-remarks-by-mary-addi-a-former-gulen-charter-school-teacher/

20. See note 19.

21. See note 1.

22. Ravitch, Diane. (2012, May 14). 60 Minutes on the Gulen charters [Web log post]. Retrieved from dianeravitch.net/2012/05/14/60-minutes-on-the-gulen-charters/

23. See note 15.

24. See note 15.

25. See note 19.

26. *Daily Sabah.* (2014, June 16). FBI raids Gulen charter schools in US. Retrieved from www.dailysabah.com/politics/2014/06/16/fbi-raids-gulen-charter-schools-in-us

27. Livingston, Doug. (2014, July 05). Ohio taxpayers provide jobs to Turkish immigrants through charter schools. *Akron Beacon Journal.* Retrieved from www.ohio.com/news/break-news/ohio-taxpayers-provide-jobs-to-turkish-immigrants-through-charter-schools-1.501940

28. Concept Schools, Inc. (2013). IRS Form 990. Retrieved from pdfs.citizenaudit.org/2015_01_EO/03-0503751_990_201406.pdf

29. See note 27.

30. See note 27.

31. See note 28.

32. Cortera Business Directory. (2015). Breeze, Inc. [Directory entry]. Retrieved from start.cortera.com/company/research/k6s0stp5l/breeze-inc/; Concept Schools. (n.d.). Contact us. Retrieved from www.conceptschools.org/contact-us/

33. Gilbertson, Annie. (2014, July 21). Charter schools: Audit finds misused, missing funds at LA network. *Southern California Public Radio.* Retrieved from www.scpr.org/blogs/education/2014/07/21/17031/audit-finds-missing-misused-funds-at-la-charter-ne/

34. See note 33.

35. Watanabe, Teresa. (2015, March 11). L.A. Unified ends effort to close embattled charter schools. *Los Angeles Times.* Retrieved from www.latimes.com/local/lanow/la-me-ln-lausd-charter-20150311-story.html; Howle, Elaine M. (2015, May 07). Magnolia Science Academies, Report

2014-135 [California state audit report]. Retrieved from www.document-cloud.org/documents/2074556-2014-135.html

36. Watanabe, Teresa. (2015, May 7). State auditor finds improvement in embattled charter chain. *Los Angeles Times*. Retrieved from www.latimes.com/local/lanow/la-me-ln-magnolia-charter-20150507-story.html

37. Howle, Magnolia Science Academies report, see note 35, p. 42.

38. Magnolia Educational and Research Foundation. (2012). IRS Form 990. Retrieved from pdfs.citizenaudit.org/2014_03_EO/95-4649884_990_201306.pdf

39. Success Academy Charter Schools, Inc. (2013). IRS Form 990. Retrieved from pdfs.citizenaudit.org/2015_02_EO/20-5298861_990_201406.pdf

40. See note 39.

41. Howle, Magnolia Science Academies report, see note 35, p. 8.

42. See note 1.

43. Fulton County Board of Education & Georgia State Board of Education. (2012). Charter for Fulton County Schools. Retrieved from www.gadoe.org/External-Affairs-and-Policy/Charter-Schools/Documents/Fulton%20County%20System.pdf

44. Saul, Stephanie. (2012, June 5). Audits for 3 Georgia schools tied to Turkish movement. *The New York Times*. Retrieved from www.nytimes.com/2012/06/06/us/audits-for-3-georgia-charter-schools-tied-to-gulen-movement.html?_r=1

45. Dixon, Kristal. (2014, November 20). School board severs ties with Fulton Sunshine, Science Academy High School. *Roswell Patch*. Retrieved from patch.com/georgia/roswell/school-board-severs-ties-fulton-sunshine-science-academy-high-school-0

46. See note 45.

47. See note 45.

Chapter 11

1. Dillon, Sam. (2006, January 6). Florida Supreme Court blocks school vouchers. *The New York Times*. Retrieved from www.nytimes.com/2006/01/06/national/06florida.html?_r=0; Brown, Emma. (2015, June 29). Colorado Supreme Court strikes down school voucher program. *Washington Post*. Retrieved from www.washingtonpost.com/local/education/colorado-supreme-court-strikes-down-school-voucher-program/2015/06/29/a382768e-1e75-11e5-bf41-c23f5d3face1_story.html; Lee, Traci G. (2013, September 13).

Louisiana Supreme Court rules Jindal's voucher program unconstitutional. *MSNBC.com.* Retrieved from www.msnbc.com/melissa-harris-perry/louisiana-supreme-court-rules-jindals-vouche; Cason, Mike. (2014, May 28). Montgomery County judge rules Alabama Accountability Act unconstitutional [Web log post]. *AL.com.* Retrieved from blog.al.com/wire/2014/05/montgomery_county_judge_rules.html; Archer, Kim. (2014, August 29). Student voucher law unconstitutional due to "no-aid-to-religion" provision, judge rules. *Tulsa World.* Retrieved from www.tulsaworld.com/newshomepage3/student-voucher-law-unconstitutional-due-to-no-aid-to-religion/article_ea454f83-4684-5b66-8c4d-efefe13fa69f.html

2. Schneider, Mercedes K. (2015, January 12). John White begs private schools to take more voucher students and offers more state money to help them do so [Web log post]. Retrieved from deutsch29.wordpress.com/2015/01/12/john-white-begs-private-schools-to-take-more-voucher-students-and-offers-more-state-money-to-help-them-do-so/

3. Postal, Leslie. (2014, August 28). Lawsuit calls Florida voucher program unconstitutional. *Orlando Sentinel.* Retrieved from www.orlandosentinel.com/news/breaking-news/os-school-voucher-lawsuit-20140828-story.html; Kinsey, Troy. (2015, February 9). Court battle looms over Florida's tax credit scholarship program. *BayNews9.com.* Retrieved from www.baynews9.com/content/news/baynews9/news/article.html/content/news/articles/bn9/2015/2/9/court_battle_looms_o.html

4. Florida Department of Education. (2015). Opportunity Scholarship Program. Retrieved from www.fldoe.org/schools/school-choice/k-12-scholarship-programs/osp/

5. Schneider, Mercedes K. (2014). Jeb Bush and his Florida miracle (well, most of it), and Jeb Bush and his miracle reforms (the rest of it). In *A Chronicle of Echoes: Who's Who in the Implosion of American Public Education*, pp. 205–238. Charlotte, NC: Information Age.

6. See note 5, pp. 205–222.

7. Burns, Matthew, & Leslie, Laura. (2014, August 21). Judge rules NC school voucher program unconstitutional. *WRAL.com.* Retrieved from www.wral.com/judge-rules-nc-school-voucher-program-unconstitutional/13911842/

8. Binker, Mark. (2015, July 23). NC Supreme Court says vouchers are constitutional. *WRAL.com.* Retrieved from www.wral.com/nc-supreme-court-says-vouchers-are-constitutional/14791349/

9. Supreme Court of North Carolina. (2015, July 23). Alice Hart v. State of North Carolina. Retrieved from pulse.ncpolicywatch.org/wp-content/uploads/2015/07/Vouchers.pdf

10. Raymond, Margaret. (2015, June 20). The effects of charter schools on student learning [Panel discussion]. Education Research Alliance Conference, New Orleans, Louisiana.

11. Alexander, Lamar. (2015). Senate Bill 1177: Every Child Achieves Act of 2015 [Legislation agreed to in Senate on July 16, 2015]. Retrieved from hdl.loc.gov/loc.uscongress/legislation.114s1177

12. Alexander, Lamar. (2015). Senate Amendment 2139 to Senate Amendment 2089 (omnibus amendment to Senate Bill 1177) [Legislation not agreed to in Senate on July 8, 2015]. Retrieved from hdl.loc.gov/loc .uscongress/legislation.114samdt2139

13. United States Senate. (2015, July 8). Roll call vote on Alexander Amendment 2139 [Legislation]. Retrieved from www.senate.gov/legislative/LIS/roll_call_lists/roll_call_vote_cfm.cfm?congress=114&session=1&vote=00225

14. Kline, John. (2015). House Resolution 5: Student Success Act [Legislation]. Retrieved from thomas.loc.gov/cgi-bin/bdquery/z?d114:h.r.00005

15. U.S. House of Representatives. (2015, July 8). Final vote results for roll call 423: Student Success Act [Legislation]. Retrieved from clerk.house .gov/evs/2015/roll423.xml

16. Brown, Emma. (2015, February 24). Arne Duncan blasts House effort to revise No Child Left Behind. *Washington Post*. Retrieved from www .washingtonpost.com/news/local/wp/2015/02/24/arne-duncan-blasts-house-effort-to-revise-no-child-left-behind/

17. Improving America's Schools Act of 1994. Part C—Public charter schools. [Legislation]. Retrieved from www2.ed.gov/legislation/ESEA/sec10301.html

18. Public law 107-110: No Child Left Behind Act of 2001. (2002, January 8). [Legislation]. Retrieved from www2.ed.gov/policy/elsec/leg/esea02/107-110.pdf

19. See note 18, p. 25.

20. See note 18, p. 364.

21. See note 18, p. 365.

22. See note 18, p. 364.

23. See note 14, pp. 280–281.

24. See note 14, p. 283.

25. See note 14, p. 282.

26. See note 14, p. 299.

27. Open Secrets. (2015). National Alliance for Public Charter Schools [Search engine entry]. Retrieved from www.opensecrets.org/lobby/clientsum .php?id=D000054386&year=2007

28. See note 14, p. 309.

29. See note 14, p. 311.

30. See note 11.

31. See note 11.

32. See note 11.

33. See note 11.

34. See note 11.

35. U.S. Department of Education. (2015, December 10). Every Student Succeeds Act (ESSA) [Video and article]. Retrieved from www.ed.gov/essa

Index

About the Author

Mercedes K. Schneider, PhD, is a career teacher. A native of southern Louisiana and a product of the St. Bernard Parish Public Schools, Schneider holds degrees in secondary education, English and German (BS, Louisiana State, 1991), guidance and counseling (MEd, West Georgia, 1998), and applied statistics and research methods (PhD, Northern Colorado, 2002). In 2015–16, she completed her 21st year of full-time teaching and has taught from grade 7 to graduate school in several states (Louisiana, Georgia, Colorado, and Indiana). After 14 years away, Schneider returned to Louisiana in 2007 in the aftermath of Hurricane Katrina and is in her 9th full-time year of teaching sophomore English in a southern Louisiana traditional public high school.

School Choice: The End of Public Education? is Schneider's third book. Her second, *Common Core Dilemma—Who Owns Our Schools?*, examines the history, development, and promotion of the Common Core State Standards. Her first, *A Chronicle of Echoes: Who's Who in the Implosion of American Public Education*, details individuals and organizations exploiting public education in the name of "reform."